SCIENTIFIC CHRISTIAN MENTAL PRACTICE

WRITINGS OF EMMA CURTIS HOPKINS

High Mysticism

Résumé — Practice Book for the Twelve
Studies in High Mysticism

Esoteric Philosophy in Spiritual Science

Judgment Series in Spiritual Science

Bible Interpretations

SCIENTIFIC CHRISTIAN MENTAL PRACTICE

By

EMMA CURTIS HOPKINS

DeVorss & Company, Publisher
Box 550, Marina del Rey, California 90294-0550

Originally published by
High Watch Fellowship
Cornwall Bridge, Connecticut, U.S.A.

ISBN: 0-87516-199-5

Printed in the United States of America

CONTENTS

FOREWORD

"Scientific Christian Mental Practice," which once more becomes available with this printing, embodies class instruction given by Emma Curtis Hopkins in the practical application of metaphysical Science as exemplified most particularly by Jesus Christ but with varying degrees of understanding by all true metaphysicians.

To those who are meeting this inspired teacher for the first time let us state that Mrs. Hopkins was a pioneer among modern teachers of Truth. She was called "the teacher of teachers" as so many of her students became teachers. She brings to the expanding comprehension of spiritual teachings, a point of view and breadth of vision that inspire with a unity of Spirit yet freedom in expression. This tribute was paid to her in Unity (1925): "Her brilliance of mind and spirit was so marked that very few could follow in her metaphysical flights, yet she had marked power in quickening spirituality in her students."

Mrs. Hopkins' gift for teaching showed itself early. Before she was fifteen years old, she entered Woodstock Academy (Connecticut) as a student and because of her genius was given a place on the faculty as a teacher.

Later we find Mrs. Hopkins again presenting herself as a student — taking the class instruction in Christian Science, following which she served editorially on the staff of the Christian Science Journal (1885) — only to find her life purpose asserting itself and drawing her into the role of independent leadership and of a great teacher. She was not only a teacher of teachers. From very walk of life — authors, artists, preachers, homemakers — came to her for instruction and she touched them with the quickening power of her illumined Soul.

Going out as an independent teacher, Mrs. Hopkins taught in many cities (among them New York, Chicago, Kansas City, San Francisco) having large classes wherever she went.

Later she founded a seminary in Chicago. It was a regularly incorporated school and the graduates were ordained ministers and so recognized by the State of Illinois. Students came from all parts of the country to study with her and go out and carry the message of healing and comforting to the people. Some of the best known teachers were graduates of, and then associates with her in the school: Charles and Myrtle Fillmore, Annie Rix-Militz, George Edwin and Mary Lamoreaux Burnell.

Mrs. Hopkins was way ahead of the times in the freedom offered students in a group activity which the faculty of the seminary became. Her innate teaching quality shows in the leadership her teaching quickened in students who established independent movements now ministering to mankind.

Among the students in a class in New York was H. Emilie Cady, whose "Lessons in Truth," published by the Unity School of Christianity, finds a vital place in healing movements of today.

In introducing the course in "Scientific Christian Mental Practice," Mrs. Hopkins refers to it as "the method of Jesus Christ put in twelve settings," and states that "the absolute meanings of the words of Jesus Christ would be taken." She further states:

"We are reasoning out the laws of the action of Mind as it conquers the universe with righteousness when we step along in ideas with Jesus . . . that action of Mind whereby all mankind would let the reign of God come on earth.

"As we understand Jesus Christ, we have His Mind. When we have His Mind wholly, we have an understanding of the apostle's injunction, 'Let this mind be in you which was also in Christ Jesus.'

"The Science pursued has four accomplishments to work out. Jesus Christ said it would give you power to preach the gospel, heal the sick, cast out bad tempers, and raise the dead.

"It is evident that the power of God is exhibited only over the highway of a true premise with its irresistible sequences.

"Take now a right premise and reason on with it until the light of understanding breaks over and through you.

"In our time we find some people healing by one means and some by another. Whenever they begin to acknowledge that God is the health of the people you will find them using less and less material helps toward healing each other. Yet you must be sure that whatever health is brought to mankind it all comes from God.

"There is a secret of healing. The method of it is nothing. . . . The practice of healing by the word lets us most quickly into the secret of healing.

"In this healing practice we have had many a thinker touching on the enchanting borders of the Science, but only Jesus who could wholly prove his words. . . . . His words would heal the instant He sent them out. . . . The Word He consecrated to healing must even now be charged with the same Spirit He felt . . . How shall we absolutely understand how to heal the sick? Paul said, by letting the same Mind be in you that was in Christ Jesus.

"Breaking open the twelve lessons of Science and receiving the ointment of the meanings is getting at the actual teachings of Jesus Christ."

In the above quotations are a few highlights of what the author states about the instruction. The facts about the author's life were gleaned from conversations with persons who knew her and from a pamphlet of the Seminary in Chicago. An index could only be partial in a work so abundant in meaningful words but we aimed for the most important subject ideas. Mrs. Hopkins says of the words, "all the time you can trace other points . . . of finer meaning than words can kindle . . . for those of an esoteric or spiritual nature." Her aim was most certainly to penetrate through the veil of "things as they appear" to the heart of Reality.

High Watch Fellowship

"Let this mind be in you which was also in Christ Jesus."

— Philippians 2:5

CHAPTER I

THE STATEMENT OF BEING

There are twelve doctrines of Jesus Christ. This is to say that the one method of Jesus Christ is presented in twelve statements or settings. A diamond has many polished facets and it takes them all to make it shine in its full beauty. The truth has many ways in which it can be expressed and all are required if some people are to believe in its beauty and brightness. Each of the twelve lessons sets forth the whole doctrine in its own way.

We will consider the first lesson. It is the first idea with which mind everywhere, in all ages, has begun when proclaiming that outside of, and greater than any power exhibited by anything in nature, or in man, is a being called God.

The first lesson in Truth is the word "God." Have you ever heard that there is a marvelous power in every word? It contains its own potentiality. You can see that if every word contains its own potentiality, then that word which all the world agrees contains the greatest power must be the greatest word. Plotinus (A.D.250) lost himself seven times in a trance of ecstasy by thinking over the word "God" in his mind. God was the beginning of all. God is the presence of all. The use of the word by Plotinus, Porphyry and Spinoza did not solve the mystery of existence for them, however. They yielded to death and feebleness, even falling into sickness sometimes, like other men and women. There was something lacking in their teaching, something lacking in their understanding of God, for the ideal of God is told as, "My words are life unto those that find them and health to all their flesh."

Jesus Christ had quite a different idea from these men, even though they loved the name of God so devoutly. "In my name preach the gospel, in my name heal the sick." "If a man keep my sayings he will never see death." What name was that which Jesus Christ used, which had such omnipotent energy that even when it was spoken it would heal the sick and raise the dead? The Name is within every mind. If it is spoken it will be like letting loose the electricity which the physicist has stored in batteries.

It has been taught from the remotest times that we have the Name stored within us as concealed energy. It can perform twelve great works, by our words, whenever we use it, even without very close relation to it. If we were to use that Name directly it would instantly work all the miracles recorded of all the mighty men of old. The speaking of words for performing cures is an ancient custom. The Zend-Avesta tells us that it is by the Divine Word that the sick are most surely cured. Sometimes the word is thought in the silent mind. It is not always by the repetition of our words that the cures are wrought. It is by the whole lines of reasoning. The study of the lines of reasoning which bring out your healing power is called the study of metaphysics. The word, metaphysical, means "above and away from the physical."

Thoughts are ideas. We study ideas. But ideas bear an important relation to each other. They make a course of reasoning. Some people study mathematics to train their minds to logical processes. But the study of mathematics does not make thoughts and words powerful to heal the sick. Some people have believed that there is a magical power in numbers just as there is great potency in words. Cornelius Agrippa of Cologne (1486), ascribed to numbers an efficacy. But no mathematician is a healer because of his mathematics. He must use the Healing Word, or the reasoning which brings down somewhat of the power of the Healing Word.

You may be filled with wonder as to what the Healing Word or Name can be. It certainly is not the word "God", for these men who used that word continually were not mighty healers. Spiritual Science does not tell you the Name. It gives you the most direct reasoning which the word "God" brings out, and consequently gives the best healing power of any line of reasoning in the world.

There are twelve points of doctrine put forth in these lessons in plain terms. All the time you can trace other points of the same doctrine, finer and more subtle, streaming under them like fires from purer altars of meaning than words can kindle. The very finest fires of meaning I cannot tell you in words; you must be of an esoteric or spiritual nature to read them while I am talking.

We call metaphysics the Science of Life, because to know pure metaphysics is to renew the life and make death and accident impossible.

We call metaphysics the Science of Health, because to know metaphysics is to be perfectly well and free from liability to sickness or disease of any kind.

We call metaphysics the Science of Strength, because to know metaphysics is to be strong beyond any strength you have ever dreamed of. Nothing is too hard for those who are strong with the strength of metaphysics.

We call metaphysics the Science of Support, because whoever studies the science finds his support coming to him in a new way, and he cannot come to actual want, no matter who would have failed if they had been put in his place. The prophecy of Jeremiah and of Isaiah comes to pass to whoever studies metaphysics without blundering in his reasonings. "Bread shall be given him, his waters shall be sure."

We call metaphysics the Science of Defense or Protection, for no ill can come nigh the dwelling of one who puts his trust in the principle taught by this science. "His place of defense shall be the munitions of rocks."

This science of Life, Truth, Love, Substance and Intelligence is for all who look into it profoundly. Outside of metaphysics the world is seeking for its life by physical performances; working at machinery, books, commerce, cooking, washing, eating, governing one another, employing one another, killing and using animals, wearing flesh and bones into the grave to make a living. But the whole system of living by material efforts is wrong. "Turn unto Me, for why will ye die?" said the Spirit. Death is the reward of hard effort to live by material actions. If you will look into the Science of Spirit you will see that your life is meant to be sustained by the Science of God and not by the science of matter.

God is Spirit, therefore it is the Science of Spirit which we are to study when we open the reasoning with the word "God." God is the name for that Intelligence which out of its own substance bestowed upon you that intelligence you now have. Intelligence is Mind. Thus it is plain that by opening our study with the word "God" we are beginning the study of Mind.

By Mind alone we are taught we are to live and be strong. By Mind alone we are supported and defended. The further on we get in the Science, the more confident we become that it is by the words that proceed from the mouth of God that we are to live. Jesus Christ taught this. He was ministered unto by angels, and said: "Man shall not live by bread alone, but by every word that proceedeth out of the mouth of God." This means that God has a way of giving freely from His Mind words that will make alive. Jesus Christ told the people that His words were Life. He spoke of the manna which the Jews had eaten while wandering forty years in the wilderness as being so far from the real bread that the Jews all died. He showed over and over again that the Word is a bread that will keep life in the body forever. "He that eateth of this bread shall live forever."

As nearly as possible, the twelve lessons which we now begin will take the absolute meanings of the words of Jesus Christ. If we take the absolute meanings, dear friends, we are obliged to say that our life needs no material or physical effort to keep it forever. It needs only the true Word of God. It is not profitable to say that our life needs no material support. It is only profitable to say that our life does need the Word of God. The Word of God IS Truth. God works only in Truth.

We may throw true words down into the arena of human life and their power will be God's power. The power of God is freedom. Jesus Christ said that all who knew Truth would be free. What do you want to be free from? Sin, sickness, death; all the evil men fear is contained in these three words. From these the Word of God sets absolutely free. Miracles of healing have been worked by thousands of men and women who taught true words concerning God in some of the statements we find set forth in order by Spiritual Science.

Each lesson has this healing strength. Keep your mind open and free to receive that lesson which fits your own disposition best. No matter what type or character you are or what disposition of mind you have, I tell you that one of these lessons strikes your key-note, and by speaking over and over the words which that one lesson explains, you will let the fire of your own native healing gift from Jehovah kindle health within your own body and in those of all your neighbors.

Elisha cured a terrible case of leprosy by one of these lessons. It was probably the second lesson. He raised the Shunamite woman's child to life by one of these lessons. It was probably the third lesson. He increased the loaves of bread to feed a hundred men. This was the fourth lesson. He would not have called it the fourth lesson, but he would have felt in his mind all the strength of the fourth lesson as we have it.

The first lesson finds out what your mind is seeking and names it. Can you name now just exactly what your mind is seeking? You would soon be set on the right track for finding what you are seeking if you could name what you want. The naming of what the mind of the whole world is seeking is the first statement of Jesus Christ, and is the first lesson of Moses. It is the foundation thought, even in the minds of the insects. It is the GOOD.

Are you not seeking Good? Why do you move your right hand? You move it to get your Good. Why do you breathe? You breathe to get your Good. Why do the stones lie still and wait? They are waiting for their Good. Why does the bird fly? It flies for its Good. Everything moves and waits for its Good. So you see that the Good draws everything. The Good which you and I want governs everything we do. Therefore the Good which you are seeking is your God.

Spinoza was called the God-intoxicated man, because he spoke the word God so much. I am convinced that if he had spoken the word Good, instead of the word God, he would have come into a nearer relation to his God.

Moses says that God (Good) created. The Good which you are seeking created you. Just that Good which you want is the combination of words which brought you forth. The honest statement that "*My Good is my God*" has the power to set the mind to a key which is nearer to its normal tone than it is now thinking. John said that in the beginning was the Word, and the Word was God. He also said that out of the Word were all things made and without the Word was nothing made. Paul said that a veil is forever over the face when the Word is read because so many untruthful things have been spoken of God.

If you take the word God for your starting point, you will

not start so near the foundation feeling of your mind as you will if you take the word GOOD. "I am seeking my Good, therefore I am seeking my God." The devout poet who wrote, "I was athirst for thee, the living God," would have found healing power beginning to stream forth into his life like a fine white fire if he had struck his lyre to the chord, "I seek my Good. My Good is my God." Therefore in the Science of Mind you may take for your first idea one word. It is the word "Good". In the science of words you may take the word Good and let it lie before you like a great white stone. It has a revealing power which the word "God" has not.

John, the Revelator, speaks of the white stone. The white stone is a word. The word is Good. It is the name of what you want. It is the nearest approach to expressing what is in our mind that Science has thus far given us. It is evident that Science will give us the inner stone if we use the outer stone wisely. As we acknowledge that the Good we are seeking must be our God, because it pulls and pushes us all the time to see if we cannot come nearer to it, we must find ourselves better and better satisfied.

The acknowledgment that "I am seeking my Good, and my Good is my God," is telling a simple truth. It is so simple that the tiniest child can say, "I am seeking my Good, and my Good is my God, because it draws and pushes and moves me on." The child who tells this simple truth is telling aloud what the little stones are whispering without words, and the little baby who lisps this simple truth will be fed and clothed by the ever drawing closer and closer to him of his Good.

If I should take the unspoken sentence which lies like a hidden jewel under the jagged covering of your thoughts about the things you do not like, I would read it, "*There is Good for me and I ought to have it.*" There is nothing but has in itself the conviction that there is Good belonging to it that it ought to have. The prince reels from the banquet hall, seeking the Good he believes he ought to have. The thief runs from the daylight seeking the Good he thinks he ought to have. But none of them speaks the simple truth about his movements. If any one of them did he would come nearer to finding his Good. God, the Omnipotent Good, works through the word of Truth. Get to speaking the word of Truth from the first to the last statement, and God will be found working for you and through you, with almighty power.

The first name of God is Good, and the first name of the Good is God. "There is Good for me and I ought to have it," says the unconscious instinct of the worm crawling at your feet. When you look at the worm and tell the truth about it, why it moves and why it keeps still, you will be in league with its life. It will feel your unity with it. When you look at a drunkard, or miser, you will say he is seeking his Good. His heart will be better satisfied the instant you speak out what his unspoken instinct is feeling. He does not say so. If he should say so his life would come nearer to being a satisfying one. The moment anybody speaks out the Truth of his life he has spoken the Omnipotent Principle.

The unconscious truth is that *there is Good for me and I ought to have it.* Nothing can kill that unconscious feeling. It is indestructible. It is omnipotent. Thus the Omnipotent Truth is kept hidden in the stillness of the mind of man and the mind of the rocks. The Omnipotent Truth shall not be hidden in the stillness any longer, and the satisfaction of the living things will come when they are told that the reason they move, or do not move, is for one Good.

In the Scriptures we read, "Prove me ... and I will pour you out a blessing." "In all thy ways acknowledge Him and He will direct thy paths." To acknowledge God is to admit we are seeking our Good. It is well to give one day a week to acknowledging that we are seeking for our Good. We tell what our Good is. Is not our Good the free life we want? Do we want a burdened, obstructed, hampered life? Out of the word Good name a good which is Good to you.

The free life of the lily is the name of its Good. As the lily works out its life problem, it is telling as plainly as it can speak that its Good is its free life. You may name your Good as your free life. When you speak for yourself you speak for the world. It is the one chord to which, if you speak it, all nature will spring free. There will be no opposition to that truth when you speak it.

You can name your Good as free health. All nature will say "Amen!", if you proclaim that the Good you are seeking is free health. Nothing wants its health interfered with, it wants unlimited health. There is a unity of feeling between you and the stones and the thief, when you tell aloud, or consciously, what they feel unconsciously about their health. The moment you feel this truth, and speak it, the chord between yourself and your neighbor chimes into one tone. You catch a new breath of health and your neighbor catches a new breath of health. Sometimes when you say to the sick man, mentally, that the Good he is seeking is his God, and God is free health, he will get well in five minutes. His mind was unconsciously groping around for the Divine Word that could heal him, and you spoke for him.

The prophet who felt there was something lacking in his life said: "We grope for the wall as the blind." It is better for us to speak our own words, but if somebody opens the door for us it will teach us to open the door ourselves. That is, if we do not speak our words and so are not satisfied with Good, another may speak, and our satisfaction will come.

When we say that the Good we are seeking is our free life, we certainly do feel the breath of new life blow through us. When we tell the lifeless plant that the Good it is seeking is its free life, and its Good is God, for God is its free life, we shall see the plant revive. Everything rises to acknowledge Truth. You see that is God, for Good is God. Sometimes you will feel the reviving life stream so hot, like a fine elixer, throughout your being, while you are naming God as free life, that whatever you touch will feel thrilled with a quick sense of pleasure. God works in Truth. Tell the Truth of God and the Omnipotent God is moving.

Nothing can resist the very first proclamation of Truth if we let it be spoken through us. There are many names of our Good. They are all names to which all the universe of worlds nod their heads and oppose not when they are named. The irresistible name is Good. The irresistible name is God. It is an idea which is in everything, everywhere, and therefore you speak an omnipresent idea when you say: "I seek my Good; my Good is my God. My Good is my free life. My Good is my free health."

Another name of the Good we are seeking is strength. All things look for strength. They love strength. The baby laughs at every waft of strength through its little frame. The insect runs and rolls with speechless delight at every quiver of new strength. The Good it seeks is strength unlimited. It wants free, boundless strength. So do you. If you name your Good as unlimited strength, you will feel free and strong at once. As you look at some feeble woman, and think further that the Good she is seeking is unlimited strength, she will let her mind shine with yours. She has felt that unconsciously. She will feel strength consciously. Everything you tell the Omnipotent Truth to, that its strength is God and God is its strength, will rise and be strong; and you will be stronger the more you proclaim the irresistible idea which all creation feels. It is only naming God. It is telling the truth of God.

Among the names of Good which we name, surely our heart-strings will chord with one which will bring satisfaction into our life. So hungry is the world for satisfaction that it has been set down that the problem of life is how to live and think so as to get satisfaction.

The sciences of man have not started their reasonings near enough to the foundation idea of mankind to obtain this end. At the word "God" many a mind rebels, because it has become bruised by trouble and disappointment. At the word that *there is Good for everyone and everyone ought to have his Good,* each mind agrees.

The principal point of truth is that satisfaction comes through Mind. Mind speaking truth through the lips, or thinking Truth consciously, can bring all the satisfaction to the world which the world is seeking. No material process can bring health. By a metaphysical process health will quicken and thrill mankind. Nothing material can strengthen people, but the Omnipotent Truth can strengthen them with all the power of Truth.

Another name for God is support. God is your support. As you turn to the right or the left, you turn for sustaining. You breathe for support. You hope for support. Thus one name for your Good is support. To tell any man who is poor that the Good which he is seeking is support, is to tell him a truth which his mind has held unconsciously always. The chords of his mind chime when you speak the Truth that God is his support, and his support is his God, because it is Good. *God works in Truth.* That statement is Truth, therefore God works for that word. It is not Truth to say that man depends upon any kind of work for his support. His work is not the Good he is seeking. God does not work in the lie which a man tells when he says he is seeking work. He must tell the Truth and God will work for him.

Support is another name for substance. Plato and Spinoza both called God the substance of the universe. All metaphysicians have called God the One Substance. The one support that man is looking for, that will absolutely satisfy him, is that kind of support which will not fail him. Let him sit down alone and tell the truth about what kind of support he is seeking. *God works in Truth.*

Everybody, nearly, tries to cover up the main purpose of his life. He tells all kinds of stories to himself and others about what he is seeking. Often he tells that all he asks is just enough to feed and clothe and house his family. Let him tell the honest Truth — that he seeks for unlimited bounty. Nothing can possibly satisfy anybody short of unlimited supply. God is the idea of unlimited supply which men keep covered so deeply within their minds. If you name your Good, do not fail to say: "My Good is my unlimited support, my unfailing support." The Good will soon bring you marvelous support. New provisions will be made for you. There is no limit to the bounty of Truth. The substance of Truth is shown by the happy prosperity which can come to you, and is sure to come, when you speak Truth.

Jesus Christ said that all who learned His doctrine would have a hundredfold more possessions in this life. Tolstoi, the Russian writer, declared that Christians do not have a hundredfold more than they would have if they were not Christians. But this is because they are not really Christians. In order to be a Christian one must tell the Truth of God. One Truth is that God the Good careth for us. We are told by Jesus Christ to take no care for ourselves. To sit down and proclaim to the universe that "My support is my Good, my Good is my God, thus God is my support," is to stir the air to work with the mountains and seas to bring us our new provisions.

Jesus Christ said we would have tribulations while getting

our Good support by telling the Truth, but he said: "Be not afraid, I have overcome." He meant He had come over all the worldly way of being supported by telling the Truth, and that it would surely come out right with us. Tribulations are the oppositions which we meet by telling the world we get our support by thinking and speaking the Truth. Tribulations are the feelings we have when we first set forth as grown men and women into the way which is exactly opposite to our former way of thinking. It is a tribulation to attempt to cast away all anxiety. It is a tribulation to give up trying to get our living by our old mind.

After practicing the saying that your Good is your support, your old business will not be interesting to you. It will leave you, yet you will have your living. By and by you will have great and wonderful miracles of support come to you. Yet, for a long time, some of those who have told the Truth about their Good being unlimited supply may not have the faintest idea where their supplies are coming from. They need to say that their Good is Intelligence. This is a truth that will soon work out. There will come a time when they will know that their unlimited supplies are in certain places, and they need have no fear of ever losing sight of the rich provision of the Good. Good is God. God is Substance. God is Spirit. Therefore your supplies are to come from Spirit. Your supplies, coming from Spirit, are Spirit. It will not be a tribulation to practice providing for yourself by telling the Truth after a little while.

Another Good you are seeking is defense, protection. Another name of Good is defense. The movements of our bodies are all with the hope of being protected from evil. To be explicit in naming our Good, which we feel is for us, we should not forget to name the Good as defense. To every living creature we say, "God is your defense." It is another chord which the unconscious mind is glad to agree with. There is a bond of unity between us and all things. Fear leaves us. Fear leaves us by telling the Truth. Metaphysicians, in tracing the cause of evil conditions, have all agreed that fear of evil is the only evil. So, by telling the Truth that our Good is our defense, we see that in every place where we proclaim that defense, there is the Good we are seeking. That Good is our God; thus God is our defense.

Love, Life, Truth, Substance, Intelligence, are names of our Good. We may tell that our Good is Truth. This will cause our lips to speak Truth. Pilate asked, "What is Truth?" The earliest Egyptians said, "Truth is God." The continual speaking for several years, by the Christian metaphysicians that "Truth is God" finally brought them to where they could see exactly how Truth is God. It is because the telling of the exact Truth about what Good is, is an irresistible energy for bringing Good to pass.

Men formerly supposed it was truth to say sickness was good for them. They thought it was something sent of God. But God is Truth. Truth is a healing principle and not a sickening principle. They found much sickness following them up all the time. As soon as we say, "God is not the author of sickness; God is Good, Good is Truth, Truth is God," we are brought to where we cannot declare that sickness is Good. Good is God, therefore God is Health.

Love is the Good we are seeking. Love is the highest name of God. Love is the fulfilling of the law. At the height of our spiritual teachings we find God covering us with love. We find ourselves loving all things and all people. Edward Irving put his hand on a dying boy's head and said, "God loves you." The boy lived.

It is well to say that God is unbounded, unlimited love. God is our love. There is an instinctive seeking of all things for love. Love is another name for life. Many a dying man has been saved by feeling his mother's soft kisses on his forehead. Many a woman has lifted her dying face and lived when the sound of her son's voice was heard calling her name. Love is God. Do not forget to say, "The Good I am seeking is Love."

The heights and depths and splendors of Love have not been told. It is the name of God which Jesus Christ used. He said it so much that little children came close to his knees. Poor neglected women followed him. Blind old beggars clung to his clothes. High dignitaries came by night to speak with Him. I do not suppose it would be possible to name the Good by the magic word Love too often. Love is not something which comes to us in any one man, woman, or child, and then goes away. That is only the sign of love. Love, that is God, is eternal, infinite.

The first lesson of the Science of Mind tells the foundation idea of Mind. It has been called the Statement of Being. Being is that which IS. It is certain that the Good that is for us is the Good we ought to have. How shall we arrive at our Good? How shall we get hold of our Good? Not by working with our hands, for countless ages of labor have failed. It is by the Jesus Christ method only. The Jesus Christ method is the Truth method. Jesus Christ means Truth. The Jesus Christ method brings the fulfillment of all our expectations. "I know the thoughts that I think toward you, to bring you an expected end." This expectation of Good has been a long time waiting for us to declare what our expectations are. To expect Good and to be very definite in the mind that it IS coming, is to see it coming.

Many people would have their Good come instantly if they could name it, and have a clear idea of how it ought to be. A little paralyzed girl heard the Paris doctor, Bouchert, praised so highly for his healing power, that she went to see him, and by seeing him she was cured. A blind woman heard a shoemaker praised so highly for his power in prayer that she went to him, and she felt Jesus Christ's teachings so plainly that soon her eyes burst open. They both had a strong and clear idea of how it would seem to be well. They felt that those men could heal them.

If you have a clear idea of how sweet life, free and unburdened, must be, look to this Science to bring you this life. And declare very plainly that sweet, free life is your Good. It will come streaming through you like the elixir vitae of the ancients. Maxwell, the Scotch doctor, caught sight of this fine, fleet life-fire that streams through all the world.

If you think that health is Good, have a clear idea of how sweet, joyous health would feel. Name it as the name of Good. Have a clear idea of what is your Good. It will come and settle upon you. It will sift itself through you. It can be lapped up by all the little tongues of your system.

The word Good is the only word that can make all things. Good with its descriptions is as high as our mind and speech have ascended. There is no spot or place where the idea of Good as ours cannot come. It is the one conviction of animate and inanimate things. It has never been beaten out of anything. Being undefeated and never to be defeated, it is omnipotent. It always knows that it is right. It is omniscience. Know it, for it knows all things. Let the magic name Good be the name of all names in your mind. It is the name that Jesus Christ comes to be understood by. After speaking over the names of the Good, let your mind add the name of Jesus Christ. There was never any other character in history who gave orders to keep repeating his name. Many people will testify how wonderfully they have been led by repeating this name.

Another thing which the name of Jesus Christ teaches is humility and willingness. It is the meekness of character He manifested which brings us the victory over evil. He said, "The meek shall inherit the earth." Once a man who had become completely discouraged determined to let his dog lead him around, for he felt that his dog was more like God than he was. He went following the dog until it led him to a wise and good woman, who in turn led him to be a follower of Jesus Christ. *The meekness of obedience is the mystery of Godliness.*

The Statement of Being was continually in the mouth of Jesus Christ. Let it be in your mouth also. Be definite when you give this statement of Good, which is the Statement of Being. Expect to see it work quickly. Truth is not slow. Truth is quick. With Truth, all is NOW. Jesus Christ said: "Now is the accepted time."

Truth does not have to make things new for you. In Truth it was so from the beginning, as the first verse of Moses reads. All Truth is waiting for you to say plainly what is your Good. The speaking out continuously what we have felt and thought intuitively, is the first movement toward demonstration, toward manifestation, toward satisfaction.

Make now the statement of Good:

> The Good I am seeking is my God,
> > My God is my Life.
> The Good I am seeking is my health,
> > God is my health.
> The Good I am seeking is my strength,
> > God is my strength.
> The Good I am seeking is my support,
> > God is my support.
> The Good I am seeking is my defense,
> > God is my defense.
> Life is God,
> > Truth is God,
> > > Love is God,
> > > > Substance is God.

God is Intelligence,
   Omnipresent, Omnipotent, Omniscient.
God is Life,
   Omnipresent, Omnipotent, Omniscient.
God is Truth,
   Omnipresent, Omnipotent, Omniscient.
God is Love,
   Omnipresent, Omnipotent, Omniscient.
God is Spirit,
   Omnipresent, Omnipotent, Omniscient.

The name "OM" was a name of God which the ancient people of Asia used to repeat, and do even repeat now. They hold their breath while speaking it. It means: Good beyond Good. Far beyond even our ideas of Good, there is Infinite Good, awaiting our words.

Hosea exhorted Israel, "Take with you words and turn to the Lord." The first words we will take with which to go to the Lord are statements of our Good. That is as high as we can think or speak.

Have some special time to make the Statement of Being. This will make you a great thinker. The mind of God will think through you. The words of God will speak through you. The joy of God will sing through you. The skill of Spirit will work miracles through you. The judgment and beauty of God will inspire you. The love of God will melt the hard lot of mankind before you. You will be so one with your words that you will be able to say with Jesus Christ, "I and the Father are one." You will drop off the garments of flesh. You will see that by speaking Truth you are Spirit, and that by speaking Truth you are Omnipotent.

God works through Truth.

If you give up your mind to Truth you are all God. Your substance being the Mind of God, by speaking Truth, you can see that no disease, neither death nor sin, can touch you any more than disease or sin or death can touch God. It is through realizing this that so many strong young students have said that God had set his own name in their foreheads. They read where Moses was told to tell the Israelites that the name of the Good which was working for them was "I am that I am." If ever the name of this Good, which is your God, comes to you, do not hesitate to speak it. All the names of your Good which you can name are right names. Write down the names of your Good which you are seeking. Think over the names of the Good which you are seeking. Speak aloud the names of the Good you are seeking. That will be naming God. And such a practice will be manifested in your life. God is not slow to come into the life of him who acknowledges the Good.

God works only in Truth. All Truth is all God.

There are students arising who give all their mind, might, and strength to Truth.

"If a man keep these sayings, he shall live forever."

CHAPTER II

DENIALS OF SCIENCE

If the statement of what is true from the very nature of our own mind is called to our attention, then we are able to see at once what is not true.

Is there a conviction of Good belonging to you now in your own mind? That is an omnipresent conviction. Everything and everybody believes the same way. You will notice that the instant you acknowledge that there is Good for you which you ought to have, the thought arises within your mind that you do not have the Good that belongs to you. You feel that your Good is absent from you. This is also a universal feeling. Every man, woman, child, stone, stick and snail feels that its Good is somewhere else than in it or with it. This is known as the conviction of absence. The conviction of presence is not uttered. That is, we feel the idea of the Good being for us, but we do not say so, and we feel the idea of the Good being absent and we keep saying so. We think that our Good is absent. We say aloud that our Good is absent.

Do you not see a possibility of entering upon your own beautiful inheritance of satisfying Good by looking this strong fact in the face? Does it not remind you that John, the wise disciple of Jesus Christ, said that without the Word nothing is made? How plain it is that you have been ready with the rest of the world to say that your Good is absent from you. How plain it is that you have been silent on the main idea that there is Good for you which you ought to have. Thus it seems that the silence of your mind with respect to Good is accountable for all the appearances of what is not good.

John, the Revelator, speaks of a white stone. Moses said

the Spirit moved upon the face of the waters and commanded, "Let there be light." Moses and John were lovers of God. They felt great laws and principles moving through the universe and tried to express them. Moses did not always speak in symbols. He said to the people that the "I Am that I Am" spoke through him. He felt the Good within himself speak.

The moment that the idea which has always lain so silently in the mind is uttered it begins to tell great things with respect to itself. This is why it is called the Stone of Revelation — because it reveals. It brings a feeling of light and hope to the mind, and this is why Moses said, "Let there be light". He felt the strange darkness of the talk around him concerning the absence of Good, and instinctively understood the gloom of the silence as to Good. Good is the name of God. The Good that is for you is your God. Do you not move toward your Good? When you wish, is it not for your Good? Thus you are governed by your Good.

The metaphysical teaching calls attention to the law that if you tell the truth about your Good it will appear in your life. It is like speaking of the relation of numbers in arithmetic until you see exactly how they work. Repeat the multiplication tables, and sometime along the way, if you have taken the steps before multiplication, you will see that it is quick counting. If you simply repeat the tables at the dictation of another mind you may have to work a long time to find how to add by the tables of multiplication. But taking the adding and multiplication together it dawns upon you what the after process means.

The Science of Mind always runs by orderly steps in the same way. The first chapter of Genesis is the Science of Mind stated in the exact order of coming forth as power, as intelligence, as substance.

The idea of the absence of Good is plainly spoken enough.

The idea of where the Good must be, and is, we are not talking about as a race. It is to the race mind that Moses addresses himself. John also speaks to the universal conviction of absence. I will tell you that between you and your Good which belongs to you, and which you ought to have, is your idea of the absence of Good.

The second movement of your mind, after telling what truly is, you will find to be the putting away of your ideas that interfere with the substance of what you are seeking. You put away the idea of absence the first time you speak of your idea of Good. Tell the absolute truth about your idea of Good. Is there any absence of it? Is there any mixture of evil with your highest idea of Good? Where do you keep your idea of Good? Do you hide it in your mind and never express it? How do you know how much light might break over you and brighten your life if you would let it come up from the hidden place in your mind — your perfect idea of Good?

It is like every other mind's idea of Good. Thus we deal with the Universal Mind when we tell that in our highest idea of Good there is no evil. We say that in our idea of Good there is no absence. The Good that we are all seeking is our substance. It must be substantial to us. It must be present with us or it is illusion — it deludes. Here then you see why metaphysicians of all ages have made two great denials:

First — There is no evil.

Second — There is no matter.

This is because they looked so steadfastly at the word God, or Good, in their mind that its native action began in them. The Stone of Revealing makes you say that there is no evil and no matter.

St. Augustine said, "There is no evil." Jehosephat said, "There is no iniquity in God." Emerson said, "Evil is negation." They did not explain that it was their idea of Good that it should have no evil mixed with it. If every man, woman and child expressed his idea of Good it would be found to be like every other person's idea of Good.

Spinoza said, "I choose to know Spirit rather than to imagine matter." Channing says that since the beginning of time, in philosophical study, men have held that all is Spirit, and that matter is but an appearance, a delusion, having no reality. Thales, the Greek, thought so. Empedocles thought so. They did not explain that it was because their idea of Good was an enduring and substantial presence that could not fail and could not disappoint. They could not tell that matter is the result of thinking that Good is absent. Matter is that appearance which results from steady silence as to what and where our Good is; we might say as to where and what the Good is upon which subject all mankind are so silent. We may say "Our Good" or you may always say "My Good," for each one of you is the unit of his own life, and all his conditions swing around himself.

Demonstration of mental science means making visible our ideas. We must make it visible that there is no evil if the idea is true. The Truth makes free. All I am expected to do to manifest the Good that is for me is to tell the truth about what and where Good is. Good is God. Thus the making of good demonstrations will surely come out into our life if we tell the truth about God.

Jesus Christ said, "The truth shall make you free." Let us tell the truth. To say, "In my idea of Good there is no mixture of evil," is to tell the truth. It is a truth which will work freedom from evil. It will show that all evil is delusion. Here is where the denial of matter hurries in. Say that in your idea of Good there is no delusion. Very soon all matter will appear as delusion. You cannot say that in your idea of Good there is no mixture of evil without coming straight to the realization that all matter is delusion, built by belief in the absence of Good, which is evil.

Carlyle speaks of the everlasting NO of this world, whereby the world seemed to be a charnal house and demoniacal till he faced it with the stupendous "NO" of his soul, and said to all evil, "I am free." In the Book of the Dead we find how the soul talks after it is not afraid of the body any more. It, the soul, says, "I never committed adultery. I never stole from my neighbor. I never told a lie. I was never intoxicated." Every known sin is pronounced NOTHING. Formerly, it was not thought safe for men to speak these ideas while walking about on this plane of existence.

Jesus Christ said that if any man would come after him he must deny himself while dealing with the world. He knew the mystic relation of boldly spoken Truth to the redemption of man from the conditions of matter. "If a man eat of the bread which I will give him, he will never die." "The flesh profiteth nothing." "The words I speak unto you, they are life." The second lesson of His life was denial, exactly as the second lesson of Moses was denial, and exactly as all profound thinkers have given denials to all claims of mortality. It all comes of putting down the idea of Good in the mind and looking at it as to a white substance or "stone," with power of revealment in it. The highest word that we know how to express is "Good." It is certain that for a progressed realization there must be another word to express what we seek, but "Good" is found to bring us out the most safely thus far.

If we put down the idea "first cause" as a foundation word to watch, it will not be long before we find ourselves knowing all about the causes of all things, whether good, bad, or indifferent. Gautama Buddha thought on "first cause" till he found out the causes of evil, and spent all his years seeking to combat and destroy evil.

Put down the word "satisfaction" in the mind, and it will tell you what will satisfy everybody. The idea "first cause" is very enlightening. It will take the mind back to the cause of anarchy and rebellion. We can soon see that it is caused by the idea religion has given to man, that we all owe so much to God. This is the wrong way to look at God, the Good. The Good owes itself to us. We have only to tell the Truth. If the Truth makes free when it is told, and we are not free, then the Truth has not been told. The Truth that the Good belongs to us is greater than the idea that we might give our time, our labor, our life, and all we are to the Good, and still never satisfy it. To tell how impossible it is for us to give enough to God breeds rebellion at existing orders. To tell that the Good asks nothing of us but to receive its substance, will rest and comfort the people. The word "satisfaction" is a great word to use, but does not show forth as quickly as the word Good. Good is the universal name of God. Satisfaction is not the universal name of God.

In all sciences we deal first with general principles, applicable to all races and conditions alike, and then later we deal with particulars as applicable to special individuals. Thus we hit upon the foundation rock of our convictions when we say, "The Good that is for me is my God."

The denial of matter has never been made satisfactorily. Notice that all the metaphysicians have concluded that there is no reality in it. They have said that it is all the imagination of our mind; but what imagination it is they have not concluded. To persistently declare that there is no matter will dissolve material conditions. It will cause a swelling to disappear if you look at it and say that there is no matter. Whatever of matter seems most real to us is the first to disappear when we deny matter.

If money is something that you cling to, and you say that

there is no matter, it will begin to disappear. If friends in the body of flesh are your idols they will get out of sight swiftly upon your putting forth the denial into your atmosphere. Such is the power of an idea held as truth. The denial of matter is the same as if you said that your omnipresent idea of God is that God is Spirit. Thus your God is Spirit.

Your idea of God must not be burdened with the transient and unreliable. Matter is transient and unreliable, because the idea of Good as absent is transient and unreliable. Sometimes the mind feels that its Good is near, and sometimes that it is far off. So matter, which is the representation of the idea of absence, must sometimes bring you great darkness or void, because of loss, or bring something that pleases you very near. The regularity of the seasons results from the periodic habit that all the race mind has of sometimes feeling that its happiness or Good is interfered with, and then feeling that its Good is near and free again.

Some people keep on the mental strain of feeling that they do not have anything that they want at all. They feel neglected, unloved, burdened nearly all the time. It is such types of mind that make an external region of barrenness and cold. Let every such mind rise and refuse to hold the idea of absence as part of the way its Good deals with it, and the cold regions would soon disappear.

The statement that in my idea of Good there is no absence of Good, compels me to say that in my idea of Good there is no evil. The statement that there is no delay in my idea of the way Good comes to me, compels me to say that there is no matter. Matter is all the hindrance we know. Spirit is free, untrammeled, unhindered, irresistible. Matter is burdened, trammeled, limited, inert. The best way is to make the two denials of unreality boldly. If you wish to help yourself you can say, "In my idea of Good there is no mixture of evil, therefore there is no evil." This is the bold first denial.

How dare you say this? Because everybody and everything feels the same about his idea of Good, but never tells it. Sit down at a certain time every day and write down on paper what your idea of Good is. Write the highest ideas of Good you have. You cannot write a stroke higher than the slave's idea of Good, but you will find that such a practice will pin you down to the truth, and it is in Truth that there is power. All the sacred books of the earth tell that God is Truth, and that Truth is God.

The bold second denial is that "There is no matter, all is Spirit." If you notice that you are opposed to any interference with your Good, you can write it down that in your idea of Good there is no interference and there is no matter.

If you will speak boldly that there is no matter, this will handle all your affairs on a new basis. If you say, "All is Spirit, nothing is matter," that is making a denial of matter. Every time you refuse to believe any statement you are making a denial. Every time you say that a thing is not so you are making a denial. Negativing what is told you, or what seems to be real, but is not real, is a denial.

Looking up suddenly from their deep thoughts, metaphysicians have declared that "there is no life, substance, or intelligence in matter." They have affirmed that all life, all substance, all intelligence is Spirit; and therefore there is no life in matter, no substance in matter, no intelligence in matter. Spirit occupies the place that matter claims to occupy, therefore life occupies the place matter claims to occupy. In the spot where matter even seems to be a dead substance the life of the Spirit is moving. Spirit is the substance where even the stones seem to be.

Spirit is pure Intelligence. There is no place where matter seems to be intelligent, is there? Yet, "*there is no absence of life, substance, or intelligence.*" If the metaphysicians had said this, rather than "there is no life, substance, or intelligence in matter," they would have demonstrated life better than they have. For if life is Spirit, never absent, why speak of "no life"? And if Spirit is substance omnipotent, why speak of substance as "no substance" anywhere, and the same of intelligence?

It was subtle agreement with absence on the part of the metaphysicians to speak of intelligence as absent from anywhere. One reason why the substance of the metaphysicians has so often failed is because of saying, "There is no substance in matter." Yet, that denial in particular cases is a very healing one. As for instance, if a tumor claims to absorb the life of the body, it will disintegrate it to tell that there is no life in matter, as well as to tell that there is no matter. If darkness seems to act with an intelligence of its own or if insanity carries on as if it had shrewdness, it is a claim of matter to be something, and to have an intelligence of its own opposed to Spirit. In such cases you can see that it is wise to say that there is no life, substance, or intelligence in matter, as well as that there is no matter whatsoever. The metaphysicians who have had their minds set upon healing disease, insanity, deformity, etc., have been successful in their work by using this denial.

In the second lesson on general principles we are speaking entirely of certain revelations of our own mind, of the Truth, as they come forth from laying down the word Good in the mind, and making it express what controls and moves us, and what we seek.

Therefore, the third denial is: "*There is no absence of life, substance, or intelligence in my idea of Good.*" Life will thrill along through every pore and cell and fibre of your being if you declare this. It will soon seem thrilling and vibrating every particle of your environment. Nothing can seem to you to be dead. If you speak often, *"There is no absence of substance,"* it will not be long till you feel how unmixed with the miseries around you is your free Spirit. No matter what people seem to be doing they cannot draw you into their network. You live your free life in Spirit as a substance of reality, quite separate from their delusions. All things take on an enduring substance in your sight. You feel supremely real. Life seems real.

If you should be in great trouble you could not get help from God by begging for help. You would get help at once if you would stand aside from your trouble, as above and greater than it. Then you would feel the help of the omnipotent God. Reality is the strength of your free Spirit which refuses to be mixed with evil.

The only cause for evil is the idea of absence. That is all the evil there is. The belief of apartness from Good is the foundation of the word evil. The idea of absence of Good had to be called something, so it was called evil. Ideas always make conditions. Thus the idea of absence, being named evil, finally made a host of phantoms of appearances called evils.

Ancient metaphysicians taught in their practice, "There is no apartness." They hit upon the most perfect denial that could be spoken. It covers all the ground of evil. It touches the cause of evil at its root. If this idea is persistently adhered to it cannot fail to make a vacuum around you into which all Good must come streaming to fill you with delight. The Truth is that Good is God, and God is omnipresent and omnipotent, thus the Good is omnipresent. If the Good is omnipresent, the evil is nowhere present, and there is no apartness. This is the reasoning. All reasoning has the effect of controlling the environment. Your whole life conditions change if you change your modes of reasoning.

Having been trained for years to reason your life out on the basis of Good being absent from you, you now begin to reason from an entirely different basis. You judge not by appearances, but by righteousness. Many conditions slip away almost instantaneously. They were built up by your false general reasonings, and with these gone they have no props. As for instance, you have poor eyesight. It became so because of some little notion you persistently held. You now give up that notion. You cannot help giving up that notion, because the new reasoning makes it impossible to think that way any more. The poor eyesight must fall away for the good eyesight to show up. Some changes occur instantly and some are more slow.

You take an entirely new basis when you say that if God is Intelligence, then Intelligence is omnipresent, for God is omnipresent. Here then you must say that there is no absence of Intelligence. Your mind may suddenly feel very clear and intelligent, or it may be startled. If there is no absence of Intelligence you are now rich with the Intelligence of God. You know all things. There, where the idiot seems to be, you must see that the Intelligence of God is present. Why does a man not seem to be intelligent? It is because of the belief the race keeps shedding over the planet that Intelligence is absent from some spots of God, or some places in God.

When the metaphysicians say there is no life, substance, or intelligence in matter, they unconsciously intimate that there is matter, but it is empty. They do not mean this, and therefore have done some very good healing and restoration of judgment by using this denial. Others have become tangled in the subtle statement and have never been able to do a single bit of healing by saying there is no life, substance, or intelligence in matter. They have believed in matter so strongly that the mention of the name made it seem present. At once it seemed to have no life, and somebody they loved caught the effect of their saying there is no life in matter, and gave up the appearance of life. So with substance and so with intelligence. Yet, that third denial of metaphysics is perfectly correct, and in your use of it may do great works. If it tangles you at all make the third denial in a simple speech, as *"There is no absence of life, substance, or intelligence in omnipresent Good."*

Carlyle felt poor and lonely and incompetent. Hardly one on the face of the earth has not had these feelings. They come from the belief of being apart from God — apart from our Good. Those who have met the feeling with a strong "NO" have routed it out of their premises. Such feelings are the NO to Good. We meet them with the NO to evil. Carlyle calls the meeting of the NO to Good with the NO to evil "The Everlasting NO." He was met so strongly that it seemed as if all nature told him that the universe was void of life, of purpose, of volition. It was one huge, dead, immeasurable steam engine, rolling on its dead indifference to grind him limb from limb. All at once he entered his protest. His whole God-created nature rose and said, "I am not thine, but free, and forever hate thee." He felt that when he entered his protest against the power he began his spiritual birth. He then began to be a man.

"All evil is negation," says Emerson. Negation is nothing-ness. The reality of being is Truth. With the Truth we set ourselves free from negations. Does it not seem as if matter were reality? Yet it is nothing. We speak the truth, and the spiritual power we have rises in its divine substantiality and every material thing becomes subject to it. Does it not seem as if there were absence of life in some things? Yet life is omnipresent. Does it not often seem as if intelligence were lacking? Yet perfect intelligence is omnipresent. Marked and wonderful changes in your life begin with your reasoning along this line.

The fourth protest we make against the claims of matter is to deny that sensation is a physical or material experience. Sensation is a faculty of Soul. Soul is God. God is Spirit, Mind. Thus sensation is a mental process. As God is omnipresent, sensation is omnipresent Good. For ages metaphysicians have called the fourth denial of metaphysics the denial of sensation. But sensation is sight, hearing, tasting, smelling, touching. God is your sight, therefore you cannot lose your sight. God is your hearing, therefore you cannot lose your hearing. God is your skill in every faculty, therefore you cannot lose any faculty or the skill of any faculty.

The main idea of denying sensation was to get rid of the sensations of pain to which mankind are subject. Grief, pain, horror, indignation, are hateful sensations. Had life been all delight, all pleasure, nobody would have chosen to deny sensation. Many, with their minds set upon sensation as painful, or ending in pain, have cured pain in patients by repeating over and over the statement, "There is no sensation in matter."

If they had trained their mind to the high truth that there is nothing to hate, they would never have come to the position where they met pain or grief or indignation, or any of the hateful sensations which all stand for the universal claim that Good in the way of sensation is absent. If Good is not absent, then the sensation of Good is never absent. "At thy right hand are pleasures forevermore." "With thee is fullness of joy." Thus the protests against the absence of Good as joy should not be that there is no sensation, but that *there is nothing to hate.*

The race mind is exactly like your mind in its willingness to make all the protests of metaphysics. It is ready to see that a course of good reasoning will bring out a happy life if a course of wrong reasoning will bring out sickness and misery.

The Roman Emperor, Claudius, kept exclaiming continually, "What do you take me for, a fool?" The idea that others were not regarding him well finally affected him so that he lost his memory, and did indeed appear foolish. People often speak of how little they know, and finally others think so too.

Socrates said that men act wrongly because they form erroneous judgments. When they learn right judgments they will act wisely and well. Nothing straightens out the mind like looking all the claims of evil boldly in the face with the uplifted conviction that there is nothing but Good, telling all things that there is one substance, and that is Spirit, only one life and that is God, only one mind and that is God.

There are five denials, corresponding to the five senses. All five might be used faithfully and not bring to pass the right state of mind. Then there are two particular denials corresponding to the sentiments and moral sense. The five which belong to the race open up great avenues of reasoning which delight the Mind, the Soul and the Spirit. The two which delight the life and love of the heart are the two which relate to your own disposition and will.

Plato's five denials did not touch his character. He rejected matter. He rejected evil. He rejected all that we reason against, very nearly on our own basis but he did not refuse his own prejudices. He had spoken of One Life, One Mind, One Good, then spoke of woman as the failure of blind nature. He could not seem to catch the principle that there is no failure in One Life, One Mind, One Good, therefore there is no distinction of sex in God. He could not rid his mind of some special characteristics. He did not seem to know that it was as necessary to free himself from prejudice as from the belief in matter. So he was always speaking of failure including failure on his own part. He worked over the ellipse to discover its significance and confessed himself baffled by the problem.

Socrates told his pupil, Alcebiades, "It is therefore necessary to wait until some one may teach us how it behooves us to conduct ourselves, both toward the gods and men." And Alcebiades asked, "When shall that time arrive, O Socrates, and who shall that teacher be, for most eagerly do I wish to see such a man?"

Jesus Christ had no prejudices. He condemned nobody and nothing. He felt that all things were under the care and protection of the loving Father. This made his life easy for him to handle. He could lay it down and take it up at will.

There were two schools of theology in Elisha's time. At one of them he found the water very brackish, so much so that the students, who were all men, complained. He put into the water some salt, and the water was instantly healed. Many a student of the highest theology, even on to the five denials of metaphysics, has failed to drink of the healing waters of the Science of Christ, because his moral sentiments were subject to what he believed to be his physical senses. There is no moral chord which must lie mute in the nature. If you are careless about paying your debts your moral chord is not vibrating to some word which you ought to hear. If you use other people's property roughly you do not catch the word which vibrates the chord of honor. If you do the things which inconvenience or weary others your sentiment of justice is not salted.

Often we see people who yield to some trivial temptation while thinking and talking high Science. It is plain that the water of their character is brackish. Hence, like Plato, we all need to meet some special claim of the absence of Good in our life; some claim so subtle that we may not appreciate its presence. A habit of running people down will run some healthy part of our body down into disease. We must indeed think and speak of all people from the standpoint of their God in them as life and substance, instead of from the standpoint of their appearance to us, before our sickness will be cured.

While the two denials we ourselves need are often very subtle, the fifth regular denial suited to the race often leads one into his own needed cleansing. Notice the fifth regular denial. It is this: *"There is no sin, sickness, or death."* Where is there no sin, sickness, or death? In God, of course. Where is God? Everywhere. This removes the sins out of our sight which were put there by our belief in the absence of goodness in people. We shall certainly see people more honorable and chaste for being where we are when we have spoken of sin, sickness, and death as not possible in a world occupied by Goodness. We shall certainly see less sickness if the idea of the people, as being of undivided wholeness of Spirit is real to our mind. We shall be utterly free from seeing death in any form, or under any circumstances, if we appreciate that in omnipresent Life there is no death. If we are not set free from ever coming in contact with sin, sickness, and death by these five denials we may be sure we have some special prejudices of mind to get rid of. Hence it is well to devote one morning every week to reasoning out why we are, in Spirit and in Truth, free from these errors.

Carlyle dates his new birth from such a denial of all that held him in bondage. You must know that sin, sickness, and death had been very real to him, that therefore he went through all these pains of consequences of believing that the Good that belonged to him was absent from him. We can generally point to the very strong ideas of men that certain Good is absent from them when we see how miserably sick or poor they are. It is the same with ourselves.

Let us reason with the Almighty as Job did. He was accused of wickedness as the reason for his bodily ills. He made the grandest protest that had ever been made in the world — "Thou knowest that I am not wicked, Thine hands have made me and fashioned me." This healed him. It restored his good.

Paul said that we should have a reason for the hope that is in us. There is a reason why we ought to be well, intelligent, blessedly happy always. Using that reasoning we come into close touch with our health, wisdom, and prosperity.

John the Revelator saw the second stone of the Temple as sapphire. This is wisdom. It is peace and health. Moses saw the second state of mind as light, brought to us by the Spirit of God. The Spirit of God is the Word of Truth. We are building the temple of our own character. If we take the first lesson of Truth according to Spirit, we lay in Zion the foundation of jasper, which is the diamond, irresistible in beauty and brightness of purity. If we take the second lesson of spiritual Truth we lay the sapphire stone of our character. Our peace and wisdom are set free.

The second lesson of Truth gives the reasons why:

1.   There is no evil.
2.   There is no matter.
3.   There is no absence of life, substance, or intelligence.
4.   There is nothing to hate.
5.   There is no sin, sickness, or death.

The reasonings of Job cover all the ground of why we may declare against those personal characteristics which make up our hardships in life — "Thou knowest that I am not wicked. Thine hands have made me and fashioned me."

Because of this, you may take your habit of scolding at people in a manner far worse than their offenses, and proclaim that as a son or daughter of Spirit you do not chide or condemn anybody. On this plan of reasoning you may set yourself free from the poverty that troubles you, or the sickness that discourages you. On this plan of reasoning also take up the other traits you are willing to name. As a child of God you cannot have a habit of hurting or torturing people by your speeches or actions. You cannot have a habit of being jealous. You cannot feel easily offended. You cannot resent the way people act with you. You are not envious of anybody. You are not filled with eagerness to be praised. You are not cowardly about being blamed. You are not penurious. You are not glad to know that your enemies are unfortunate. You do not feel discouraged when you have tried and do not succeed.

Take some two evil tendencies you have, as a consequence of believing in the absence of Good, and tell God that they are in truth no part of you, because God himself fashioned you in the spirit of his own nature.

It is one duty we seem to have laid out before us as a race, that we reject the idea of the absence of Good by the word of truth boldly spoken concerning Good as omnipresent. This teaching goes forth from the mind in a mysterious influence. Sickness falls away from the people we meet. Death comes and looks into our homes, but hurries away like a dream. Sin falls from the character of our neighbors and they do not seem the same to us anymore. Our own sickness soon sinks into the sands of nowhere.

Try the denials of metaphysical reasoning and see if you do not feel a new freedom. Light on your pathway will break the deepest gloom. You will find something to live for. You can take these denials and dissolve your hardest trial. Take one of your own trials and say that in Truth it has no reality whatsoever. Say that as God fashioned you out of his own Goodness you have never had any trait of character which could result in absence of Good. Tell now that you reject the common feeling of the absence of Good. As God is not absent, Good must be here.

We do not need to wait to be free. As God is free now, so we are free now.

CHAPTER III

AFFIRMATIONS OF SCIENCE

The text of the third lesson of Spiritual Science is, "God saw the light that it was Good." God is Mind. Light is Wisdom. Mind perceives that Wisdom is Good. Mind understands the Good.

You will perceive, as you go on thinking of first principles, that it is your nature to be happy and powerful in proportion to your ability to appreciate what is Good.

If a beggar child, looking through an open gateway into a beautiful garden, is filled with pleasure at the sight, forgetting his misery for a moment, he has given his own character a new vigor of goodness and has increased the strength of his life in some metaphysical relation of mind to life. He has unwittingly given himself a treatment for prosperity.

You will note that, for the most part, the heart dwells with grief upon the contrast between its own lot in life and the bounty and happiness it realizes to be near it, and yet far from it. The heart may still cling to its misery while it is observing happiness. Here is where the office of denial comes in. Denial is elimination. In Science we are taught the value of elimination. The secret of freedom is in knowing what ideas are prejudices and should be dropped out of mind.

Between *om* and *presence* is the little syllable *ni*. Between *om* and *potence* is the little syllable *ni*, — abbreviation for two Latin words. *Ni* stands for *nigellum*. *Nigellum* means nothing. *Ni* stands for *nihil*. *Nihil* means nothing. So, between Om, the Mind, and its rightful possessions of power, place, and Science, or Wisdom, is the claim of darkness, or *nigellum*, which

48

is negation, standing as if it were something, while it is nothing.

Thus, between your mind and the attainment of its supreme bliss is the everlasting "ni," or the very bold assumption of nothing that it is something. By dropping the claims of misery, you step through the valley of the shadow of the apparent reality of misery, into the reality of blessedness divine.

Now this "ni," which lies between you and the presence of your Good, is as apt to be one of your virtues as one of your vices. If you are one who takes pride in never speaking or acting from impulse, and who feels a sort of contempt for people who act impulsively, your virtue is the claim to be something when it is nothing.

Does God take pride in never speaking nor acting from impulse? Let that pride in your virtue be eliminated from your character. Here the apostle Paul on the subject: "Though I bestow all my goods to feed the poor, and though I give my body to be burned, and have not charity, it profiteth me nothing." It is "as sounding brass, or a tinkling cymbal." It is well to act with discretion, but your virtue becomes as sounding brass if you take pride in your discretion.

Suppose you are very prompt in paying your debts and take pride in it, speaking scornfully of people who do not pay promptly; this pride in your virtue hides the virtue. One good day you may believe yourself unable to pay your debts, and if it causes you to be more lenient with people who are careless you will pass the shadow "ni" that stands between your mind and its satisfaction — present, so near, yet with the distance of a personal trait between.

In our last lesson we named these "ideas of absence." We called our protests against them "denials." We spoke of the two particular traits of each human being. These are not innocent traits. They are the habits of thinking which belong to our manner of believing in the absence of our particular good. They are strong men, armed to the teeth, with the determination to stay by us as long as we live. Take yourself in hand, and, looking up to heaven, resolve to reason your special traits out of your life.

Prosperity is the acknowledgment, either consciously or unconsciously, of the presence of God. He who is prosperous has eliminated from his mind some idea which the one who is seemingly not prosperous still holds on to with tenacity.

We are often surprised to see how prosperous liars seem to be. It is because they have eliminated a belief in absence, which leaves a good opening for what they wish for to rush to them. Some liars make good healers on the same plan. They have dropped the one belief in the absence of Good which the poor healer holds on to. The liars get their hardships in some other way than the absence of abilities. They may have some incurable malady in their own body, or some member of their family may be afflicted.

There are seven thicknesses of the claims of negation standing between every mind and the security of its Good. Five belong to us in common. The last lesson should have given you a clue to the claims that seem to master you, but over which you are in reality master. You can see that the claim of being ungrateful for your possessions, or for your education, or for your lot in life as it is, when met by you, melts down and leaves you the master you were when you first came forth from Om, the Divine Mind.

So it is with selfishness, enviousness, jealousy, revengefulness, anger, etc. They are no masters at all, yet they seem to be our masters. So is it with all negation to Good which faces mankind. There is a metaphysical, or mental, process for meeting them all, and utterly dissolving them, as the sun dissolves icebergs. In place of each protest that we make — that is, in place of what we deny — we put the statement of a great Truth.

What is it that abides here, or where your sickness seems to be? Is it not the fullness of the riches of God? The bold insistence upon what IS here, or there, in reality, has been called affirmation.

All science has affirmation and negation. In the science of numbers you subtract what is not wanted from what is wanted. In the science of geology you say, "This is not aqueous rock, this is not igneous rock." You show as much wisdom by negation as by your affirmations. One tells you that this is a picture of Napoleon and a dear friend wounded in battle. You say, "No, it is Aeneas bearing away his father, Anchises." One tells you that sin is a terrible evil which God permits. You say, "No God is the only presence, and tolerates no other nature in his realm but his own nature." If you protest, all sin will seem like a dream of the night, not worth rehearsing.

There are five affirmations belonging to the negations we make, to which I will now call your attention. These are the five Wise Virgins of the object lesson of Jesus. They are called virgins because they are the most simple and reasonable statements the mind can make when telling why the negations of its Good are not reasonable. The two affirmations that belong to you each in particular we will describe under the miscellaneous affirmations. These affirmations are all mentioned in the Book of the Dead. Your two special affirmations are not virgins. They are strong defenders and providers. They are the strength and wisdom of your own life, in its unique relation to all life. As your mother cannot do your eating for you, nor your breathing, so no one can charge you with the strength of your own denials and affirmations.

John the Revelator said that the third foundation stone of the Temple was chalcedony. Our character is the Temple, or the Holy City. The chalcedony is the love stone, translucent like the opal, always gleaming with the purity of the diamond and the heavenly blue of the sapphire, shone upon by the hot sunshine of a light that never fails. There is upon the earth no chalcedony stone like that one John saw, gleaming with the white light of primal Truth, of the omnipresent, omnipotent, omniscient goodness of God with blue flashes of wisdom and unchallenged peace, and the red gold of love, of truth, and goodness, set on fire by challenging negations. Without this stone, character is not glad and strong and fixed and secure.

There is no use making the affirmations until we have made the denials. You will see people affirming that they are God, who are quite willing to do ungodly deeds. This is because they have not met the everlasting "ni" of Carlyle with the irresistible NO! They have not taken their unreasonable prejudices by names and told the reasons why they are free from such claims against them. The strange part about the claims of negation is that, whatever they are, everybody seems to see them. So the two mighty appearances of evil in man, not being met by denials, or bold reasons why they are not realities, leave the character making great religious professions but badly inconsistent therewith, and they fill their neighbors with disgust. When the right denials are made, the affirmations will be exceedingly hot and effective. James, the half-brother of Jesus Christ, said, "The effectual fervent prayer of a righteous man availeth much."

The photographer, in a yellow glass room, has light and heat enough for fixing beautiful pictures upon his films, but still there is a mysterious something lacking, and he cannot take the photograph in such light. Thus, in bringing out the answers to our prayers, the actinic ray, which is the cutting, pungent ray of denial, is as necessary as the sun-ray called actinic is necessary in bringing out the images in photography.

The day set aside for denials gives the mind a clear draught for the finest affirmations to blaze hot on the firmament of our daily life. If a great fire is smouldering under a house, it will never make a bonfire of the house until an opening is made somewhere for a draught. If a powerful steam pressure is set against the machinery of an engine, it will not move a wheel until a valve is opened for a vent for the steam. So the mighty Truth, filling every mind with its energy, waits to move through the sluice-like ways made by scientific protests, like Carlyle's energetic "I am free."

"Let your light shine," said Jesus Christ. He would not have the great Mind, with which we are all stored, hidden under a bushel. He would have our Mind free. It is a good denial of evil to reason out, as Carlyle did, why we are free. We must then affirm our nature, and hold on steadfastly to our affirmations.

The race religions have talked about one Word, somewhere in the universe, which contains all the potency of all denials and all affirmations. Jesus Christ used that Word, evidently, but only to the ears attuned to it was its tone clear enough to be heard by man. So, as nobody received it, he told them to repeat His Name. If you will repeat the name of Jesus Christ you will, step by step, come into His quality of mind. Then you will, step by step, become cognizant of the divine nature charging your being. You will feel a delight in your substance. You will see how the wisdom of God is your wisdom. You will see that your wisdom is God. But you will never realize this till you have given free vent, or clear passage, through your mind, for the powerful pressure of the God Mind to speak and think through.

The syllable "ni" which stands between "om" and "presence," is the thick wall of belief in the absence of Good. It is sometimes called the dark river. It is often called a veil of flesh. It is sometimes called a bridge, over whose mysterious claims we are to walk into the presence of our Good, or over which our Good comes to us. Many men who have accidentally, as it were, stumbled upon the denials of Science, have made some of the affirmations with good effect. They did not make the personal denials. You have seen that personal cleansing is as important as general doctrine.

David cried out, "Cleanse thou me from secret faults." You would, like Carlyle, give a reason why there is no reality to the appearance of faults. To the great Om, which is the pressing intelligence and wisdom of your own mind, you would say, "Thou knowest that I am not wicked, for thy hands fashioned me." You would take your selfish disposition, and to the great Om, or Om Mind, you would say, "Thou knowest that in Spirit and in Truth I am not selfish, for thy thought sent me forth, thy mind thinketh my life, thy hands fashioned me."

It would not be long, after wise and earnest denials, before you would be uttering mighty affirmations of Science, and your life would be consistent with them. Certain of the great Greek philosophers illustrate this truth. Pythagoras, in the sixth century B. C., made certain of the denials of Science. Especially he saw that sensation is mental, not a physical exercise. After determining thus, he found himself affirming that our soul is an emanation from the Universal Soul, and partakes of the Divine Nature. The soul in man is the self-moving principle. Anaxagoras, born in 500 B.C., said that matter is only the result of ideas. Soon after this he had to make an affirmation on the subject of matter as being absent, and Spirit as present. He said the force which shapes the world is not in the nature of matter. It is not impersonal force. It is Mind. This Supreme Mind is distinguished from matter by simplicity, independence, knowledge, and supreme power. Plato, a century later, found that evil is a way of believing and not omnipotent. This denial opened the way for him to affirm, "God is Goodness." A denial and an affirmation always seem to match each other.

When Jesus sent his messengers forth, He sent them in pairs.

You will see, by reading over the characteristics of the men, that one was positive, while the other was negative and receptive; as, for instance, Peter and John. Peter was impulsive and positive. John was trusting and yielding, and therefore coincided with all the eloquent impulses of Peter.

Jesus Christ spoke His sentences with negation and affirmation, as, "Call no man your father upon earth, for one is your father, even God." "Come unto Me, all ye that labor and are heavy laden, and I will give you rest." He put His negations sometimes as if they were realities, as, for instance, He seemed to be admitting the reality of labor and weariness in this quotation, but He called flesh nothingness, so He was not making a reality of its operations.

A young man who was seemingly very sick indeed, said suddenly, "Satan, get out of the way! God Almighty, do your work!" Now the young man had been brought up without any belief in Satan, so he was only meeting a condition of unreality by a name applied to the whole "ni" of the whole world, to the whole run of evil in creation. Jesus often called our belief in the absence of Good by the name Satan. Job called it Satan.

A strong Scientist said he had to meet all his lack of supply by a strong negative statement, or form of expression, or his mind would not work it out into view quickly. If he was requiring money he never said, "I am supplied with all I can use." He said, "I do not need money." And thus he made a clear way for his bounty to come to him. Some people who cannot sleep will fall into peaceful slumber by saying, "I do not need sleep." For, you see, they made the word "need" a great reality. It is the name of their belief in the absence of Good.

The belief in absence takes many ways of exhibiting itself, and clothes itself in many words. Some of you may have the belief in the absence of Good take the form of being grateful that you are so much blessed, more than others. There is no point where one is blessed more than another. It sometimes flatters our vanity to have people tell us how much more of Science we know than they know. Be not deceived into admitting it for an instant. All are partakers of the Divine Mind in equal potency and might. If people cling to us it is because they have not learned to appreciate themselves. When they realize that their understanding, or their wisdom, is good, they will not depend upon you for anything. It is evident, if they do lean upon you, that you ought to think towards them and for them in a way to turn them toward their own relation with their own divine nature.

If you watch yourself, you are likely to discover that you lean upon someone, for companionship or strength or sympathy. Emerson prophesied that the high laws to be taught in the future would teach mankind to find themselves self-companioning and self-strengthening. This is discovery. It comes with the affirmations of Science. It is evident that you must see, as Divine Mind, that your own nature is self-companioning.

Successful men and women, along any line, have borne about within their own minds strong, native affirmations. Sometimes they took them as children. They are hardly aware how important a part in their lives their positive conclusions have played. High resolves made in intense feeling have been like oak trees. One of the Popes told how, as a boy in the field, he decided to be Pope of Rome. Euripides, the son of a fruit dealer in Greece, took some lofty resolve, as a boy, and rose to be the friend of Socrates. With him the glory of the Athenian stage descended into the tomb, says the historian. Virgil, a baker's son, lifted his thoughts on high, and they took him to the plane of such ideal concepts that, when he had written his poems, the Roman people would rise in the theatres to show him the reverence they paid their Emperors. Epictitus, a Greek slave, put the thoughts of his young mind to noble principles of life, and though he was deformed and sickly, his noble affirmations lifted him free from being the slave of a cruel master to being the honored companion of lords and princes.

The young man's ideals wait for demonstration on the heights of affirmation. The mother, whose tired feet touch the hills of light, shall say, "My God is rest." She shall see that her thoughts are good. The care-burdened father shall sight the port of the heavenly city of "Well Done," and God, his God, shall take away his care. "And they shall be mine, saith the Lord of hosts, in that day when I make up my jewels and I will spare them, as a man spareth his own son that serveth him."

The hill-tops of delight are the true meanings of affirmations. They cannot be reached except by clean feet and pure hearts. All the way of life, with beautiful health, beautiful judgment, and happy success, through spiritual doctrine, lies open to him who, commencing with the jasper stone, feels the love gleam of the chalcedony, the third message of Jesus — "God is Love."

The five universal affirmations are:

1. My Good is my God. My God is Life, Truth, Love, Substance, Intelligence — omniscient, omnipotent, omnipresent.
2. In God I live and move and have my being.
3. I am Spirit, Mind, Wisdom, Strength, Wholeness.
4. The I AM works inevitably through me to will and to do that which ought to be done by me.
5. I am governed by the law of God and cannot sin or fear sin, sickness, or death.

Set apart a morning each week to making your mind touch the mountain peaks of the most noble thoughts. They have many ways of being expressed, but these have the substance of them all.

Your own two affirmations, which, if you would use them,

would lift your life out of bondage, must be sought out and
spoken by yourself. If your life seems turbulent, you had better
speak of peace. If your life seems defenseless and unprotected,
tell of the defense and protection of the Most High God. If you
seem to fail in everything you undertake, tell how your God can
take the small and insignificant things of human seeming and
glorify His own name and nature thereby. It is not to the seeming failures of your life you must look for your reputation
among the angels of light, but to the purpose you have held.

"What matter smile or frown,
If angels looking down
Shall each to other speak of thee
In tones of love continually,
Until the name on earth but seldom heard
Hath come to be in heaven a household word."

There is no storm of adversity that can shake your name
through the ages, if your affirmations are lofty enough concerning the dealings of your God with you.

There once was a woman who held on and held out that she
must cast all her care on God. She would never admit that she
got her support from any other source than Almighty God. She
would not admit that her life was assisted, or kept, by any other
means than straight from Divine Mind. She feared nothing and
nobody, because the everlasting God was her rock and fortress.
From being the child of adversity and misfortune, in the seeming, all the conditions of her life grew easy and bright. She
took as a principle to hold in her mind, that the yoke of Jesus
Christ is easy and his burden is light. You may take any position you like and hold on to it, until it makes your life demonstrate it. It will be your own affirmation.

Many people change their affirmations. You can add to your
affirmations, but you should not change them. You may explain
your affirmations, then the repetition of them will help you.

Let us explain the first affirmation that makes the first denial. "My Good is my God." "My God is Life, Truth, Love, Substance, Intelligence — omnipresent, omnipotent, omniscient." Why do we each say, "My Good?" Because we are each the unit around which our Good swings. If we are right, entirely right, in our relation to our Good, and we can explain how we secured our Good, we can tell the world how to attain its Good.

Jonathan Edwards made a noble discovery under this point. He said he found the supreme plan to be that he should attend to the salvation of his own soul. He put the idea crudely, and spoke in the language of his time, which called the exhibition of our divine nature the "salvation of the soul." You can see for yourself that your soul does not need saving; it needs to be made visible. The power of your soul shows itself upon the least little exhibition of determination not to believe in the reality or power of evil. On any plane of thought you will find that the resolve to be on the side of good and right will win victories for you. Health will come plainly into sight. Prosperity is certain to come to you. Happy life comes to you.

Why do we say, "My Good is my God"? Can we not see that every move we make is to get some good to ourselves? Do we not breathe because we think it will be better for us? If you wish to stop breathing, even that will be because you think it more comfortable not to breathe. You feel deeply that there is Good for you, so all the time you do your best to get that Good. It makes the Good your governor. It makes it the governor of your life. Thus it is your God! It is for you to choose to make your God either the most high principle which Jesus Christ taught, or the incidents and happenings of your everyday lot in life.

Whatever draws you toward it, making you think it can satisfy you, governs you, and is your God. This is the reason so many have stood upright on their feet and said, "I am my own

God." They thought it better to be self-ruled or governed, than to be governed by appetite for food, hunger for praise, search for home, quest for health, hope for friends, etc.

It is very safe to say, "My Good is my God." It is then our privilege to say *what* is our Good. We have a natural tendency to love life itself. We may have been displeased with our conditions in life, but we do not mean life itself when we are telling how we hate our life, if it is hard and disagreeable. No, we mean we hate the conditions of our life. We do not think that the free elixir of quickening forever, which breathes like a fine wind through the universe, is not Good. So we look straight toward the free, fine elixir that breathes through the universe, and we say, "Life is Good, Good is God, thus life is God."

It is natural for our mind to love truth. "What is truth?" asked Pilate of Jesus. Whether he spoke jestingly or scornfully or sincerely makes no difference, the fact remains that every man, woman and child would like to know what is really true. There is, even in the mind of the most devoted religionist, always a doubt as to the absolute truth of what he is talking about, when he tells that God was so angry with the world that His Only Son had to take the part of a scapegoat of the Jews, in order to pacify Him for the world He had made having turned out so badly. It seems strange to see educated, noble looking men, standing on high platforms and proclaiming such a childish-acting being as the Jehovah of Goodness. They doubt it in their secret hearts. But nobody doubts that the free fine Spirit that breathes intelligence through the rocks and through mankind is God. This is Truth.

The speaking of this truth leads on to other truth. We seek for absolute Truth; thus our God is Truth. Jesus Christ said, "I am the Truth." He meant that he spoke the Truth. He also said, "I am the Life." He meant that he understood the fine, free, undivided and eternally abiding Life, that fills and swells and breathes, like a wind of delight, through all the universe. Truth is Good. Good is God. Thus God is Truth.

There is an uplifting strength which comes with acknowledgment that God is Life and God is Truth, that does not come to the man who says his Good, or his God, is his beer or his horses or his billiards. The face and form show what the thoughts proclaim as your Good. What have you sought after? That was your acknowledged Good. It has marked your face and form. Take a true thought in your conscious mind and say it, either silently or audibly. Soon you will mark your face and form with another light.

Moses said that the acknowledgment of the right and true God would be like a wind moving across the face of the waters for the light to break over. Waters are conscious thoughts. If we have occupied our thinking mind with what we shall eat, drink, wear, and such subjects, we are in a dark state of mind. It is the Egyptian darkness. If then we begin to occupy our thinking mind with the subjects we call divine principles, we feel the glow of On High shining either suddenly or slowly over and through the mind.

Again we name our Good. We keep on naming our Good. We say our Good is Love. We do not mean the selfish clutch of some human being upon our time or attention, our body or our thoughts; we do not mean the clutch we sometimes feel upon the time and attention of some other human being. We do not mean the clutch we feel toward money, toward food, toward home, toward animals or friends. No, we mean the free, fine life of delight, that streams with kindness and mercy and gentleness and entrancing beauty through the universe, and draws, with its irresistible kindness, all things and all people to love it and feel its love.

"I drew them with the bonds of love and they knew not that I healed them," said the goodness of Divine Love, that never clutches at us, nor is caught by our hungry clutching. It is the Most High Good, nameless in the life of man while he seeks material good, and nameless in our thoughts while ever we think there is some power operating against us; nameless in our thoughts while we believe there is something good absent from us; nameless in our mind while we think we have inferiority or hardship or suffering or loss. The Most High Good is Life, Truth, Love. There is a wonderful uplifting energy in the words "Most High God." The mind is lifted to higher feelings of truth and love. The Most High Good is higher than any good we have yet realized. So we speak on the lofty heights of our highest words. Out of the reach of words we have the Love that draws the universe, and keeps all things seeking and seeking it, but never finding it, until the mind meets the great plane of unreality, and strikes it with the omnipotent NO!

"Yea, I have loved thee with an everlasting love: therefore with loving-kindness have I drawn thee." It is the true and eternal Substance that woos us with its everlasting love. To lay hold upon your Good is to be satisfied. Then there will never be any feeling that what we love and are satisfied with will leave us, or fail or disappoint us. God is Love. Love is God. God is eternal. Eternal Love is God. When we love somebody, and then later do not love, it is only that we have a mental feeling of absence. It shows that while we felt the love, we gave no word to it — that it was eternal God.

It is by use of the right word to all things that they show their real character and do not hide from us. The delight that we now feel in the little glimpse of the feeling called love is a foretaste of a substance that we have here at hand, hidden only by our feeling that our Good we were to lay hold upon is absent.

One and another of the world's great thinkers have found that there is a shadow system gathered over us that is a great, dark something, hiding us from the Good we are seeking. If you study into the matter you will see that it is all a mental state. Rise, as Carlyle did, and proclaim your freedom from the claims of your incompetency and ignorance. It will vanish, and you can stretch out your hand and lay hold of some new good each moment.

You will first notice your freedom from sickness. Then you will see how much better you get on with people who seemed before to be hard and ugly. You will notice that your own disposition is better. You will soon be more prosperous. Many things will change in your favor that hurt you before. It is the only way offered to mankind to change by a method at all worthy of the idea of the easy yoke and light burden Jesus promised, by accomplishing great works through a doctrine.

To some it seems an easy task to sit down alone by themselves and reason out their freedom. To others it seems almost like nonsense. The reasoning seems right enough, but its basis is so different from that of the world that it seems that there is a fallacy in it somewhere. To such we recommend the fact that many have stumbled upon the process without knowing they had touched the keynote to all power of God for all men.

For instance: a Russian General once said that when it seemed as if his body were too sick or weary to undertake the hard tasks of the day, he would say to it, "You must be strong and able; you cannot be sick or feeble. Do as I wish you to do. Be up and about your business." Soon he got his body so trained that it would rise from a great claim of misery .

The father of Henry Ward Beecher would say to his overtaxed mind, "Go out, every thought. I will have none of you in my mind; I will shut the doors and lock you all out." After awhile he could shut out every thought. Napoleon Bonaparte could do the same thing. If it is hard for you to fasten your mind to a treatment, such as this, write down just what you would like your body to do and be, and read it over at intervals. Read it aloud. By and by you will accomplish with your body exactly what you wish. We are entirely built up and moved by our thoughts.

In the "Theologia Germanica," a religious book written about the time of Martin Luther by an unknown writer, we read that if any practice in religion seems at first hard and almost impossible, one should persevere in practicing it, until it becomes easy and natural.

In this statement of what God is, we say, "God is Life, Truth, Love, Substance, Intelligence, Omnipresence, Omnipotence, Omniscience." Everything that is evil seems present enough. That which we call good may seem to fail us easily. Presence which endures is Substance. That which we can take hold of, and keep, is the kind of Good we would have. Paul tells us to feel after God. God is Substance. God is Good. Our Good is Substance. It is a very good part of the statement of Truth to say that God is Substance, present with us. Our Good is substantial presence. For people who believe that their Good is absent it is a helpful word. There is no poverty, no lack, no loss, no want in this word Substance. Our God is near as Substance.

If you are one who believes that you are absent from your beloved friends, this part of the statement of Truth will bring you great satisfaction in some marvelous way.

Nothing is out of reach of the power of these statements. After awhile they come around with their fruit like seeds to fruitage, or like planets to their orbits.

It must not dismay you if you do not work with your mind as quickly as others. There is always one thing in which each one of us is quicker than others. It is a great practice to offer glad praises that God has made the way of the Holy Spirit through you so successfully. There is a self-supporting power in the Holy Spirit which, when you let it operate unhindered through you, leads straight to your substantial support. People will think you fortunate, but it will be simply because you have thought on a high plane of provisions till you have opened a gateway of mind. Support is Substance. Skill in action is Substance. If you can do things skillfully you have the substantial action of the Holy Spirit. The Most High Good lets fall the easy touches of her all-powerful fingers. Give glad, joyous praises every night, before going to sleep, to the Most High Good, that the Holy Spirit fills your thoughts with ardor, and fires your affairs to splendid achievements.

Your Good is practical, substantial satisfaction. You must be satisfied in mind to be utterly satisfied, must you not? If the beggar child, looking through the window into a home of plenty, and forgetting her physical misery because her mind is so happy, can keep that up for five minutes, she can cause her mind to draw someone to feed her body that very day. Suppose you multiply your soul's delight in the knowledge that God is the very substance of the things you want, by a number of degrees more than her delight, the arm of the Lord is not shortened that it cannot save you from every want.

God is Spirit. Then you see the Substance you long for is Spirit. Very well, be spiritually happy, and the material shadows, the affairs of your life, must be happy. This is the process of intelligence. We have to use our intelligence to be acquainted with our Good. God is Intelligence. When we know God we have touched the very substance which can inform us how to work each minute wisely, so as to be clothed and fed and housed and healed, without any other process than simply knowing God.

To know God is to be God. We are exactly like what we know. Does it not take intelligence to know intelligence? The more we can appreciate that the mind is God, and that it is the only intelligence there is operating through the universe, the more we know in and of ourselves. It keeps fixing the mind to new intelligence to say, "God is Intelligence." The Psalmist wrote how the mind of God is forever saying, "Acquaint now thyself with Me and be at peace." In you is all knowledge. By saying that God is Intelligence, that God within you begins to show forth through yourself great wisdom, along some line. You may be very wise in healing the sick. You may be very wise in speaking in public. You might suddenly be able to speak in many languages, as did the apostles of old.

The words applied to the Most High Good, as "omnipotence, omnipresence, omniscience," will enlarge your sphere of action, by lifting your mind away toward the heights and depths which do contain God, the eternal changeless Principle. You are the mind that stands back and uses great words to express your ideas about the Most High Good. Do not get entangled in your own words. You are greater than any words you ever used. At present you use words to approach unto your own Good. *There will come a time when you will not use words.*

The Eastern mystic repeats the word "OM" by drawing in his breath and speaking the word twelve times. Then he holds his breath and repeats the word twenty-four times. Finally he feels that he himself is "OM". To feel that Om is your substance, your life, your mind, is greater than to feel that the words you say are OM.

The only words you can speak and be identified with, wisely, are, "I am my own understanding of God." These words bring you face to face with the highest of yourself. You can be identified with your own understanding of God. Understanding, as far as you have it, is the Mind of God. It is perfect as far as you have it. To speak of it as yourself increases it within yourself. People who speak of God as a wonderful being sending calamities are not exhibiting their understanding of God. They are hiding it.

In you is the understanding of God in perfection. Speaking of your understanding intensifies it. So, the second affirmation, which is, "In God I live and move and have my being," has always meant "In my own understanding of God."

There is a great intensifying of fine intelligence in the mind that stands up and identifies itself with its own understanding of God. No word can express your understanding of God. You are it. Live in the second affirmation much, "I am my own understanding of God," or this one, "All that God is, I am." It balances the denial, "There is no matter," for understanding is not material, it is spiritual. And what understanding of God you really feel, or really show is all the substance you show. Your understanding is your substance. This is true of everything. Its only substance is its understanding of God. This leaves Spirit the only substance.

The third affirmation is, "I am spirit, mind, identical with God, wisdom, strength, wholeness." This is your understanding, which is the same substance that God is. If we have called God Spirit, then we are also Spirit. If we have called God Mind, then we are also Mind. If we have called God the Universal Breath of Life, then we also shed abroad the Universal Breath of Life. It will seem to cause fine, free nature to make itself felt through you in power. Wisdom will beam from your countenance. Did not Aristides tell Socrates that his presence illuminated him with wisdom? So, all who let the Spirit be themselves, as it is God, will show the same spirit as God. So, all who let the Mind be themselves, as it is God, will speak and think the thoughts of God in wisdom. There will be no loss of mind, no weakness of mind. Thoughts will flow free and strong. Thoughts will shed abroad healing. Thoughts will reflect their thinker. That is, we mean by reflect, that they will shed abroad the Mind of God by wonderful thoughts, which can accomplish great and wonderful things.

All power is given unto Mind. All accomplishments are given under the power of thoughts. The world will uncover from its shadows of grief and sin by right thought. The world has covered itself with pain and poverty by wrong thought.

The fourth affirmation is, "God works through me to will and to do whatsoever ought to be done by me." That is true. Our understanding does all that is done for us. We are clothed and fed and housed and healed, we have all our blessings by our understanding. This is God. If we would have these marvelous works increased or perfected, we must intensify our understanding. This is being more of God. We may be all of God or we may be as little of God as we please. Being free to speak what we please, and thus free to make our understanding show forth great or small, free to make our world, we therefore make what we now experience by our understanding of God.

If you put up with many small annoyances, thinking that by such conduct you smooth things out, is it not your understanding of Good which causes you to act that way? If you would have your conditions perform to please you better, you must understand a larger Good. Whatever you do, and whichever way you turn, it is certainly by your understanding of Good. The statement, "God works through me to will and to do that which ought to be done by me," can be put in this way, "My understanding makes my world according to itself." Either way of putting the affirmation will perfect your understanding. Yet, when I say, "perfect your understanding" I do not mean that your understanding can be perfected. What I mean is that you have never loved your understanding enough. There is nothing you can be so well pleased with as your understanding. Watch it, and give it credit for all the Good you receive. You will soon love it, and this is loving God. Thus you will be in the same idea with God who saw the light that it was

Good. It is the mind seeing that its power of understanding is Good, that brings it all its Good.

The fifth affirmation, which matches the fifth denial is, "I am governed by the law of God, and cannot sin, cannot suffer for sin, fear sin, sickness or death." Do you remember the fifth denial? It was, "There is no sin, sickness nor death." Why do we call them regular denials and affirmations? Because they are those reasonings which, step by step, come forth after saying that first foundation sentence, that there is One Power, One Presence and One Mind. That One Mind, which occupies all things, says there is Good. The conviction is understandable, thus all-powerful. The Good is. The Good is God. Thus God is. There is One Mind and that is Good. Thus God is Mind. There is One Power and that is Good. Thus God is Power. There is one everywhere present idea that is Good, thus God is omnipresent as the idea of Good. After reasoning this way from your own mind you cannot help making the denials of Science.

Remember, denials mean rejecting the appearances against Good. Appearances against Good are the negative of Good. This we meet by denying the evil and proclaiming the Good. It is as if something denied the Good. We meet the lie with the Truth. We meet the appearance with reality. We meet the claim of absence with the truth of presence. This we have sometimes called the omnipresent "No." We have called it universal negation.

Logic is mental reasoning. We are reasoning out the laws of the action of Mind as it conquers the universe with righteousness, when we step along in ideas with Moses and Jesus. All mankind sets out to overcome evil; to overcome ignorance, pain, sickness and grief. But it is by instituting other forms of ignorance, pain, sickness and grief, that all achievements of the earth are wrought. Wars and hardships, and cruelty of

man to man mark the great works of the world. By way of
Jesus Christ there is peace on earth, good will to all men.
It is by taking hold of a doctrine which, by thoughts and words
of a certain character, lets all things come to pass as God wills.
It is that action of the mind whereby all mankind would let
the reign of God come on earth, and be glad to let it come.
Their whole nature is changed by seeing the reasonableness of
the reasoning.

The fifth affirmation is the same as saying, "I govern my
world by my understanding of Good, without sin, sickness, or
death. I understand God, therefore I love God." You certainly
do govern your world by your understanding of God as Good;
and if you have agreed to say that you see how it is possible
to get along without sin, sickness or death in your world, it
is your privilege to say so. You realize that you are governed
by your understanding of Good. This is your understanding
of Good. This is your God. It is God. It is all the God there
is. It is Principle — high Principle.

He who knows the unreality of sin does not fear it nor
grieve about it. He who knows the unreality of death pays
no attention to it. To him there is no sin, no sickness, no
death. To him there are other affirmations easy to believe.
He can say with the Psalmist, "With me is understanding! I
am strength!" He can heed the Voice that came to the prophet,
"Say not, I am a child. See, I have this day set thee over the
nations and over the kingdoms." You will feel that you are a
transcendent nature. You cannot help feeling that all power
is yours to use. You cannot help using your divine wisdom
and power. You cannot help understanding Christ, and as you
understand Jesus Christ you have His mind. When you have
His mind wholly, you have an understanding of the apostle's
injunction to let the same mind be in you that was in Jesus
Christ. Then you will understand how so many Scientists have

spoken of their divine nature as God, and you will see that it is through not yet understanding that others have criticised them. Your nature is God. Your possessions are power, wisdom, and substance.

Between you and your possessions lies the claim of the absence thereof. You proclaim your right of way, and down falls every evil. Try it, and so prove your divinity. It is written in the Scriptures, "Prove thyself." We prove ourselves. By uniting with our power we are married to God, our Good. We are identified with our understanding. This is marriage. Jesus Christ was married to God in that He was united to His understanding.

All your noblest aspirations are to be fulfilled by being in full understanding of God.

Set apart one hour, or one day, each week, to affirm your divine relation to God — your God.

CHAPTER IV

FOUNDATION OF FAITH

The words "Omnipresence", "Omnipotence", "Omniscience", grant revealing. The dividing syllable "ni" between "Om" and "presence" means nothingness or absence, as explained in Lesson III.

If a principle is nothing to us until we know it, this principle of the value of words in relation to our lives may seem to be unreal until we watch the difference which knowing the nature of words makes in our lives.

We silently speak the words omnipresence, omnipotence, omniscience. Soon we feel larger and more powerful and wiser. Perhaps we do not see that our duties increase. Our power to carry on large affairs enlarges. Our judgment is better. Perhaps we do not see all this quickly.

The Brahmins attained to great power and wisdom by meditating much on "Om," their name for God. The presence of the "Om" is Substance. They dealt wisely with the great negation, except in some instances. When the claim of the ages met them, saying that Brahma had made woman without a soul, they did not say, "It is not true, the soul of woman is Brahma as the soul of man is Brahma, for He knows no partiality." They neglected other negations in the same way. They did not meet them with the right "NO". In our own time we have similar things left undone which we need to do.

There is always one perfect way of meeting every situation and every affair so as to adjust it rightly, and see it come out well. Carlyle tells us, "The situation that hath not its duty, its ideal, was never yet occupied by man". In your life problems

every one of them has a way, has exactly ⌐
with, so as to have it come out right at or

There is a way to raise the dead instar
to heal the sick instantly. There is a way
in all art, science, and language instantly.
far as known, we are conscious of putting i ⸺ ⸺ needed and
leaving out some non-essentials. We keep our mind's eye fixed
on the Science, with our whole mind, that we may drop what
we do not need from our statements and bring forward what
we do need.

If a Scientist has a sickness which he cannot meet with
prompt nullification, he has not touched the keynote to his own
power. If he has poverty or grief which he cannot make leave
his premises, you may not scorn him, you may simply see that
he has not touched that sentence which, if he would speak it
as truth, would heal him of poverty or grief.

The main thing to do for a demonstration is to notice what
sentences work quickly in your behalf, and use them altogether.
They have revealing power, and will quickly put you on the
track of your right line of thinking. This is wherein the orderly
arrangement of the Science is, so far as we have it, of the
greatest benefit. It follows the order set out by Moses, and
is so arranged that we can tell on what line of thought we are
strong, and on what line we must add to our strength.

The first (Lesson I) is a statement of foundation principles.
The second rejects whatever contradicts those propositions. The
third rallies every idea that confirms them. The fourth tells
our relation to them, as to why and wherefore our lot in life
is as it is, and may become what we please.

Jesus Christ called this fourth lesson "Faith". He did not
say, "According to thy denial or according to thy affirmation
be it unto thee", but, "According to thy faith be it unto thee."
Moses said, "Let there be a firmament in the midst of the

aters." "Ment" means mind, from the Latin word "Mens."
We call a firm mind "Faith."

If you see a tailor cut up a long strip of broadcloth, you
know he will bring forth a beautiful coat from the apparently
useless cuttings. This is confidence in the correctness of a process. We see the sick child receiving the right thoughts of a
practitioner or healer, and we commence to believe, although
there is no sign of healing as yet, that the healing has begun.
We have this confidence in our life conditions when our affirmations are working.

Paul noticed that the people who accepted the Christian
ideas had moments of great exultation, then they suddenly fell
into deep depression. He said, "Call to remembrance the former
days, in which, after ye were illuminated, ye endured a great
fight of afflictions." He saw how often it happened. Moses
called trials "water". We have it in poetry and song to this day.
"When peace like a river flows over my soul, when sorrows like
sea billows roll," etc. Again, "The waters of sorrow are drown-
ing my hopes." Then is the time, says Moses, when we must
show firmness.

He who shows firmness in the midst of surging miseries
solidifies a firm character. He makes a substance of his mind.
Faith in the success of Good, when evil seems to be harrowing
your life, will act like a gallant ship plowing the stormy main.

People often know the "promise" passages of the Bible
by heart, but when trouble strikes them they have no confidence
in them as absolute Truth. Just once holding on to them when
you are in trouble would give you a good start in faith. Holding on to the great principles set forth in Scripture, while you
are in trouble, will invigorate your character marvelously. It
is the very mystery of godliness. How sure people are to come
out right who have a strong, honest confidence that they will
come out right! It is a perfect proof of the teachings of Jesus

Christ, "According to thy faith be it unto thee." As a result of your being certain that the thing which has come surging over your life cannot hurt you at all, soon the perfect condition will show forth, and things will come out right.

Bacon said that he had never made up his mind that a firm conviction that things would turn out right helped them to turn out right. He thought it helped us to bear things cheerfully, but was not certain that it affected conditions. We will not take Bacon's shaky uncertainty of the Omnipotent. Jesus said, "Thy faith hath made thee whole." It is rather strange that Bacon did not have confidence in the wisdom of Jesus, enough to take His teachings for granted, whether he himself had proved them or not.

We must know what we are to have faith in. We are to have faith in God, said Jesus. Thus we have faith in the Good as cutting out our life conditions just right for us, no matter how much evil there seems to be operating against us. God is Life. Thus we are to have confidence in Life as the outcome, no matter how death may seem to act. Life will win. We must be firm on this point. God is Truth. We must believe that the truth about the Good will act anyhow. We must be sure of it. We speak boldly that our patient will live. This is the truth about Good. Moses said, "Be firm." Paul said, "Stand." Jesus said, "Thy faith hath saved thee."

Truth about Good is God. You may go away out of the room from the sight of what death seems to be doing and tell the Truth. Truth is God. God is omnipotent. You will strike the life key of the patient and he will live. Every man, woman, and child has a life key. You have the skill to touch it and turn him into free life. So with the truth about any situation. Tell the truth about your child, about its goodness. Its goodness is God. No matter how much evil may sweep over that child be firm in saying, "All is well, God reigns, my child is good."

Tell the same truth about health. Be very firm. Tell the air around you that health is God. Sickness is not God. God is all. Sickness is nothing. Then be firm. Say nothing else. Stand to it. Allow no other idea. That is Truth. Why should anything but Truth interest you. Why should what seems to be sickness baffle you and fill your mind, if the Truth is God, and you have the Truth in the possession of your understanding?

Begin today to practice this: Look into your life, look it over and see what you lack. Then tell the truth about it and be firm. See how it will come out. Faith means, to be firm. Faith brings things out all right. Firmness on the side of evil is stubbornness. It opposes Good. As evil is not God, there is not a particle of power in evil. You may argue that the child will die because death seems to be acting, but the man who sees that Life is Good and is firm, will beat all your ideas of death, even if one hundred thousand doctors are on your side, for death is not God; Life is God. Lies are not God; Truth is God. Stubbornness to bring out death, or keep a person sick, is not God. Firmness to bring out health, because health is Good, is God. That is, Faith itself is God. Hence we have Jesus telling us "Have faith in God."

We have a mental quality which can increase faith, so that the whole world does as we say. It shows Good at every turn. It drops its evil appearance at every turn. We become very firm in Good. We do not give a farthing for evil. We laugh at it. We ignore it. It is nothing. We are so firm, so steady, that all things are seen by us as God made them.

There is one thing about your firmness that I wish to speak of. It is this: You need not try any experiments of putting your will on the patient, nor against evil, nor for Good. You may only tell the truth about God. The Truth is its own will. It is the omnipotent Will. You might get weary trying to exercise your will, but you would become strong from being firm. The truth that you speak asks only your announcing it and standing by it.

There is a generation of faith, like the generation of electricity. We speak the truth about the Good as sure to come out in our life or in our work. We stand firmly to the truth. It goes out stronger and stronger as a power to drive back the belief in and appearance of evil. We do nothing but speak the truth and stand to it. If we feel confident one moment that all will come out right, just because a little appearance for the better shows up, and then our heart sinks the next moment because a bad appearance sets in, we are unstable. We are judging by appearances and Jacob said to his son Reuben, "Unstable as water, thou shalt not excel."

Firmness as to Mind, or Good, being the power, does not make the Good come out right — it makes us see the Good in its true light. All is Good in reality. We have power to see things in reality. We see things in reality by being firm in our minds. The firmness of our minds as to Good is the original substance of all things. Thus substance touches substance when we speak the truth to the sick man. He is drawn out into sight as well. He is exposed as alive.

Firmness to any principle will expose a power. More than that, it will expose the very thing you seek in it. If you have, for instance, set your mind to heal heart disease, and are sure that there must be a remedy, keeping firm to that idea and seeking for the healing of heart disease, your mind will get firmer and firmer, till one day it feels a quickening certainty. At that moment you may be handling clover leaves. You give some clover leaves to the patient and he gets well. Then you insist that the clover leaves made him well and cured him. But it was the new quality of your own mind.

Firmness developed a new working efficiency. You might have been handling camphor-gum at that time and it would have been the same. While you keep your mind and heart intent upon healing heart disease those clover leaves will obey the streams of healing energy that quiver forth from your soul. When you have withdrawn your thoughts, or the influence of your mighty confidence has passed into another realm, the clover leaves will no longer cure.

Paul's aprons and handkerchiefs served to cure people, because radiating from him went a buoyant confidence in his own principles. Shaky and feeble people felt the confidence of him as a brace. It took hold of that concealed substance within their own natures and it recognized itself.

All great remedies discovered by man have owed their curative energies to the continuous confidence of some firm mind. When that mind left the remedy it would not work. It is for this reason that the faith should be set on God. God is eternal. Faith in God being generated on the earth, everything and everybody will breathe it, and it will touch the substance of their life and unite them to eternal cure.

Abram was working for the power of faith and suddenly received it. He had an "H" from Jehovah's name inserted within his own, and he became Abraham, Father of the Faithful. This was the mysterious old-time way of expressing every mental quickening by calling it a direction straight from the Lord. So it was indeed.

All the liberating of the inner fire within us to operate on the world without us, by laying hold of its substance, is the speaking of the God voice within us. This voice may come from the God voice without us, as it did to the prophets. If we feel that around us is God we may hear a voice from the bushes, like Moses. We may hear a voice from the air, as Samuel did. We may hear a voice from the clouds as Jesus Christ did. If we contemplate the God within us we shall feel the voice within us, and it will be as audible as if it were without us. Whichever way we may hear it we seem to turn our faith in that direction, and so our strength comes from that kind of faith. If we are determined that ALL is God we shall not be limited to the voice within nor the voice without. Everything will bear witness that we are in God. Then there is no seeking, and no command to be firm. We are firm and fixed in our eternal Godhead and power.

This Science pursued has four accomplishments to work out. Jesus Christ said it would give you power to preach the gospel, heal the sick, cast out bad tempers, and raise the dead. Every time the waters of opposition float over us we stand firm, and the Good comes into sight.

The fourth idea with which this Science deals is the doubt that the Good is working to prove itself quickly in our behalf. This doubt has a rushing and overturning action with us. You all know what it is to fear that you are not going to have things come out your own good way. This is doubt. It shows that either consciously or unconsciously you have been taking some high thoughts of God. Likely you have thought of God from a much higher standpoint than your minister or preacher or anyone ever spoke to you. It was so much higher than the world that when the trial came you could not reconcile the conditions with the great goodness of God, which you felt to be true. So you doubted that Good was cutting out the pattern of your circumstances to please your heart. Here is where you are to remember your highest thought of God which you have ever held. Hold it firmly. If need be you may speak over your truth rapidly and constantly, so as not to let any other idea be spoken by you, even in thought.

Nehemiah, the builder of the walls of Jerusalem, would not listen to anything but his own ideas of the presence and power of his God; so he succeeded, to the astonishment of his enemies. Ezra built the temple in conjunction with Zerubabel, when neither of them would listen to one word against the power of Jehovah to take a feeble and weakly congregation and out of it build a mighty people.

Miracles are nothing to the power of this faith or firmness, when it is once liberated in you by your firm holding out for the omnipotence of Good, for the omnipotence of the truth of Good, for the certain action of the principle of Goodness. This was so plain to Jesus that he said one grain of faith would move a mountain. Faith is a self-increasing property, just as jealousy is said to be. The jealous person, you know, sits down and imagines a whole sequence of actions. He then feels so strongly that he acts upon his feelings and does dreadful things. His jealousy feeds itself by his thoughts until it handles him entirely.

Faith in Goodness will feed itself and increase itself in the same way, till we rise and work miracles by reason of it. We do not seem to handle our faith. It handles us. We become faith. We always were our faith. It is, in its intrinsic nature, God himself. So, one name for God might be Faith.

In pure spiritual doctrine we have an axiom for the science of denial in its relation to environments. It is that mind is as free as it has courage to deny. Looking around us we perceive that what our mind determines the environing circumstances demonstrate. We are as free from evil as we refuse to think about it. Whatever of evil we think about, that we are mixed up with. Whatever we positively will not think about we never get hurt by.

There is another very beautiful axiom. It is that mind is as great as it has courage to affirm. This also will demonstrate in the life. "I will be Pope of Rome," said a little boy, and he was. "How did you become so great?" they asked Sir Isaac Newton. "By intending my mind," he replied. An intention is a strong affirmation. "I will be an artist," said a child. He could not even draw a plain picture well. Yet, he became a wonderful artist.

For this fourth lesson there is an axiom which is very true in demonstration. It is that mind will certainly demonstrate as much greatness as it has courage to stand by its intention. It is not so much by what we do as by what we think that we stand by our affirmations or intentions. For instance, no amount of dosing with drugs, or rubbing, or poulticing, could avail to cure your patients. But your mind holding firmly on to its denials and affirmations is certain to cure them, though you do not lift a finger.

Euripides, a Greek dramatist, was one of those thinkers of the far past whose axioms have come down to us. About 450 B.C. he said, "One right thought is worth a hundred right hands." And so it is. A child's prayer can do more to clothe and feed a family than its father's daily toil; exactly as your treatment in a sick room will do more in curing than a hundred doctors' best prescriptions.

In all great lives you will see that it was what they did when some storm of adversity struck them which made their characters count. Nehemiah never flinched when they told him that if he stayed outside the Temple he would be slain. When they threatened him he arose and said, "Should such a man as I flee? I will not go in!"

Paul sang praises to God in prison, Silas joined him, and a great earthquake shook the foundations of the prison at the sound of their singing. Certain tones have power to shake rocks, to crumble walls, to lift weights. Paul and Silas thought only of omnipotent Good, and it shook off their bonds. It opened their prison doors. This way of treating exile was so different from the way Seneca acted, who was exiled about that time, and wailed and lamented so abjectly that his high-sounding phrases seemed a mockery.

There is always once at least when we are called to stand steady to our principles. In one of the Bronte novels it is spoken of in beautiful language, that we do not know the value of our high principles and laws until we test them in trial. Take this night your hardest trial and put some denial and affirmation before it. Then from that hour stand by your denial and affirmation. Stand firm. This is your faith that builds character. Nothing is sure at all in your life until it has been put through the furnace, which is the meeting of the opposite to it with its noble steadfastness to itself.

"There is a spirit in man, and the inspiration of the Almighty giveth him understanding," says Job. This spirit in man is his God. The inspiration is his breath of God. The God within and the God without are united by breathing. But the external breath of air into the lungs is only a symbol, a hint of the true breath which right thoughts can give, if they are put forth and taken in at the moment of intense experience called trouble. It is equally powerful if in a moment of great joy one keeps firm to the same great Truth. Firmness is poise, balance of character. Balance, poise of character is a great healing quality. We become healers of disease according to our poise of character.

The thoughts of Good within us are opposed to the beliefs of evil that seem to swell and surge without us. This makes an apparent conflict. If the firm will stands by the Good "the middle wall of partition" is broken down. Paul speaks of the thoughts of evil, which make seemingly evil conditions and surroundings, as the "middle wall of partition," because between our good thoughts and the world of reality is our line of false thinking which reports such ugly things to our mind. It is the mystery of the word omnipresence over again. "Ni" is the middle wall of partition, yet it is nothing. It is the "No, you are not good," which faces all people. When met by the

"No" of your proposition of the irresistible Good it falls away.

It is the same with many of the words of Scripture, whether we have before observed their wonderful possibilities or not. Take the word "Ho" in the sentence, "Ho, everyone that thirsteth". Students have been surprised to see how appropriate it is to the sentence, outside of a mere exclamation. H-O were the two letters which in ancient alchemy represented water. In modern chemistry they use the formula H^2-O. But it was an expression far beyond the simple first sight of the word.

It is the same with all Scripture language. Take the word "firmament" — firm to God in all things. It has the full meaning of a mind firm to holiness, firm to goodness, firm to God in all things. Firm to Good when evil appears, firm to life when death seems near, firm to health when sickness seems reigning, and so on — a mind striving to set itself free in steadfastness from the waters of these trials.

The "A" which divides the word "firm" from the word "ment" is the angel in the sun, of whom John the Revelator speaks. When he seems dark he is Abaddon, according to the Hebrew tongue, or Apollyon according to the Greek tongue. When he is the dark angel he is the angel of the bottomless pit. But it is only in misunderstanding that he is darkness. In understanding he is an angel and archangel of light and life and joy. It works out in human character as the forces which are said to follow men as the sun follows them, or as the night follows them.

The first force or quality for which this "A" stands is approbativeness, and this is very strong in all mankind from early childhood. The second is amativeness, which comes later. The third is ambition, which comes in its fullness still later on. The fourth is acquisitiveness, which is yet later. When the character is in the light, these four are seen to be: First, artlessness, which is innocence; second, attractiveness, which is beauty and judgment; third, aspiration; and fourth, ascension, or the complete absorption of the mind and life in spiritual themes. The transformation of character from the first four to the last four comes when we meet temptation with the right spirit.

One may say, "I cannot help being afraid when I see sickness showing its mastery over health." Yes you can. No man is ever tempted beyond what he is able to resist. There is always a way of escape from the greatest or least seeming evil. One may as well say there is no Omnipotence as to say that he cannot help what it is his very omnipotent nature to throw off easily.

One may say the drunkard cannot help drinking any more than a child can help crying. This is an insult to the omnipotent Spirit resting within him. It places a man where he is not divine in nature, but is Satan. It puts him in mind of where he must be restrained. It is siding with the great "ni-hil" claim against him, which comes as, "You are a weak-willed fool." You must not side with the claim that man is too weak to resist drinking. You are the weak fool you say he is, for we are what we accuse our neighbors of being.

Some say the sharp-tongued scold can no more help her hateful words than a child can help breathing, because it is her nature born with her. Who told you that anybody had a mean, wicked nature? Did Jesus say so? No, he said all came forth from God. Stand firmly to your Jesus Christ principle that ALL are strong, that ALL are well. Stand in the waters of seeming and see the real nature come smiling up.

Some say, "I cannot help crying when I see my best feelings, my generosity, my kindest efforts insulted." What is that omnipotent spark within you for, if it is not the Principle to be agreed with when the waters of grief come rolling toward you? That is the way to talk.

There is no seeming temptation that is too great to be met

with the Good and put down into the nowhere and nothing. The woman who speaks sentimentally of how the poor drunkard cannot help his drinking, and with condoning smoothness puts up with him as a weak thing, will be severe enough with her own children. The man who sentimentalizes over his drunken partner will vent his rage on his wife and daughters. It is because they themselves do not resist their own weaknesses. Hence it is part of the right action of the mind in its relation to environment that we take one half day to changing that old angel of accusation of weakness into the angel of ascension, by saying, "*I do not believe in a mixture of good and evil in the world, or in myself. All is Good.*"

There are not two sides to this question. There is only one side. There is only one Being to make your convenant with, and that is Omnipotence. To make a covenant with, is to agree with. We agree with Principle by declaring that we believe in it.

Did you ever say that it was your feeling that justice and right would sometime be done in the world? Did you say that the time seemed very long? Did you think that it would be far ahead in the millenium time of the poets and prophets? Tell me why you thought the time for the triumph of Good to be far ahead? I am sure you are judging by appearances. Why do you do so? Can you see that when making a choice as to whom to believe, you chose the poets and the prophets rather than Jesus Christ? He said, "This generation shall not pass away until all be fulfilled." If He was speaking to the people, can you not see that He meant that if they took His doctrine they would see the fulfillment of their words in their own day? He said, "This day is salvation come."

It is certain that when you put out great words of Truth into the air you may expect to see them come to pass any moment. Notice the way these texts read: "Immediately his leprosy was cleansed." "Immediately he received his sight."

"He lifted her up and immediately the fever left her." "Immediately she was made straight and glorified God." "And immediately he was made whole." "And immediately I was in the Spirit." The idea of Spiritual Science seems to be entirely of instantaneous demonstration, if the words of Jesus are believed, rather than the ideas of the poets and prophets.

The whole fact of demonstration rests upon wise choice. Today, if you will choose the teaching of Jesus Christ, you will be based in mind, you will know where you stand. A good base of mind is a good healing power. It is a better policy either to believe in something entirely or disbelieve entirely than to be up and down in changes of feeling about matters.

A business man who believes in nobody is a certain man to deal with. You are sure he will show no favors, so you do not whine and shake around where he is. You stand up and keep your eyes on your own affairs. A business man who believes in everybody has exactly the same effect, only that he braces you to believe in yourself, because he believes in you. Then agree with some principle. Stand to it. Here is a commandment of Solomon: "Keep sound wisdom and discretion: so shall they be life unto thy soul."

Hear this idea of the power of faith: "The Lord shall be thy confidence, and shall keep thy foot from being taken." When the Lord is your confidence you will never find yourself at all deceived by the ways and speech of men and women, though they be very brilliant, if they speak outside of the Principle that demonstrates healing and goodness and life.

Do you remember two pieces of statuary by Thorwaldson, the Danish sculptor, which he called Day and Night? On the breast of the woman, who symbolizes Night, repose twin babes, Death and Sleep. So limp and terrible looks the little figure of "Death", so absent from life looks the little baby "Sleep." On the shoulders of "Day" smiles the child of quickening life.

Life and joy and vigor laugh in every curve. One is the symbol of unreality and the other is the symbol of reality. In Truth there is no sleep and there is no death. All is life. Life at its joyous height is the rest of God, which sleep tries to symbolize. Life at its sweetest charm is the peace which night tries to typify. The promise is that there shall be no night there in that life of Truth we are told to live. Neither shall there be any death.

There is no fate that can come up to face you with defeat. You were not made for failure, no matter who you are, nor how much you know, nor what anyone has told you. God is your prosperity. God, the Most High, is your defense. God, the Absolute Good, is your friend. Do not heed that high-sounding poetry which reads that: "On two days it is useless to run from thy grave, the appointed and the unappointed day. On the first neither balm nor physicians can save, nor thee on the second the universe slay." It is good poetry but it is not the Truth.

Error is put in very bright packages of beautiful words, but it is better to have a mind of your own. Do not convenant with the principle of limitation to believe in it. It is the teaching of Jesus Christ that He has, by His doctrine, set before us an open door which no man can shut. We have unlimited power.

If we do not use that power it does not alter the fact of its being our inheritance. We have a store of unlimited wisdom. If we do not draw upon it, that does not alter the fact of its being ours. We may tell how little we know. We may complain of our feebleness, but that touches not our strength. We have exactly what we say we have, so far as appearances go, but appearances are nothing.

Principle is so generous and full of faith that it takes it for granted, if you say you are ignorant, that you surely must want to be ignorant, for man's word is his own to do with as he pleases. And a man's word is the weapon with which he cuts out his destiny. Or it is the stuff out of which he builds his life. If you have the use of all wisdom by saying, "I am wise," and the use of all ignorance by saying, "I don't know anything," you are rather ungrateful if you choose to complain. In the years of travel through the wilderness the Israelites provoked the Lord with their complainings. Complaints increase the conditions.

You may hear people who profess to have confidence in the Holy Spirit, telling how badly their stomach feels, how weak their limbs feel, how heavy their head is, how blue they feel. They do not show any signs, by such drafts on the ethers of blankness, that they have any communion whatsoever with the Spirit. Do not take your ways of thinking or acting from them. Look to your own relation to the Spirit. When anyone speaks on the side of evil you will say, within your own mind, "I do not believe a word of it." Thus you will be on the reality side, and will call them out of their sleepiness, for all talk on the side of death or weakness is sleep. There is no life in it. The subjects which interest the mind are the stuffs out of which happiness is made or not made. Only one theme is full of life and beauty and increasing strength.

Let me tell you the twelve effects of thinking of the Spirit: You will have life, health, strength, support, defense, thinking faculty, wise speech, ability to record well your ideas, joyous song, skill in carrying out your principles, beauty of judgment, and great love.

The musician thinks he is skilled at the piano because he practises hard. Not so. It is because he has in some moment covenanted with the spiritual feeling or ideal that stirred him, and it has come forth so far as to lead him to be willing to practise to give it more freedom. It is certain that if he really knew that it was the Holy Spirit expressing itself through him, he would see that it is not his practice but his free mind that enables him to be a good musician.

It is the Spirit that doeth all things. It is never anything else but Spirit that does all the good that is done. All the beauty of life, all the love of life, all the kindness of life, is of the Spirit. The Spirit is God. David says that God proclaims, "I have made a covenant with my chosen." The chosen are those who speak in the Spirit. They have chosen to speak on that side, and that covenant God will not annul. He will not break it. It is His promise that, "Thy seed will I establish forever, and thy throne to all generations."

It is ours to choose our principle. It is the way of the principle we have chosen to deal with us according to itself. Jesus Christ said, "His ye are to whom ye have yielded yourselves servants to obey." He also said, "No man can serve two masters."

John the Revelator called the fourth step of Science the fourth foundation stone of the City of Peace. We have great peace in the Spirit, there is no turmoil whatever in the Spirit. If there is turmoil it is a signal that we have tried to believe in both evil and good at the same time. It cannot be done. When turmoil comes before you, make haste to say, "*I do not believe in a mixture of good and evil, I believe only in Good.*" If the turmoil is within your own mind, you will make haste to say, "*I believe that my God is now working with me to make me omnipresent, omnipotent, and omniscient. I believe only in the Good as ruling in and with my life. I have the faith of God.*"

It shows that you have to make some decided choice in and with your mind. It is the experience which comes after realizing some great ideal in spiritual life, which your human lot seems to be far from carrying out. Its symbol is the emerald stone, symbolizing that the choice on the side of Good is made.

Joel, the prophet, was looking over the people of the earth, and when he realized how we see principles and how we judge of life, he cried out, "Multitudes, multitudes, in the valley of decision." That is, not yet decided. Goethe wrote, "Choose! choose well! Your choice is brief and yet endless." The choice is ever before us, for evil always seems very real and very powerful, until met with the Truth.

Our way of believing deep down in our convinced mind is our faith. We are sure to speak out from that faith. If we talk against our faith, that is, do not quite believe that the health principle is most powerful and yet we keep on talking for health and will not admit that we are afraid of the sickness, we surely will find our faith coming around to the side of omnipotent health. This is the way of entering into faith by a straight line of procedure. If, when we are trying to talk for health, and talk for prosperity, and talk for wisdom, everything seems against us and everything hurts us greatly, we must put great vehemence into our saying, "*I do not believe in sickness, I believe in health. I do not believe, or think, that misfortune has any power whatsoever. I believe in prosperity and success.*"

God is working, as we put deep feeling into the circumstance. For instance, if you feel grieved, you must put as much feeling into your declaration of faith as you have grief in your mind. The two states of grief and of vehement words of faith will act together to form a new base in your character. They are like silver in solution, which a certain kind of acid can precipitate into fine flakes of silver again. So the right circumstances are hidden in the solution of your grief. You put strong words into your feelings, and a new state of mind comes forth, which is a great power. Even in the daily life you can prepare the soil of your mind with a certain set of ideas which will go beforehand like a King's Guard and cut out or down all the trials in your way.

Your own radiance of mind, engendered by your noble thoughts, will go like protecting fire before you and stop calamities, stop sickness, stop the tongues of your seeming enemies, and do all things for you. It is the Spirit that goeth before to guide; as it is written, "I will guide thee with mine eye." All your days of ease from sickness and calamity should be filled with words and thoughts which have this protecting power.

Divide your days into statements that can accomplish miracles. Take Monday for one kind of thought, Tuesday for another, and so on. And when Thursday comes around, why not take that day for discussing or meditating upon the fourth lesson in Science, since Thursday is the fourth day of the week's activities.

This law of thought concerning spiritual doctrine is the law Jesus Christ taught. That is why it has been called Christian science. If you will look up the history of art and science, especially chemistry and physics, you will see how often practical usages of great principles are named after the men who first used the principles.

Jesus Christ taught that we may uplift our life by uplifting our thoughts. Jesus Christ taught that the only uplifting thoughts are the thoughts of God. The true thoughts of God were given to us by Him. We now take them and resolve them into twelve definite propositions, which are not only in the same order in which He expressed Himself on spiritual matters, but are the actual processes of our own mind, as soon as we give it freedom. The statements usher us into a new realm of life.

We find that it is not spiritual nobility to be brave in warfare, nor to be able to cure the sick, nor to be able to rise above temptation to do wrong. By thinking wisely ahead of these circumstances we never come into them. If you say in a moment of anger that you are unlucky, and that brings you a stroke of hard luck, can you not see that it is no special credit to you to get bravely out of the mess into which you have deliberately plunged yourself by your words? Can you not see that you would be far more noble to do the right thing beforehand? Getting bravely out of a mistake is just like putting your hand into live coals and then asking us to praise you because you are a good surgeon in cutting it off, and so patient in bearing the deprivation or loss of your hand.

We make our own conditions. And this brings us to the preparation of our feet with the Gospel so perfect that we never enter the seas of misery. Paul said, "Have your feet shod with the preparation of the Gospel." The new covenant which it is prophesied in the Scripture the Lord will make with his people, means this agreement with the Spirit, by which Spirit is to do all things for us, and we do nothing for ourselves, our only relation to the perfect way being that we agree to leave ourselves entirely in its keeping. On this account, if you will make your covenant with the omnipotent, eternal Spirit, to do all things, and you will do nothing but trust it entirely, you also will be that people with whom the prophesied covenant is made. You will find it mentioned by Jeremiah in his thirty-first chapter: "Behold, the days come, saith the Lord, that I will make a new covenant with the house of Israel. And the whole valley of the dead bodies shall be holy unto the Lord; it shall not be plucked up, nor thrown down any more forever."

Paul writes of this new covenant in the eighth chapter of Hebrews. Here he shows how wise the covenant will make mankind, and how happy and free. It is heaven here and now without fighting or waiting any more for it.

Jesus Christ is called the Mediator of the New Covenant, because He teaches that by His principle we have an easy yoke and a light burden. He does not praise hardship or suffering. He praises faith and freedom. It will help you into a mighty understanding of Spirit to covenant with Spirit for the action of the Holy Spirit with you in this perfect fashion.

Do not covenant with the Spirit for pain or suffering. In Spirit there is no such manner of dealing. The Pietists (1700 A.D.) told the Spirit they were willing to suffer. The Spirit never asked them nor anyone to suffer, but, as they covenanted for suffering, they got it. A certain pastor of an English mission was very much pleased that he got his expenses paid by praying for them, and had about $14.00 left over. As all the wealth of the earth was offered him you can see that he was not especially honoring God by having such a little bit at his disposal.

*Sit down by yourself, and honestly and lovingly say:

I hereby covenant with the Holy Spirit for my life, and I will do nothing to preserve my life; my life is the life of the Spirit.

---

*The covenants, or agreements, are stated from the standpoint of the principle of Truth. Mrs. Hopkins points out the relation between Truth reasoning and action in the following quotations:

"One does not have to strive to carry out his Truth by stopping his factory when he hears that all clothing should be made out of the Word of Truth. No, he sees that his knowledge is all the power he needs to exercise. He need not stop eating to show how long God will keep him alive without food. His knowledge will regulate his actions. All should be accomplished by the irresistible action of Principle." — Bible Lesson 49

"In Truth there are no criminals. In Spirit there is no need of prisons and reformatories. Spirit and Truth are all. Shall we then close up our prisons and reformatories? Our first duty is to know the Truth about them. "Ye shall know the truth and the truth shall make you free." It is not for you to try to change the externals. You are

I covenant with the Holy Spirit for my health; and I will do nothing to preserve my health; my health is the health of the Spirit.

I covenant with the Spirit for my strength, and I will do nothing for my strength; my strength is the strength of the Spirit.

I covenant with Spirit for my support, and I will do nothing for my support; my support is the providence of the Spirit.

I covenant with the Spirit for my defense, and I will do nothing for my defense; my defense is the protection of the Holy Spirit.

I covenant with the Spirit for my mind in its perfect thinking, and I will do nothing for my thoughts; my mind is the mind of the Spirit.

I covenant with the Spirit for my right speech, and I will do nothing for my speech; my speech is the voice of the Spirit.

I will do nothing to fix, or record, or write my Truth

---

to know what is true. This is your whole business in life. Knowledge of Truth is its own demonstration. All things are coming to the world by its knowledge of Truth." — Bible Lesson 43

"Labor not." Ought a man sit down and fold his hands while his children go hungry that he may meditate on spiritual doctrines, seeing that all labor is the sign of living under the curse. No. He must keep swinging his hammer and balancing accounts till his knowledge of Truth takes those tasks out of his hands. Spiritual knowledge itself does the turning and over-turning. It is subtle in its workings. It is so secretive that the eyes and ears take no cognizance of it. But by and by its mission is visible." — Bible Lesson 43

"There are two ways of denying evil and matter, one intelligently, and the other blindly. One of the first propositions of Christian doctrine is that there is but one substance filling all space, all places, all things. As there can be but one omnipresence of cause this substance every-

unto the earth, for my record is the record of the Holy Spirit. I say, as Job said, My witness is in the heavens and my record is on high.

I covenant for my joyous song of life, and will do nothing to be joyful; my joy is the joy of the Spirit.

I covenant with the Spirit for my demonstrations of efficiency and skill in rightly doing all things, and I will do nothing to perfect myself. My efficiency is the working skill of the Holy Spirit, according to the words of Jesus Christ, who said, "The words that I speak unto you I speak not of myself: but the Father that dwelleth in me, he doeth the works."

I covenant for my judgment in its beauty, and the beauty of judgment; and I will do nothing to make myself greatly good in judgment; for the Spirit is my judgment.

I covenant with the Holy Spirit for my love, and will do nothing to make myself loving or beloved, for all is the Holy Spirit now acting with irresistible goodness through me.

---

where present is God. God is good. Thus all is good. Then there follows the necessary negation to such a promise, viz., then there is no evil. The intelligent acceptance of this reasoning has the most straightening and purifying effect upon character. The blind acceptance of this reasoning causes people to act exactly like Jehoiakim. Whatever appetite of passion or temper they had before they now say it is good because there is no evil. Now that one little turn of metaphysics contains all the law and the gospel. It makes all the difference between light and darkness. The one who says his conduct is good when it is manifestly bad is as much a believer in evil as he was before he spoke the words. For demonstration is the accompaniment of truth understood." — Bible Lesson 32

"Take now a right premise and reason with it until the light of understanding breaks over and through you. . . . Reasoning based on pure Principle is like sunlight to the mind and life." S.C.M.P.

This will make it easy for you then to say, from the depths of your heart, "*I do believe that my God is now working with me and through me and by me, to make me omnipotent, omnipresent, and omniscient. I have faith in God. I have the faith of God.*"

This is the fourth lesson in Science. We are hereby taught about being fixed in an eternal choice. This is a lesson in faith, with an explanation of why we have a reason for the faith that is in us. It is a lesson in the covenants. Look up all you can find about the covenants of the people with God, and see how much more beautiful the covenants of Jesus Christ are than any of them. "I came down from heaven, not to do mine own will, but the will of Him that sent Me."

Our own will says: "Believe with the world." God's will says: "Believe in Me."

CHAPTER V

THE WORD OF FAITH.

There are three ways of dealing with the principles announced in Truth. There is the deep thinking which the mind exercises respecting them. There is the speaking them forth which we do not hesitate to do. There is the careful recording of them, which is writing down what we know of them. The next is living them, which we are sure to do if we think, speak, and write them. It is by faithfully doing all these things with Spiritual doctrine that we accomplish the works of the Spirit in us.

Sometimes a practitioner of healing is astonished to find that he has cured a half-dozen people of very miserable conditions, and yet those cured patients will not speak of their cures nor urge other people to be cured by the same means. It is because the practitioner has not recorded the miracle on paper and caught the principle as it were to abide in his house so firmly that when a patient is cured it is a fact so present in his consciousness that he cannot forget it and has to speak of it.

Cures are the works of Truth. Cures or works are wrought by faith. That which we have faith or confidence in is our mental character quality, and goes through our thoughts, through our writings, through our speech, to others. If we do not write down our thoughts we leave out an important part of our way of shedding abroad our healing quality. There are certain writers who have not yet come into their stream of consecutive, careful, thinking power, but they can write the truths of the Science, and through their writings they convey a sweet healing. After awhile the writing of their thoughts leads them out into consecutive thinking and then they heal by mental reasonings.

Peter told the Christian converts to whom he wrote letters that they ought to have a reason for the hope that was in them, and be able to tell that reason. The telling of that reason has been the means many times of healing those who told it, as well as those who heard it. To say to a man with a lame foot that he is a spiritual being entirely, and that as Spirit it is not possible to be lame, is to touch perhaps the only chord in his mind which could influence the foot to be well.

There is always one chord in every mind which is capable of responding promptly in the cure of the one ill that threatens you or anybody. It is when this healing chord is not struck that people continue in their old sickness.

There are twelve ideas with healing power in them. There are thousands of ways of presenting these twelve ideas. Sometimes a practitioner of healing will find that he cannot make his thoughts train his body by positive or direct statements. He has to come to his nature by negative or indirect processes. For instance, he cannot make his thoughts work out his affairs aright by saying, "My prosperity is satisfactory to me." He has to say, "I do not need prosperity. I do not need anything." It is all a matter of belief. Thus we often hear people telling about having a "belief" of this or that malady. It sounds strange and affected, but quite expresses the state of affairs. If they are strictly in the faith of Jesus Christ they do not believe at all in sickness. They do not permit themselves to believe in any doctrine which makes sickness.

It is not yet known very widely that certain religious beliefs make sickness. For instance, a belief in Satan makes some people ill. The belief in an end of the world by fire and brimstone makes others sick. A belief of a personal God on a great throne in the skies makes people sick. If one has strong belief in inheriting conditions from his ancestors, it may be the whole mental cause of his physical disorder. Thus, thoughts which move in the mind make the body, as waters moving upon the land change and form the land.

It is to this that Moses refers in his statement of the principle that thoughts arrange and formulate outward conditions. Notice that he says, after the mind has been firm in the Truth, "Let the waters be gathered together in one place, and let the dry land appear." Let it be plainly seen what you believe. It cannot be hidden out of sight, really. It is a certain law that is enunciated in the text, "According to thy faith be it unto thee." What we believe is written out on our bodies, and we cannot hide the handwriting.

What the waters do is plainly seen by the land. It is not especially interesting to symbolize spiritual thoughts and their results by land and water, and stars and stones, but it is record of one thing surely, and that is that as the stars and the earth act they each and all act, and each and everything symbolizes the mind.

The great minds of the world have felt that the study of matter has not done them any good, only to teach them that such knowledge profiteth nothing. They are convinced that all things have an inner significance, and it is that inner significance which it is worth while to know. The things themselves have no value apart from their divine meanings.

A celebrated physician was once speaking to a thoughtful woman about the influence of faith in the cure of disease. He said that he believed greatly in the effect of a powerful faith, that it had often accomplished what regular prescriptions had failed to do but he did not believe that faith itself could be studied and understood, because of the prejudices of mankind which would interfere with such studies.

"I feel that Jesus meant we have a right to freedom from prejudice with all the rest of our liberations, when He said,

'The Truth shall make you free,' " said the lady. This unconvinced doctor shook his head.

Here is where our fifth step in mental action, our fifth lesson in life Science, finds us. Do we believe Power operates through all things? Yea. Do we believe that Power can be understood by us? If we can honestly answer that we do believe the Omnipotent Power can be understood, do we believe it is worth our while to give all our mind and all our strength and all our life to finding out how to deal with it?

It is certainly the Jesus Christ doctrine that we take no thought about what we shall eat, how it shall be prepared, where it comes from, what it costs, what we drink and wear, where they come from, how they are made, along with other subjects which interest the people who look to phenomena or material things. He would have us know all things, have all things, without trying to have them; and be filled with power without long practice in science or art, and so on through the list of worldly ways. It lies often to our choice how far we will undertake to follow Christ.

The choice sets our mind to a keynote. This keynote we always strike when we meet people. They feel our mental tone. They feel it with their mind. If they have thought along our lines they respond gladly. If they have thought quite differently they feel mentally opposed to us. But if we do not change our base, do not falter in our faith, there will be a constant sounding of our tone that will break down their opposition. They will come to respond with their own tone which is like ours. They will be healed. They will be uplifted. Our mental conviction that evil is nothing real, causes evil to falter in their feelings. Our mental conviction that Spirit is the only substance will spiritualize them. The more firmly we hold to our own thoughts, the more the conscious reasoning which we keep thinking will change and alter their conditions.

Our own conditions will change for the better, and still on for the better, world without end.

Our words along the nature of our faith make our faith a working principle. The waters of a river might be walled up into a great basin, but if a channel is made for that water, it flows down over the lands and makes them fruitful. Thus our words are the outlet of our faith. Our words in the silence of our mind are as potent for good as our spoken audible words.

If our faith were small, and we should keep talking, keep thinking, keep writing ideas absolutely true, our faith in those words, which lies hidden in our nature, would finally come forward. If we did not greatly believe something, but should keep speaking it, or thinking about it, we would construct an artificial faith in our words, and make conditions like our persistent ideas. You will remember that Napoleon talked much of what he would do in case of defeat. So his defeat came at Waterloo.

Jesus Christ taught the importance of the word. "By thy word thou art justified and by thy word thou art condemned." "If a man keep my sayings he shall never see death."

Two ministers of the old school of theology were accustomed to call themselves miserable sinners, and also to tell that there is a dreadful place prepared for sinners. One of the ministers came back, it is told, after he had passed through what is called death, and communed face to face with the other. He said, "I am condemned to a place of burning, and justly too." He tried to say more but could not. We know why. It was the justice of the law, that if it is as we speak that we are condemned, then he who had said that miserable sinners, of whom he was one, must all be burned, must honorably share the fate of the rest of the sinners. He had not really had faith that he should burn, but the waters of conscious speech fixed the lands or settled the places of his lot. So we are told to guard our heart's thought. So we are told to watch our tongues.

Some minds quickly translate their thoughts into actions. You, yourself, may have a habit of fearing some little thing and it keeps coming up till it finally begins to seem real. For instance, you fear that the old pain in your head may trouble you if the railway car is warm, so you open the window and yet your head aches. Now suppose you had risen in mind with calm self-poise and said, "I am not a victim of headaches, I do not believe in them; neither do I believe in material causation." You would have, by your very words, compelled things to be as you said. You would have been free from pain.

You, yourself, are the arbiter of your own destiny. Why give in to the old ideas? Old ideas are old beliefs. You are not obliged to believe that you are a being liable to misery.

This changing of all events by thoughts is called works. If the faith is good we do not have to take many conditions in hand specially. They take care of themselves and let us deal with the principles. As for instance, if your faith is established in Truth, you will probably find people will be well and easily recover from their maladies from association with you, while you keep on thinking the twelve propositions of Mind Science. On that day which you devote to the fifth proposition you ought to see people very well, without especially thinking for their particular health. If they are not well you must speak specially to them.

Do you remember the fourth statement? The fifth is like unto it in showing how we make our own happiness or unhappiness so far as this phenomenal world is concerned. The Spiritual or Real World is not changed by our words. It is the same changeless good yesterday, today, and forever. All our faith, all our reasonings, are to the end of opening our eyes to see the Real World. From the standpoint of Truth it is thus with us always. From the phenomenal standpoint we have chance and change and unhappiness. The fifth statement is:

As Divine Mind, which I am, I preach the gospel, heal the sick, cast out passions, raise the dead. I work the works of God, who works through me to will and to do that which ought to be done by me, according to the doctrine of Jesus Christ: "The words that I speak unto you, I speak not of myself, but the Father that dwelleth in me, he doeth the works."

Such an affirmation makes you realize that you have nothing whatsoever to do, for do you not see that if the Spiritual world is already perfect, if that is the Real World, you do not really have anything whatsoever to do? *Thus the highest working power is the power to see that we have nothing to do.*

Our demonstration of this will come out in many unexpected ways. For instance, we are in hard straits with our business affairs, and we insist that it makes no difference to us in reality. This may show out in our power at healing, or in our bodily health, before it shows in our affairs. Even at their best what are our affairs? They are symbols of our real life. If they please us they are pleasing symbols, but nothing is real except Spirit. So this idea will come step by step to make our environments right. We cannot fail while we are daily speaking the lofty principles of that Kingdom on the earth, though not of it, which will come up before our vision more and more.

We were not made to fail. We were not made to be burdened. Probably you will notice that the fifth lesson seems to take away our own management of things. It is therefore the great lesson in meekness. It touches most nearly that word of Jesus Christ, "Not my will but thine be done." We are willing to submit to the law of our words. We are willing to give up old words to let the Word of God be spoken in us and through us.

God hath given the Holy Spirit the speech and thought of the universe. In us is the Holy Spirit. We let it speak and think through us; then we are like John on the Isle of Patmos. We cannot realize time or people or events. They come and go as we hasten nearer and nearer to our sight of the Heavenly City. If we speak of preaching the gospel, we mean telling the world of the spiritual Kingdom — speaking from the Absolute standpoint. If we tell of healing the sick, we do not mean that there are sick people, we mean that we see people more nearly as they are. If we speak of casting out passions, which are called demons and devils in Scripture, we do not mean that there are devils or demons. We mean that we see the Holy Spirit in mankind instead of passions and tempers.

We mean the same by raising the dead. There is no death, yet we speak of raising the dead as a work of Science. How is this? We mean that we see life where we have believed in death. If we should say all the time, "I see life; I see Health; I see strength; I see prosperity," and so on, we should mean exactly what we do by saying that as Divine Mind we heal the sick, cast out demons, raise the dead.

There is only One Mind. That Mind is the source of all thoughts. We think the first thoughts of that Mind when we think according to Jesus Christ. All other thoughts are no thoughts. All other words are no words. Thoughts and words not in Science make thicker and thicker fictitious conditions. They are all subject unto us.

Do not fail to keep some of the words of Truth running in your mind continually. It is well to have the Truth ideas running because they lead the mind out into the events of the day.

If we are involved deeply in thinking mathematical problems we would not carry a healing presence. If we were the greatest musician that ever lived we would not carry healing power by our scales and chords; but at the first trump of the doctrine of Jesus Christ within our mind we are filled with healing presence. It works through us like a fine fire of sweetness.

There will come a moment when we appreciate how closely related our thoughts are to our world. We will see that our reasonings based on the premise of matter being real, are not enduring, as to the conditions they have made. If we have spoken of riches as being the possession of material things, and then reason why we should have riches, we are talking entirely of nothing. Riches are the presence of the Holy Spirit in us. All reasoning based on that premise is solid reasoning and will demonstrate in good symbols.

Swedenborg thought so much upon God that his face shone so that sometimes his servants were afraid of him. Do you suppose he asked that his face might shine? No, he was thinking beyond faces. Mme. Guyon, the French Pietist, could heal the sick wonderfully. Do you suppose she asked to heal the sick? No, she asked to be married to God. This meant she desired to give up her will entirely to the Divine Will. She had a few wrong notions of what the will of God is. She said God's will is that we suffer great tortures of mind and body to discipline us. She thought it was through suffering that God perfected his people. If all miserable conditions result from miserable ideas of God, it is no wonder she had miserable conditions.

Other religious people had miserable conditions. They had them as the outcome of their mistaken ideas of God. Job's friends tried to persuade him that it was God who had afflicted him. He denied it. That is our duty also. We deny the being of a God capable of afflicting people. Guyon, Fenelon,

a'Kempis, Luther himself, all ignored the doctrine that according to thy faith so be it unto thee, as related to human experiences, and accepted what others taught them. Luther never
seemed to apply the Doctrine to the persecutions he received
from mankind. You remember he was so unhappy by reason of
the ill-treatment and maligning he received from people that he
was in the depths of despair a great deal of the time. Now and
then Luther agreed that faith could heal the sick. He himself
healed the sick sometimes by the prayer of faith. He had the
same privilege in the matter of stopping persecutions. Faith
in Good, as God, will stop persecutions, poverty, sickness, sin,
and death.

The greatest mystery about the goodness and intelligence
of the Pietists was their ignoring the Jesus Christ idea of God,
already implanted within their own good intelligent minds, and
taking the teachings of other men about the ways of God. After
having announced and intensified the idea of faith as the keynote to demonstration, they believed the most outrageous things.
They are our examples. By their lives we see how faith in evil
operates as well as how faith in good operates.

An accepted writer on the dominant theology of today says
to the world that the sufferings of good men are not explain-
able. He thinks some might be called discipline, some just
chastisement, but the rest are out of the reach of reasoning.
Yet he well knows the principle that according to what we
believe so it all happeneth unto us.

Environments are works. Our works are the activity of our
faith. There is one state of mind which indicates no settled
conviction. It is called in the Scripture, "The fearful mind."
John the Revelator said the fearful mind would enter the lake
of fire. He means by the lake of fire the troubles of this human
experience, and the experiences that follow on after the human,
called the astral or after-death state. This again signifies that

as long as our confidence in Spirit is not yet fixed we must suffer. Yet suffering is still no part of God's plan with us. It will still be our own state of mind.

Is it any part of the principle of mathematics that we should get off the track by saying five and three equal ten? Yet it is the way mathematics acts every time. God is the life principle. Go contrary to it and off the track we get. Yet in the pathway of our easiest mental powers is our fearless confidence. This fearless confidence we must enter into. If at first it requires what seems to be an effort, what of that?

There was a book written in Luther's time in which we are told that in the practice of trusting, only the good could happen unto us. We might find it almost impossible, but if we would persevere therein we should find finally it would be the easiest thing for us.

A Frenchman of long ago took up the idea of being married to God. He became so unified that all things he asked for he got. He did not ask for persecutions, so he never got them. He asked for death and he got it. There was nothing wanting. What we ask for, in faith believing, we shall surely get. Jesus taught this. But Jesus would not have us ask for death. "My words are life," he said.

Because the world works out its homes, its health, its friendships, its prosperities, on the plane of believing in evil need not make you work out your home, your health, your friends on that basis. This is the only point in Christian doctrine wherein strict reasoning compels us to sever from the best religious ideas of even the professing Christians of all ages. We do not believe in trouble. We do not believe in pain. We do not believe in poverty. We do not believe in sickness. We do not believe in our fears. Only joyous prosperity can come to us. Only plenty and abundance can come to us. Only health can come to us. Only safety can come to us.

Algazali, a Mohammedan, said that faith is the point of contact between God and man. Abraham joined himself to God by faith. Faith is God. Our substance is our faith. We have only so much substance in us as we have faith in the Good. We can control our destiny only so much as we have faith. We have the use of all faith. We can lay hold upon all the faith of God if we please. The disciples cried unto Jesus, "Lord, increase our faith." He said unto them, "Why are ye fearful? Be not faithless, but believing." If this great confidence were not something we could easily secure, His orders would make the Christian way just as hard as the preachers have made it. He never called His way hard. He even made healing the sick easy for us all. "All things are possible to them that believe," He said.

Very soon His disciples got so strong in faith that they wrought miracles. Those to whom they preached wrought great miracles also. For three hundred years there were great works of healing brought to pass by the Christians, then slowly the ministry of healing ceased. It came to be a sign of power in Spirit, and sometimes people not high in church office could heal better than the high officers. This aroused jealousy. Jealousy is not a healing quality, so they entirely stopped healing ministries, first in the high church dignitaries through feeling jealous, and second in laymen through being forbidden to heal. The true faith gives freedom to all men exactly as to ourselves. You can tell when you have true faith by the pleasure you take in seeing others successful and prosperous in their own ways.

It is human nature to wish to compel others to do as we think they ought to do. It is divine to see that their own way is their true way. One man thinks he ought to be allowed to have plenty of air in his office. So he has it. He thinks his clerk ought to keep his office full of fresh air, simply because he thinks it is best, while the clerk's mind is inwardly rebelling that he cannot have his own way about his own office. Now that employer might be wondering and mourning over his not working out one of his hard places right. He cannot bring it around. He has not the slightest idea that he is a slaveholder on a small scale.

Slaveholders have always one hard and undemonstrated proposition of their own religion. They cannot for the life of them see why, when they try so hard to be Christians, it happens so miserably with them. People who hold tight rein over children often wonder why they are held from prosperity and good health. Some cannot heal well because of it. "You must not drink water now! You must not eat so much!"

We hold tight rein over our friends. We do not like them if they go out or come in, when we wish they would do differently. If they associate with people we do not like, we drop their acquaintance and grieve them. Then we wonder why our health is poor. We wonder why we do not do good healing. Give all people absolute freedom in your own mind. This will cause them to do right exactly.

In Norway the merchants leave their wares in booths and write on cards that people who wish the articles may leave the price in the box and the merchant will come and get the money at the end of the week. This freedom from suspicion causes the buyers to leave the right change. They do not steal. There is no question that giving our neighbors freedom from our ideas of them, that they need our counsel or need to do our way, will cause them to do right. Right, which is Good, which is God, acts only through freedom.

If I am of a mournful type of mind, I am thinking that the Divine Mind has disappointed me in some way. This suspicion is a kind of blot between me and the sight of good health in my patients. If I hate tobacco, or hate rum, or hate any man or woman, I put up a dark steel-like screen between myself and the sight of good health in that patient I am trying to cure. If I think the doctors of medicine are in great error because they think that healing is possible by the use of drugs, I stop some energy of the Spirit from being free through me. I am the one to tell the Spirit how free it may be, but the Spirit never acts through accusation. Doctors think the healing power acts through drugs, and you think the healing power acts through words. All the time that healing power is operating through that one who has confidence in the Good as health.

God acts through confidence in Good. God acts through freedom, because the feeling of freedom is one form of confidence in Good. God acts through our toleration of doctors, because toleration of the rights of others is a sign of confidence in Good. Any act and thought, any feeling which evinces confidence in Good, will have the power of God acting through it at once. This compels us finally to have our confidence in the law of the Good itself, not in the drugs themselves, not in words themselves, but in God, the Good. "I take my refuge in thy order, Om," said the Brahmin. So we take refuge in the way God works.

It is customary for us to say that we wonder why people do not accomplish more with their religion. We speak sharply of our clergymen because they do not go down out of their pulpits into the hospitals and prisons. It is belief in respect of persons. It is a sign we believe God has given the ministers more power than He has given us. If we feel there is a work to do, we may be certain we are the very ones to do it. We see that crime increases and we want it cured. We say so. That very speech or thought is the signal for us to cure the crime of the world in the thoughts of our own mind.

We may be keeping books, or keeping store, or keeping house, with our hands, but our thoughts are free to go and take down the hand of the man who is going to strike. We may go on the free thought to the hungry child, and lead him straight to the house, or place, where he will get all he wants. We have no time to waste condemning people for not doing great works. We must get on about our own business.

"All crimes shall cease
And ancient wrongs shall fail
Justice returning, lifts aloft her wand,
And white-robed innocence from heaven descends,"
says Milton. He put this blessed state of affairs afar off into the future. Why did he do this, do you think? He did not know the law of speaking from what is *now* in Spirit. He did not know affirmations.

We may keep the health we would like still ahead of us, by thinking we are going to be well sometime. Aeneas of Lydda was always expecting to be cured sometime. Peter came near him. Peter never believed in waiting for anything. It would do you great good, if you have always been thinking in terms of the future, if someone who believes in doing everything NOW, should speak scientifically to you. You would spring at once to a sight of your benefits. Also you would yourself, all alone, catch hold quickly, if you would put the word "Now" into your affirmations and denials, into your statement of faith and into your working affirmations. The Truth is NOW.

People often wonder, while looking at the phenomenal world, after speaking scientifically, why things do not change for the better immediately. What is the phenomenal world? It is the unconscious mind of the world. What is the unconscious mind of the world? That which the conscious mind has made. What is the conscious mind? The thoughts we are aware of while we are speaking them. Our bodies are the register of past thoughts consciously thought. Bodies are machines which are going around with the affairs of our life mechanically. If we set them to the conscious tones of our true words, they will be quickly respondent.

When people's bodies do not quickly respond to their scientific statements, we may know that they have set their bodies hard to great positive and determined errors. Their bodies will not quickly respond to the touch of their spoken words, though these words are very earnestly spoken. It seems as if they must actually begin to make new bodies. It is the same with affairs. They are machines which register our past ideas. We speak Truth once or twice and then wonder why the affairs do not change at once.

When we speak Truth and feel thrilled to our very feet by a cool fire of feeling, we may know that from zone to zone of our being our unconscious mind is shaped toward Truth. We shall not fail to see our bodies and affairs exhibit the thrill. There is the order, according to Christian Truth, to transform our bodies by renewing our conscious thoughts on the plane of Truth. Truth will utterly build over the brain. Some begin to build at the brain first. Some begin at the bones. Some have actually begun with their hair. That is, they have changed its color or nature. It is told of a woman whose ancestors were colored, that when one of her children had the kinky hair of her race, she spoke to the hair and it became straight at once. Some touch their environments first. Even the winds obey their words. Some tell coffee and tea that they cannot make them nervous, and the coffee and tea became harmless.

The best way to fasten our scientific statements into our conditions is to give a reason why the scientific statements are true. Tell that in reality your body is Spirit, the coffee is Spirit, and therefore all it can do is to inform you of some new and sweet law of God.

Some of the very first Scientists gave for their reasons why material food could not hurt them, that matter could not hurt Spirit. They being Spirit, the material food could not possibly affect them, and so on. The later students would not accept that way of reasoning, because it implied more than one substance. The first Scientists did do beautiful healing, however, by such ideas. They would look at a man who thought his food hurt him and mentally tell him that, being Spirit, nothing he could do could hurt him. Food was harmless. Then aloud they would tell him to eat his dinner without fear. The food never hurt him after that. He was utterly cured of indigestion.

In their classrooms they were told that their physical bodies were nothing at all — pure unreality. Matter in every form was unreality. This is true. We are Spirit. We do not need to show material bodies at all. We may show only our spiritual body, which is our true nature. We may see all things as Spirit. This is our privilege now. As Spirit, which is Mind, we think what we please. In the Absolute we do not think anything about bodies, or matter, or affairs of earth. You can see that all conscious thinking about such things is no thinking at all. The affairs of earth, as they show up materially, are nothing. The conscious thought that made them is nothing. Only by so much as we realize Spirit is there any substance to our thinking. Only by so much as we realize Spirit are all things real. Every realization of Spirit brings our bodies out from their unconscious machinery into their glorious reality and freedom.

Jesus Christ could manage matter in all its forms instantaneously, but He did not teach anybody else to do so. He taught what to think that would eventually result in instantaneous demonstrations. The disciples could do everything but save themselves from persecutions. We take the conscious teachings and train ourselves till our machine-like bodies spring to as quick intelligence as our consciousness itself.

People were perfectly astonished when they first found that there is as great intelligence in the feet as in the brain. There being no material brain, no material feet, all being the Spirit of God, who is this that dares say that one part of Omnipotent God is more intelligent than another? It is "no-mind" which is called the conscious mind. What is wrought out by thinking of material things as reality? Your bodies, of course, with their troubles and pains. But as it was "no-mind" that thought these things, they are nothing. They must disappear. They disappear for the true conditions to show out.

Even thinking the truth about numbers will change the shape of the head. The mathematician will keep thinking and thinking about numbers till he seems almost discouraged, he is so far away from his right answer. He keeps on calculating, however, and some day his mind is capable and strong in numbers. His very head has changed its shape. His face looks different. He did not ask to change the shape of his head. He did not expect it would happen so, but it did.

So you, by repeating the twelve propositions of Life Science, will change your entire life conditions. You must consciously think what is true. This is what Moses called the waters of being. You will soon be what is true in all your looks and actions. These are your fixed estates. These are your mechanical tablets, your records. If you can set the red blood coloring your face by a thought, you can also straighten your crooked bones by your thought.

When you rise into the highest thoughts you can write, or think, or speak, you see your body as a white glory of beauty, as transfigured by your thoughts as Jesus was transfigured by His thoughts. Yet, He was not really changed. Peter and John and James had been saying the words He had told them, and suddenly their eyes were opened to see Him as He is. So your eyes will be opened. So your mind will perceive things in their reality. So your own body will show forth its hidden beauty like unto the transfigured Jesus. John called this accomplishment of the mind, the sardonyx stone of our Temple of Life.

Every stage of this manner of reasoning has power to heal. From the ways of the first Scientists in their earnestness, to the ways of the new Christian Truth healers with their determination, there is healing power in the Truth, whether you ask to be healed or not. There is power, and there is beautiful prosperity in the Truth, whether you ask for them or not.

Keep one early morning every week for the fifth word of the Truth of Life. Let us close our lesson with it. You will find your thoughts going out to their works with obedient kindness if you keep this saying faithfully.

As Divine Mind, which I am, I can preach the Gospel, I can heal the sick, I can cast out demons, I can raise the dead. I work the works of God, who works through me to will and to do that which ought to be done by me, according to the doctrine of Jesus Christ: "The words that I speak unto you, I speak not of myself, but the Father that dwelleth in me, he doeth the works."

CHAPTER VI.

SECRET OF THE LORD

It is said of a Western physician that he always spoke so encouragingly to his patients that every family liked to have him enter their house, because he radiated courage and buoyancy. He always told people nearest death that there was no reason why they should not get well right away. He lost some of those cases, speaking from the standpoint of appearances, but their loss did not seem to affect his practice at all, because other physicians who looked melancholy and hopeless lost more than he. He had no high standing as a school man, but drugs administered by him had more healing qualities than the same drugs given out by studious book doctors.

The constant affirmation to his patients, "You will get well; you are better off than you have been imagining," finally became his whole mental state, and his presence radiated it like sunshine. It was his independent mind, shining by its own convictions, which shed healing. Had he been swayed from idea to idea by his fellow-physicians, learned in the shadow system of drugging, he would have been sometimes like what he read in books and very seldom like himself.

We are told of General Ben Butler that when he entered a room or restaurant, though nobody knew who he was, there was about his presence that which finally attracted attention and a general certainty that he was a strong and great man. There are people who do not strike us as beautiful to look at, who yet uplift us and command our admiration, even while they are doing or saying very little. There is something about some people which wins their way anywhere. What is it? It is their

116

way of independent thinking, according to their own convictions.

There are ways of handling your thoughts quite independent-ly of what seems to be going on and of the opinions of others, which will make you a lofty soul in the feelings of people. It is not too late to begin that way of handling your thoughts, even if you are now seventy or eighty years in the world's belief. You should have a systematic mode of reasoning with power in itself to quicken you into a bright and clear under-standing of Principle.

You will not start out with your noble ideas for the sake of the respect and attention of mankind. You will start out with the noble ideas for their own sake. It is the nature of every man, woman, and child to choose great themes for the mind, if those themes are started within them. This the twelve stones of the temple of Divine Science, or the twelve lessons of Jesus Christ, are sure to accomplish. Nothing like their mar-velous potency was ever discovered in the line of reasoning. By some of them we find ourselves enabled quickly to dis-tinguish right from wrong, in places where once we would not have detected differences.

Paul said, "I had not known sin but by the law," when he found how quickly his mind detected error. Your judgment of affairs will be quick and accurate. But this you will notice, that while you can instantly separate chaff from wheat in affairs, the evil, or imperfect, does not hurt or disturb or anger you, as it did formerly.

The denials of Science have the double effect of dividing off the erroneous promptly and making it harmless instantly.

The fifth lesson showed the law of the word — showed how essential it is that even after faith is established the speech and thought should express the faith constantly.

Many people keep their faith so secret that it does not work outwardly. Emerson spoke of the unreality of evil. He spoke of the omnipresence of God as his faith. But he said that the gods overload with great disadvantages those whom they would compel to do mighty tasks. He said this so powerfully that it affected his human lot powerfully. He lost his family. He had great opposition to meet. He had softening of the brain, or a strange loss of mental faculties. This was his overloading to keep pace with his words, for he was great and must therefore take his own drugs for greatness.

It is this law of the word which carries the faith into quick and irresistible action. Moses told his people, after they had been wandering forty years in the wilderness, to keep all of the words of the covenant with God, and do them, that they might be prospered in all their undertakings. Notice how like our lesson it runs — the covenant first — then keep the words thereof, then prosperity. Jesus called prosperity the Kingdom of Heaven.

"God saw that it was good." God is Mind. Mind sees that all is Good. What it sees and smells and tastes is Good. Nothing hurts. Nothing offends. This is the power of the covenant kept with God. We covenant with death and receive death. Isaiah prophesied that there shall be an action of Spirit with men sometime whereby their "covenant with death shall be annulled and the agreement with hell shall not stand." All the refuge of lies shall be swept away. Then comes prosperity.

"Judgment also will I lay to the line, and righteousness to the plummet." "Behold, I lay in Zion for a foundation a stone, a tried stone, a precious corner stone, a sure foundation; he that believeth shall not make haste." Read the twenty-eighth chapter of Isaiah and see how it fits the lesson of Science in the best way Isaiah could interpret his own prophetic feelings. Nobody need strive or haste for his prosperity if his faith is fixed, and his words keep repeating his covenant.

There surely comes a moment when the full power of the

words comes surging through us. The power comes *through* the words — the power is the Kingdom of God. You remember Paul said, "The Kingdom of God is not in word but in power." So we really do not see and hear and smell and taste and feel that all is Good until the sixth lesson of Science has come with its meaning and potency.

It is not until the power of the word has come that the word is worth while. The word is a pathway to the power of God. The great interpreter of the Bhagavad Gita is Mohini M. Chatterji. He says, "The powers of Deity are beyond description and enumeration, yet both description and enumeration are needed for the benefit of the devoted."

Hosea said to his people, "Take with you words and return unto the Lord." We hear people telling how useless words are, because it is the power of God that accomplishes all. Yes, that is true. But it is the revelation of mind and the experience of mind that it is over the pathway of right words that the devoted come into their demonstration of power. You will notice a great difference in your power if you say that everything good that happens in your life is a demonstration of the presence of the Holy Spirit.

Your acknowledgment of it will affect you mysteriously. It will not alter the fact that every good and perfect gift cometh from God, as James told his friends, but it will alter your relation to the good in appearance. I do not tell you that in reality anything is altered, but in appearance everything is altered.

Maybe you think you have such a miserable life that you cannot be thankful. That cannot be true under any circumstance. Paul said, "Every man has his proper gift of God." He told Timothy to stir up the gift that was in him. So there is some special gift native to you alone. The thoughts engendered by the repetition of the twelve statements of Science will stir up your own gift. They will open up a way for you to exercise that gift. Everything will yield to that gift stirred up in you. The third lesson, you remember, was full of praises and thanksgiving. Such an attitude of mind is very clarifying. Jesus always gave thanks before He wrought a miracle. He never attempted to raise Lazarus to life till He had given thanks. So far as externals went, He had nothing to be thankful for, except that He had the gift of God in him stirred up, with all this gift roused to its highest power.

Yet He let himself be used exactly as if He had no power, in order to show each man what to do under all circumstances. He taught us to use the highest and loftiest affirmations when events are lowest and darkest with us. He said, "My God, my God, how Thou hast glorified me!" when He was being crucified on a cross of shame. People looking on said that He cried out that God had forsaken Him. That was the human or natural way of looking at the glory of the presence of God. There was the same misunderstanding of his glory when the voice from heaven spoke of glorifying Itself through Him, and called Him the Beloved Son. People said it thundered.

It is evident that the power of God is exhibited only over the highway of righteousness; over the highway of a true premise with its irresistible sequences. What premise is nobler than, "God is all?" What is nearer irresistible sequence than to proclaim that if God is all, then that which is not God is nothing?

If I am, what must I be? Must I not be God in substance, nature, and office? And if the I AM of me is God, then that of me which is not God is not the I AM of me. It is nothing. Then as flesh I am nothing, and as Spirit I am substance. The rest of the reasoning based on the first premise is exactly as righteous. If this is true, then I must believe it. If I am the Truth in my substance, I must believe in myself. I must have faith in my own Truth. I must be the word of Truth or my words are nothing. By the utterance of this reasoning the power of God is expressed. It is by the word of the Lord that the heavens were formed and all the hosts of them. This is prosperity when we speak the word in power,

It is time when we, as Mind, put forth our perfect senses. The senses of Spirit are called seeing, hearing, smelling, tasting, feeling, exactly as we speak of senses. "Thou, God, seest." "Thou hearest." "God saw that it was good." "Taste and see that the Lord is Good." The character which thinks strongly in the right way will feel a pleasure in life entirely unknown to one whose ideas are wrong.

And this sight of things by reason of true premises is something all can learn. On a desert island, a man kept saying, "Living Water!" while his companions were mourning about their thirst. There was no water there, but still he kept saying the words, "Living Water.". . Finally he felt that he must dig for water. The rest laughed at him, but he was persistent in spite of their jeers, and he struck a spring of water so powerful that they had to pull him out suddenly or he would have been drowned. It was the same with the fishermen who obeyed Jesus Christ and cast their nets on the right side of the boat. It will be the same with us if we persist in the high true way of thinking; keep speaking high and noble Truth.

A Japanese youth suddenly found himself gifted with miraculous healing power through constant praise of Deity for all his blessings. It took several years to accomplish it, but he did it. He was cured of consumption in its worst form by that one practice. The power of God came to him. It is sometimes called the Holy Spirit, and sometimes understanding. Its symbol in the life temple we are building is the sardius stone, which is the glistening or shining stone.

Understanding is a clear seeing of how works are performed. If you were found to be full of healing power and should know how to use it, you would be pleased. You would see that the healing power was good. If you were found to be full of genius for writing books and should understand how to write them, you would see that your genius was good. So God sees all things in the universe as things He understands how to use for His own glory and satisfaction. It is all good in His eyes.

Swedenborg says that the angels looking at us see only our good, our evil they behold not. It is to this absent evil and present good that the study of the Divine Mind leads us. We become like what we study. The sight of our mind is the girth of our powers. While we see good, we are powerful. The instant we see evil we are paralyzed, for the darkness of our mind is come. Half the globe sees the sun and half sees the shadow. It is the prophecy that all shall be light some time. This is the external appearance of the state of mind which is to prevail through seeing all things good.

There are two standpoints to look at in the propositions of this Science before the demonstrations are achieved. One is the material or human, and the other is the spiritual. While one is studying the Science for the sake of the body, his business, or intellect, his words are like shells filled only with desire. He will strike a moment when he will see that the Science is to be studied for its own sake, that its ministry may bring him its gifts in its own order at its own judgment. The Science is not a new enterprise to make money by, nor a new patent medicine, nor a new phosphorous for increasing brain forces. It is for its own sake. It is for the expression of the soul.

The soul is careless of money, careless of business, careless of bodily conditions, though it shines over these with beneficent prosperity to them. The doctrine of the soul is that while knowing all things, and doing all things, it is identified with nothing; it is absolutely free. To the soul there are no works to be done. Yet all works are done by the presence of the soul. The soul, as it is called, is the Divine "I" of each man, woman, and child. When it is prominent there is a radiation of power from the mind and character. The mind that best causes the soul to shed abroad its power is the mind that is absorbed in the study of Principle.

The mathematician who studies mathematics for the sake of a seat in the university is not a successful mathematician, he is superficial and external. D'Alembert, the French mathematician, looked with great coldness on a young man who solved some abstract proposition with a view to a seat in the academy. "You will never secure it with that motive in mind," he said. The young man was not making mathematics his goal, but a seat of honor.

Shall the Science of Spirit be less jealous? It is to be studied for itself, not for its external performances, for in keeping your eye on external works you can see that the works are your goal, while the goal ought to be the Spirit itself. The Spirit being looked at will give us its substance. This is the meekness of Spirit, that while knowing it does no works, it kindly overshines the operations we call works.

The earliest teachings of Buddhism show that it is our part in life to stand aside and let the Spirit within fight for us. Yet we fight the battles of life as though we, ourselves, external as we seem, were fighting them. He who best stands aside for the soul to do his work, while yet he does all, is as though himself were doing all, and is most powerful in overcoming and outdoing natural defects and unkind destiny.

There are certain practical ways by which we are to read the Science of Mind. For instance, we do not fast in order to become spiritual, but often fast because we are spiritual. One does not speak true words in order to become spiritual, but because he is spiritual. If he were not already spiritual, it would be false to say, "I am Spirit." It is because I am Spirit that I say so. The appearance may be that I become more and more spiritual, but it is only that I more and more show forth my real nature.

I do not say I am health in order to become healthy, but because I, in my Divine Truth, am Health itself. I tell the Truth about it. I do not say I am wise in order to become wise, but I tell the Truth, I am already Wisdom itself.

I do not say I am owner of the universe in order to get hold of great possessions, but because it is true that as Spirit I am the possessor of all.

In the Scripture we read of the angel of life and death, time and eternity, spirit and matter, who is the angel of mystery, crying with the roar of a lion. Then the seven thunders uttered their voices. The lion always typifies the strength of purity. Pure Truth is spoken. It touches the mystery of life and death, time and eternity, Spirit and matter, and immediately all materiality thinks it is to be advantaged because health, strength, support, defense are named as the result of Truth. But this is its bitterness, for the words of pure Truth cause materiality to disappear.

The pure Truth is spoken like itself, not like what it is commanded to do. Thus the premise being utterly independent in Spirit, will rouse the native energy to express itself, and we have a great and mighty character evolved.

We do not take the premise that there are any sick to cure or any sinners to reform. But as Spirit our energy makes nihil of sin and sickness. We do not take the premise that our brother needs to be cured of swearing or stealing. We say he is free to do as he pleases. This takes off the burden of our heavy supposition, and he feels free to cease swearing and stealing. This is more like the way of the Spirit than if we were to take the solid seeming premise that our brother needs reforming, and cure him of his habits by treating him.

Do you catch the strong metaphysics of this idea? It shows that cures are often the result of a strong will coming against a weaker will and overpowering it. Thus it is that it is more like Spirit to cure sickness, ignorance, and death by being in the Spirit where there is no sin, ignorance, or death, than to rise in the power of an antagonistic feeling and overcoming. "My Spirit shall not strive and cry."

To the Holy Spirit, all the life of the universe, all the joy and skill of the universe, is given, and one does not have to beg for it or work for it. It is so. That is all. This stately standing place is ours. The greatest miracles may be wrought out under the most unpropitious circumstances by holding to the loftiest ideal you can conceive of faithfully.

Miracles are prosperity. They come for every type and kind of religious feeling which is addressing itself to its highest. Luther begged the God he described to have the men at the Diet of Nuremberg grant toleration to Protestantism. Suddenly he ceased praying as a beggar and shouted, "We have won the victory." He was many miles away from Nuremberg, but his words burst over the situation with their power.

Right in the place where we now stand we may work miracles. There is nothing in Scripture about running away from duties that lie nearest to hand. Shakespeare, the student of phenomena, noting how certain types of mind act with environments they have wound themselves up in, makes one of his characters obey the fiend within him, advising him to run away from his obvious duty. But Scripture says, "Stand thou in thy lot to the end of thy days. Stand and see the salvation."

There are two standpoints then from which to view all things, to ask questions, to talk. One real, the other unreal. There are two kinds of faith. Take the faith of the two ministers believing in the burning lake for sinners, and believing themselves sinners; that was expressed faith. Believing not that they themselves ought to go into that lake, yet never saying so; that was unexpressed faith. We ought to trace our logic to its deepest practical outcome. This we ought to do by definite speech or thought. It will bring us up from the deeps farther and farther till the push of the springs of truth within us is externalized. Jesus called it, "A well of water springing up into eternal life."

At each purer realization the world takes a different turn in our feelings. It shows its best to us step by step. The lily in the night looks a different object from the same lily in the sunlight, yet it is the same lily. So this world in which we walk looks so different by this nighttime of thought. It will be the same world when the sunshine of pure Truth strikes through our minds in its glory.

Here in our midst abides the glory of God. Here all is Good. There is a state of mind in which, if we get into it, we shall see what Jesus Christ called "The Kingdom of Heaven." There has always been a teaching in the world that there is a Kingdom of beauty and goodness near at hand. How to enter it, or how to see it, was the mystery. The people of the past fasted and prayed and limited themselves in every way in order to see it. Still it seemed afar off. Stephen saw it, just as he was breathing his last breath upon earth. Jesus walked therein always.

Moses took the Israelites through the wilderness with such thoughts in his mind as the Kingdom near gave him. Their shoes and clothes lasted forty years to symbolize the enduring Kingdom of the Good.

Now and then in the wilderness spots of this earth, there are sights and sounds vouchsafed to the simple of heart which show that the less our mind, with its earthly descriptions of life and love, touches anybody or anything, the more we may see of heavenly things.

A young man of seventeen or eighteen years of age went from Germany to seek his fortune in Africa. He used often to wander in the sands alone, hiding himself behind clumps of bushes when the Kaffirs came toward him. He says he used often to see on the sands ahead of him, beautiful cities with mosques and minarets and towers and wonderful homes. Going on and on he never found these cities. They are not in Africa. He has traveled over many countries but has never seen any cities like them. No picture of spots on earth represents such scenes as he saw when, as a simple youth, he wandered alone to make his fortune.

The same kind of untouched cities may have been seen in the untrod fields of the far North. Many a long-neglected spot of earth, not touched by the thoughts of man as he now thinks, has suddenly exposed some scene to the traveler in the early morning. It is promised that cities shall spring up in the deserts, and roses of tropical clime blow where not even a grass seems to thrive. This will be the new way of thinking which now comes with Science. It opens our eyes to see things as they are.

Intellect and matter call this idealism. It is pronounced transcendentalism. But under the reign of intellect and matter limitation is continually put upon even the power of God himself.

Have you ever heard of learned men saying that a sick child must die? Did you ever hear of Jesus saying that a child must die? And he who feels most of the Mind of Jesus thinks most of life. He goes to the child and cures him. He does not agree with intellect or matter. He is practicing transcendent teachings. They are all of unlimited, unhindered, untrammeled spiritual vitality, force, health, protection, provision, here and now, by the union of the mind of man with the Mind that is God.

The Mind of man is the Mind of God.
The Life of man is the Life of God.
The Soul of man is the Soul of God.
The Spirit of man is the Spirit of God.

Mind, Life, Soul, Spirit, are names of God. They are the Substance of God. They may represent to our way of thinking very different things, but being all names of God, they are one.

The Science of Mind must be the Science of Life. The Science of Soul must be the Science of Spirit. There is no matter, so there can be no science of matter. Therefore, he who studies, trying to establish a science of things material, must be forever baffled.

There is a call in every heart for something that will endure. Only Spirit is eternal. All the study of snails and asteroids in which you can spend your time must cease with extreme age. The brain fails, whose cells have been the dry and dusty storehouse of material facts; but there is no old age in Spirit. The brain that is cleared to its tiniest cell of the facts about comets and earthquakes, gleaned from observations and histories of matter, will revive and renew strength and buoyancy, till there is no sign of a material brain in sight. The clear light of Mind, shining with the understanding of eternal Truth, glows like the aureole of the supernal visions of John and Jacob.

Though this has been proved only a little way, it is strong enough, when once begun, to lead those who are ready to risk all to the marriage of their life with the life that is God, to persevere.

> "He who hath led thee to this way,
> Still on the way will show;
> He who hath taught us of this way
> Still more will make us know."

Jesus Christ took the premise that from God, the Father, He

could call all power unto himself to use at a moment. He did not use all that power. He used as little as He could help. When He used very little power against the soldiers they fell on their faces. He needed no guns or swords or bows or arrows to fight for Him. He needed not to answer their taunts or questions. He stood aside from the ways of matter and intellect. David stood aside from the ways of warfare when he slew Goliath of Gath. He was the forerunner of Jesus. We will stand aside from the methods of the world in every particular, and thus be forerunners of those who will come after us.

"How far have I progressed by standing aside from the ways of the earth?" we will ask ourselves. No man shall ever hear our answer to him from his own standpoint when he speaks of evil. No day shall hear our complaint when it shows us death or foolishness or evil or sickness and tells us these are our lot. We will look up. We will think on high. We will trust to the Spirit of God.

David spoke to the Philistine giant of his age as we are expected, in the Science of Spirit, to speak to the giant-like apparitions of poverty, failure, sin, sickness, death, old age, and weakness. He said to the Philistine, "Thou comest to me with a sword, and with a spear, and with a shield; but I come to thee in the name of the Lord of hosts, the God of the armies of Israel, whom thou hast defied."

Does not the shadow system of pain and discouragement, from the study of matter, face us with defiance of the teachings of Jesus Christ concerning eternal life, eternal health, eternal intelligence, here and now?

There is a heart, a quickening secret, to the teachings of Jesus Christ, which few have touched as yet. It is called in Scripture, "The Secret of the Lord." Note that He ascended and descended at will. With the air spheres for stepping stones

He arose into heaven, and came again and again to the sight of his people. We read that He appeared thus to them. He was seen of Mary Magdalene and Mary the mother of James with other women, and unto the two on their way to Emmaus. He was seen of the twelve disciples. He was seen of about five hundred at once. Then James saw Him. Then again all the apostles. And Paul testifies that he too saw Him. He came through the walls to greet His beloved people. He was the irresistible Spirit. It is worth while to obey His directions insofar as we can find them recorded.

This Science is the nearest primitive Christian doctrine of any being spoken on earth now, but there are some words yet to be spoken. There is a secret not yet revealed to mankind, even in this Science thus far. How can we tell? We know by the signs. "By these signs shall ye know when ye are my disciples." Though these signs are partially manifested they are far from His demonstration. Therefore, as Spirit, we must rouse our whole being to proclaim that we do understand the Secret of the Lord concerning life, health, strength, support, and defense, without material means.

By the utterance of this word of the Inner Spirit, breathed deep into us all by the Spirit of God, we shall catch these thoughts beyond our thoughts, which whisper the secret of healing of the world. We shall speak those words beyond our words which tell the secret of Divine Love that can raise the dead.

The sixth lesson deals with the Secret. Its message is all about the quickening power of the Spirit in understanding. We tell of a mathematician that he understands numbers. We praise Euclid and D'Alembert for their splendid understanding. But theirs was not the understanding that makes and keeps alive. It was their manna in the wilderness, but it was not the bread of the true Science. We praise the musicians who startle

the world with their sounds of glory, but one by one they drop
into the grave and only the echoes of their songs are left.
Theirs was not the Secret of the Lord. They knew not music
in understanding. Like the manna the Jews ate, it fed their
minds with what promised to be life, but it lasted only a
season. The bread that Jesus gave is so alive that if a man
eat thereof he shall never die. This Secret He gave to the
world, and He said, "Abide in Me." "Keep my words." "The
Holy Ghost will come in my name."

Sometimes to repeat the name of Jesus takes us closer and
closer into His Mind, where the living Secret rested. We speak
of that Spirit within ourselves which is exactly like His Spirit,
and of it we say, "I understand the Secret of Jesus Christ." It
is not in order that we *may* understand His secret that we
speak, but because, as Spirit, we *do* understand. It is the Truth
of Spirit we speak — Spirit works only in Truth. It comes
forth in freedom over the highways of Truth.

If you watch all the writings of the devoted and spiritually-
minded of all the ages, you will find them speaking sometimes
of Spirit as the reality and sometimes of matter as the reality.
That was because they had not their revelations or thoughts
in perfect understanding.

In Genesis we find the first chapter telling how perfect are
all the creations of God. They are Good. Perfection cannot fall.
Can God fall? Can Goodness become badness? Can strength
become weakness? Yet Moses tells in the second chapter how the
perfect son of God fell from his high estate of goodness into the
dusty sinfulness of Adam. He is speaking in these two chapters
from two standpoints, one is Reality and the other is unreality.
Christ, the Spirit, is Reality. Adam the dust man with his
world is unreality.

Both these natures come calling our attention, even within
ourselves. One is pure Adam nature, with its erroneous ideas

of God and Life. The other is our Christ nature, with its faithful ideas of God and Life. One is our substance, the other is our shadow. One is our real and the other is our unreal. We abide in the Light by acknowledging only our Christ nature. We are torn in the conflict of change, and ups and downs, by acknowledging two natures. We abide in the darkness by yielding to the idea that we are matter and intellect. Intellect is the Adam intelligence, naming all things by material names, telling of them as matter. Intellect will subside in meekness when we give utterance to Spirit — when we admit that the Spirit is all in all and the only Reality.

Understanding this we put ourselves in the ranks of spiritual being, fearless, satisfied, and powerful. We understand the way of our life. We understand God. There is no study that can bring forth this fearless, capable mind, except the study of the fearless Spirit.

By the study of Spirit we become acquainted with Spirit and realize that the trees are in reality Spirit, whispering great secrets of how to be happy and free. We realize that the men and women on the streets of restlessness are Spirit. In Truth they are walking secrets of the splendor of God. We know that all that is real is Mind thinking such thoughts as demonstrate goodness and health.

All that is really thought demonstrates health, goodness, and peace. That which demonstrates otherwise is the shadow of thought — the Adam claiming to be real but never real at all. True thought demonstrates intelligence, and somebody is wiser when we think a true thought. True thoughts demonstrate in peace, and somebody is at peace when we think Truth. "Acquaint now thyself with Him and be at peace." "Taste, and see that the Lord is good." "Perceive in thine heart that there is only God. Thus shall thine eyes see thine own kingdom." Every sense faculty shall be quickened, intensified, extended out from the Central Fire which burns within us, till we perceive as the Divine Mind wholly. To God all is Good. To Mind all is Mind. To Spirit all is Spirit. To Soul all is Soul.

"As God I perceive that all is Good," says the Divine One within us. "As Mind I perceive that all is Mind," says the Divine Mind. "As Spirit I perceive that all is Good," says the Holy Spirit within us.

John the Revelator could only see this sixth movement of Science through our thought as a shining stone in a foundation. It is indeed a foundation principle, which, being understood, makes life another thing quite from what it was when we had not the doctrine of Spirit in understanding.

Take now a right premise and reason on with it until the light of understanding breaks over and through you. With the sixth light of Science we are prepared to meet the world with our own free independence of thought, able to make nothing of its worst appearances.

CHAPTER VII.

THE SPRING OF LIFE

The seventh separate statement of Moses is, "Let the earth bring forth." Earth here means mind. Let the mind bring forth. What can mind bring forth except thoughts? But Moses is talking entirely of the Divine Mind in man. It is not acknowledged by us as the only Mind and thus is hidden entirely. Hide it not. That is letting it bring forth.

Immediately we uncover the Divine Mind in man, it shows action in making fresh life in everybody and everything we meet. It brings out their original health. It strengthens them wonderfully. It brings provisions and bounty to them. It brings them defense and protection from accidents, from trouble, from afflictions. But all its ministry is only showing more and more nearly what is already worked out in Spirit. Remember this: Even healing is not healing, because Mind needs no healing. Our saying that Mind is given its freedom is also a statement of appearance only. For as God is free, so Mind is free.

Moses is using a figure of speech entirely in saying, "Let mind do thus and so" — for the Spirit, which is God, which is Mind, has its own way entirely. We are to see Spirit. We can see Spirit. And the more of Spirit we see the more perfectly we see things.

The man appears sick to you because you see him that way. If you let your Spirit tell what it sees there will be no talk about sickness, no discussion of what is distressing anybody. All things are waiting to be looked upon by us as they really are. Did you ever notice how you feel that the one who realizes your worthiness seems to understand you best?

Take the old Lord Fauntleroy as an example. Little Lord Fauntleroy thought he was generous and good. He really believed it. He praised his old grandfather. Everybody else condemned him. Consequently the grandfather would say, "Ask little Lord Fauntleroy. He knows me, he will tell you what I will do." Now, even if the old Lord Fauntleroy had appeared to all other people to be savage and ugly, his soul was generous and good. The little child saw the soul. He could see nothing else. This is true of everybody and everything. They feel that in Truth they are Good. So they who see them as good, please them best. Here is where it probably seems impossible to you. You think that the beastly characters we read of must not be called good. You see very plainly the faults of those you meet every day, and it is impossible for you to call them good.

Moses and Jesus teach the same story. Let it be of the soul you speak. Let Spirit utter itself. The evil disposition, the greed, the appetite of mankind, is all unreality. It signifies how far we are from seeing spiritual Truth when we see evil. You can see for yourself that if God the Good is omnipresent, then that which is not good is not present.

It is a tenet of the most ancient religions that what seems external exists not at all. And wherever we find profound thought and feeling, we find men thinking the same way of outward and external things. Nothing exists outside ourselves, as to what seems outside. When we realize God we are sure to say we feel God. The realization is within ourselves. We have supreme power over and with our realizations.

All realizations of Good externalize in good. We train our realizations first. Then, as phenomena or the world that folds us round comes second, we deal with our world secondly. In this Science, there are six lessons devoted to the Self Mind alone, that is, devoted to the realization of God in the soul. And there are six lessons devoted to our relations to the world.

There is no religion which has not, in one way or another, taught that "As a man thinketh in his heart, so is he," and, "By thy words thou art justified." The words we speak and the thoughts we think constitute our breath of mind, as the air constitutes the breath of nostrils and lungs. There are words which exhilarate the mind, as there are airs which exhilarate the body.

The Japanese believe that praise of all things will exhilarate first the mind and then the body. A young man in Japan, named Kurozumi Saki, in 1814, became very gloomy through complaining. Complaining and praising are two separate processes. They bring very different results. He had breathed in the spirit of gloom till he was in deep-seated consumption. Their theological term for gloom is "Inki." He suddenly resolved to cease mourning. It was hard for him not to complain at first, but he was one who could hold to whatever he had made up his mind to do, and he began to praise everything and everybody. He went on for some years, breathing into himself an entirely different set of words. He began to be very cheerful. His consumption kept growing worse, but he did not heed it. He kept on praising everything he thought of. One night, just as he supposed he was breathing his last, but while he was praising the early rising sun, a sort of buoyant ecstasy seized him. His breath grew deep and electrifying. He straightened himself up from the ground, where he was prostrated on his face, and found that he had breathed into himself the elixir vitae, the vital breath of health. The Japanese call it "yoki," the spirit of cheer. He was more than well. He was buoyantly quickened. His very breath was a healing vitality, if he breathed on deformed or dying people. His fame spread abroad into all lands. He was a miracle worker.

There is an elixir in the words of Truth. Keep them going continually. They will change your entire life and change your powers. You are a miracle worker by inherent right. Give your soul the chance to do all your thinking, all your speaking.

A young man had a cancer in his nose, which had gone so far that there was no material remedy. He betook himself to prayer. There is always God waiting for us to depend upon when we come to where we find that nobody and nothing else can help us. He had prayed and prayed and still no signs of healing, when he suddenly felt the cheerful elixir of his Spirit breaking through him, and he was healed.

In the Bible we read, "In the morning sow thy seed, and in the evening withhold not thy hand for thou knowest not whether shall prosper, either this or that, or whether they shall be alike good." Again we read, "Let us be not weary in well doing; for in due season we shall reap, if we faint not."

Agassiz was a great student of nature. He felt that there were secret springs within all forms which he would like to understand. When he did, it would seem miraculous how some other new points of interest would come up to lead him on. It is the very way the Spirit of God works with us, if we set out to make ourselves one with it.

A young Catholic priest in Germany, about two hundred years ago, was so buoyant and cheerful in spirit that when he spoke in a loud and authoritative tone of voice to a sick man's disorder to disappear, and commanded health to appear, they obeyed him almost instantaneously. He would wet his finger on his tongue and make the sign of the cross over the sickness. The saliva on his finger was a symbol of erasure. The up and down stroke of the cross means that nothing has any evil power. The right and left stroke of the cross symbolizes that the Good now reigns. If they did not get cured at his first order, they did at the second or third. He was persistent to his own ideas. The howlings of the people did not disturb him. He lived his own life alone with the Spirit.

Why should you say that God has afflicted you, if saying such
a thing makes your breath a disease breeder? Why should you
say that you feel unhappy, if saying this shuts up a gate against
the breath of the spirit of the morning of joy? Are you not a
chooser of the thoughts you shall think? Have an hour in the
morning for some special message to the world, or about yourself. Have an hour in the afternoon for some words of Truth
to the world. These words will come to fruitage. No matter
if you have a special tendency to some grief, or your way is
lonely and hard, tell the way of the Spirit so often that she comes
stealing through you and you become a health giver and a
cheer bringer.

Sometimes you may find yourself seeming to be sick. Nothing
has happened to you, yet you are sick. You have caught some
of the world's false beliefs in your thought. Maybe they are old
notions you used to think which are just showing themselves.
No disease comes from material causes, although we say so
when we talk as the world talks. All is in thought first. This
Science deals with the thoughts, just as Jesus did, and then it
speaks of externals.

Learn to get exactly right ideas, and you will after awhile
educate the world by just thinking Science. You do not have
to tell a man that he has no disease, that he never took a chill,
etc., when every bit of him is sure that he had been in a draft
and that he has influenza. You treat him silently. You need
not talk all the time about any point in Science, but you may
know the Truth. Jesus said, "Ye shall know the Truth, and the
Truth shall set you free."

A very strong mental healer was afraid of damp drafts
before she was in the Science. She was already past sixty years
of age, according to symbolic reckoning, and she kept taking
apparent colds whenever a damp draft struck her. She was
sensible enough not to say a word in the presence of a draft,

except in her mind, for her words had not power apparently to annul drafts. After awhile her mental feeling got so strong that drafts never affected her.

Do you think that it was primarily the draft which gave her the sign of hoarseness so often? No, it was the fear of certain people. She had always been the kind of mind that has someone it fears all the time. Certain people always have something that they are fearful of. Look them squarely in the eye of their mental face and you can trace it every time to the fear of some person.

It is well, said Jesus, to agree with your adversary quickly. That is, while you are alone with yourself, take up that man or woman and settle the question decidedly that you are not afraid of them. They cannot enter the sphere of life where you dwell. Your thoughts push their evil down and leave the Holy Spirit of them free to do you great good. Much of material misfortune can be traced to dread or fear of people's influence or opposition. You may lead your own free life in mind, and it will unconsciously rebuff every hurt. The hurts may at first seem real, but as the mind puts out its wings stronger it blows even the memory of evil away as a chaff. You rise out of the reach of the things that frighten you. You forget the feelings of repugnance. You drop even the memory of the things that brought it on.

Sometimes the way to meet hardships that have clung to us for years is not by saying that they are nothing at all. It is by stopping and finding the Holy Spirit of them. A young Scientist had a bronchial affection which never yielded at all to calling it nothing, though other parts of her body had quickly healed through telling them that nothing could ail them. One night she faced up the hoarseness which had kept her whispering instead of speaking for about three months. She said, "You seem to stay around me as if you had nowhere else to go and belonged here. Now I feel that you have some good mission to me. God sends me a message by you, and I have been snubbing you and treating you badly. I will do so no more. As God, with good for me in your presence, I bid you welcome in love. You may stay with me as long as you please." In the morning the cure was wrought. She found out that it was true that it was a message of goodness for her, for her gloom of mind had left her. She touched the same principle which the Japanese worked upon so many years, viz., rejoicing in the things instead of mourning about them.

If I were to be asked directly as to the quickest way for a Scientist to get his healing power going, I would probably say, "Praise everything and everyone in your mind, and as far as your mental convictions will demonstrate promptly, speak these praises aloud." If it should be through fear that you did not speak audibly about things, you must redouble your thoughts, and speak a few times to your seeming discredit. If you are timid about telling people that they are well NOW, I would advise you to run the risk of your pride of name a few times, and say, like a Denver doctor, "I do not care if you do seem to be sick, I don't believe in sickness, and I think this is all imagination. You must be sitting up by the end of an hour and well by tomorrow." It is different with different states of mind, however.

Your timidity is often because you are afraid it will not come out right, and people will think you are foolish, and tell others so. Can you not trust your reputation in the hands of Truth? Which do you suppose had the larger practice, the cheerful, buoyant doctor who always told his patients that they would get well, or those who tried to be sensible and judge by appearances? Why, it was the one who told everybody that he would get well, whether or no, and laughed cheerfully. His presence to cheer was an elixir for the family, and they sent out their cheerful feelings and buoyed up the sick man's mind, and he caught the vitalizing sparks of electric cheerfulness. You must break over the bounds you have put upon yourself sometimes.

But again, so much of denial of the patient's seeming malady is talked out like an intellectual problem that patients do not catch healing, they catch fear. Perfect love of your Science takes away your fear, and after a while you do not talk Science much, you heal by some hearty, simple, cheerful word, that bubbles over from constant thoughts of health and life, irresistible spiritual vigor, and unhidden goodness in everyone.

There was one doctor who, it was reported, laughed his patients well. Everything they said and did amused him so that he laughed uproariously. Patients would get to laughing in spite of themselves. He would sit and roll up bread pills, or anything else that came handy, and tell the patient that he was more scared than hurt, that he was resting up a little and would be all right soon. He took many a seemingly dying man and laughed him back to life. Change the groove of the patient's mind .

Doctor Abercrombie went to visit an old schoolmate, and found her seemingly breathing her last. "Do you remember the crow's nest?" he asked her, in his buoyant, boyish tone of voice. She smiled. He said something more. Not as if he were urging or coaxing her to think of old school days, but as if they were something to remember. It brought back to her fainting mind the memory of her springing, happy girlhood, when the birds sang in the summer trees, and the boys and girls played and laughed in the orchards. That change of mind cured her.

A great healer once said that he always kept his mind dwelling on the enchanting airs of summertime. He remembered how the chirp of grasshoppers and the far away song of birds and brooks sounded. Then he would feel the soft flakes of health. There is a faculty of your health whereby it loves to drop down into your mind and distill like the dew through your flesh.

Thus God has chosen the weak things of this world to confound the mighty. But you do not have to watch anything or anyone for your health. God is health. Ever present with us is God, the health of the universe. You need not depend upon any physician or friend for your strength and courage. God is Strength.

"Though all around thee courage fail,
Do thou be strong.
Though all around thee doubt prevail,
In faith move on."

It is the dependence upon outside help, or even what seems to be outside help, which the Truth takes away. We learn to see God in the sick man as health, because we know that as health God is there. We learn to see strength in the feeble man because God as strength is there. Our strength rises and goes forward to mankind, because we know that our strength is God. It goes forth just by our knowing that it is so. Tremendous strength is tremendous health. Thus John the Revelator calls the effect of certain denials "beasts", which is a word for strength. There is an atmosphere of uplifting about one who knows he is strong in Spirit. He realizes that his soul is always rising on the wings of aspiration above the conditions of his lot. You may breathe strength itself by talking to strength itself. The Holy Spirit is strength. God has given to the Holy Spirit all the strength of the universe. If you praise the Holy Spirit for this strength you will be surprised how it will take hold of you. Some morning or some eventime its energy will thrill you.

You will not find any timidity about telling patients how the snow flakes of healing are falling around them all the time, if your heart is sure of it; but you will be wise enough not to speak of such seemingly impossible process if your heart is full of certainty, for you will see that your presence is all the speech they need.

Do you think you must say something audibly or mentally to sick people? Bind no burdens of necessity around your neck. If you have awakened in the early morning with right thoughts for the day, just keep still when your first case comes in, or when you see her or him. "Wait on the Lord." "Stand still and see the salvation of the Lord." "Stand aside in the battle and let the warrior within thee fight." "Wait, I say, on the Lord."

There was a young practitioner who had spoken mighty praises in the morning of the way God, as the health and salvation of the people, would work through her to will and to do. She was not as yet a successful healer and it troubled her. She meekly acknowledged that God was doing great things for her and through her and by her, even though she had not seen it so. Her first case that morning was a lame man. She felt divine compassion for him, but had no thoughts, for she felt that if God did not manifest through her she could not make Him do so. And this held her silent, almost helpless, as if she were nothing at all and God were all. All at once, quite unexpectedly to herself, she told him to throw down his crutch and try to walk across the room. He obeyed at once. He found that he could limp without his crutch very well. She had him try two or three times more and he was cured. It seemed as if his flesh and muscles drank in the elixir of a new mental atmosphere. Very likely he was thirsty for the waters of the refreshing God presence, with nobody's thought to interfere with him. (Lameness is a pretty sure sign of a mind interfered with). This little woman made herself so silent that the voice of the Spirit could speak to the waiting soul of the man.

There are ways of thinking about your environment which will make you like a harp in the fingers of love, so enchanting will be your silent mind to the world-hurt traveler, so blessed will sound your voice to the bruised child of human hardships. You need not worry about whether you shall speak or not. You will have your feet shod with the preparation of the gospel if you take the fresh morning for giving thanks and glad praises unto the Spirit, and speak forth with freedom some lesson of Science.

In the Science there is really no need of studying the symbolic language of Moses, as we have done. We know these great principles without going back over the ages to past men's thoughts. But we are inclined to look through the files of thoughts which have run through men's minds and made them famous or made them miracle workers. Moses was a miracle worker. What idea did he hold which made him work miracles? The mind of the man is expressed in his writings. This is true of all miracle workers. If they spoke aloud words, what did they say? Their healing power was God. God with them, in them, through them, is the same God of whom we seek to get the high healing knowledge. There is a secret of healing. The method of it is nothing.

The Japanese breathed upon his patients and they were healed. The German priest made the sign of the cross and cried with a loud voice, "In the name of the Father and of the Son and of the Holy Ghost, let the devil appear." He meant the disease. It was his expression for evil. He wished the evil to show itself plainly that it might get out of the way entirely at his order. Then he made the sign of the cross in the air, and again he cried with a loud voice, "In the name of the Father and of the Son and of the Holy Ghost, let the disease be gone." Then to the patient he would say, "From this time forth be healed." In our time we find some people healing by one means and some by another. Whenever they begin to acknowledge that God is the health of the people you will find them using less and less material helps toward healing each other. Yet you must be sure that whatever health is brought to mankind it all comes from God. Material methods are apt to turn the mind away from remembering that it is from God that all health comes. So, practitioners have resorted to thinking out great reasonings about God's presence as a healing presence, and the results have come out in good health and invigorated life with as sure certainty as by any other method. The more spiritual the feeling the practitioner has while healing the patient, the more certain is permanent cure.

There is something about reasoning about the presence of God, and telling about the character of God, which makes the cure affect other needs of the patients besides bodily disease. They are often turned from their old habits. Very often they become attentive to divine ideas and entirely change their tastes.

Scientists become very particular about leaning on the word of God alone in curing sick people. Zoroastrianism, a religion older than Brahminism or Buddhism, has for one of its principles that one may heal by herbs, another by the will, but it is by the divine word that the sick are most surely healed. The practice of healing by the word lets us most quickly into the secret of healing. But, it is no more the words that heal than it is the herbs, for if it were the words themselves one would heal by using them as well as another. We all know that one may use the words faithfully and not cure the case, while another may use the same words and cure the case in a few minutes.

This has led students to talk of faith in words as the healing power of mind. But if words do not cure unless we have faith in them, faith is the curative principle and words are nothing. It is the same as urging us to have confidence in nothing at all to tell us we must have faith in words to make them work, for words without faith are nothing at all. That is no way to instruct mind. It is running it around in the same circle with herbs for its weapons or words for its weapons. Either one must have faith in them to accomplish anything. If you examine it closely you will see that healing is brought to pass by *faith in health*. The good practitioner has his mind fixed definitely on something which to him is Good. It comes right through the appearance of evil by his mind being fixed on it. All his words about health just express his feelings as nearly as possible. The more perfectly his words express his feelings, though he is only thinking silently, the more real the health of his patient seems to him. Thus you see it is not words that heal, yet it is while words are being spoken that the feelings go forth as on highways and touch the sick. Yet it is not feelings that heal, for people often feel strongly that their patients are cured and they are not cured.

There is a secret spring to the healing practice that has never been taught, except this Science by its reasoning will keep touching it with each one of its lessons. By going over and over the lessons we come nearer the healing feeling. There is not a practitioner of the Science cure who has struck the spring with the touch of such perfect understanding that he works out his cures as accurately and surely as a mathematician works out his problems. Old age, palsy, rheumatism, grief, poverty, overtake them, and they have their match, for they have not beaten their own particular adversary.

The healing Science is like an unexplored and underscribed territory. Columbus discovered America and brought it to the notice of the civilized world so practically that others coming after him could describe it exactly. The healing lands have been discovered for ages, but there are only twelve pieces of information given concerning them.

Nobody could tell what was to be the secret of prosperity in the new world discovered by Columbus. But today we know the secret of American prosperity is its plenteous gold, coal-beds, gas wells, timberlands, grain lands, reliable climate, its river courses, its building stone, silver deposits, pasturage, salt wells — all on a material basis, but the foundation for material opportunities. The enterprise and efforts of men in Europe and Africa had nothing to encourage them, but in America they had all. Yet for ages America lay unknown, though possibilities were within her borders. Norway keeps her records of one who discovered America long before Columbus, but he made no lasting impression in the minds of his contemporaries. He brought home no marvelous products to substantiate his reports.

So in this healing practice we have had many a thinker touching on its enchanting borders, but only Jesus who could prove His words. We need therefore to believe most in Him who proved most. Wherever we are found disagreeing with Him we will simply take His word on the subject and keep it as Truth. If we are inclined to speak slightingly of any practice of healing, we will remember that He condemned none, because the secret of healing was known to Him. His coat would heal whoever touched it. But do you think the coat, before He charged it with healing, had any curative energy in it? His words would heal the instant He sent them out, but those who knew Him best used those words and failed. The word He consecrated to healing must even now be charged with the same Spirit He felt. How shall we get His Spirit? How shall we use the omnipotent Principle He set before us? How shall we absolutely understand how to heal the sick? Paul said that by letting the same Mind be in you that was in Christ Jesus. He exactly agrees with Moses. Let the Christ Mind speak its way through us.

Now the Christ Mind thinketh no evil, is not puffed up,

is not angry, is not vain, is not critical, is full of praise. Here again we come by another line of thinking right upon the same idea of praise which has made so many healers successful. Also I will call your attention to the fact that after a short time vain or critical or proud thoughts seem to stop the healing power of those who at one time were quite strong workers. The vain mind does not feel praiseful toward others. This state of mind has no praiseful feeling toward even God. So we make a practice of praising everybody and everything, and above all giving daily thanks that God has done such wonderful things for us in Spirit. We take the twelve statements of Science and sanctify the day with two of them particularly each day. Through such practice the secret of healing is coming to be an open secret. We feel it becoming more and more the inheritance of the world.

Once a practitioner, who had a woman come asking to be cured of catarrh, put down her head, and silently let the Spirit speak through her as I just told you. Then she waited a moment, and to the woman she said, "I pronounce you free from the thoughts of other people. You think your own noble thoughts. You are free, whole, cleansed, and good. You are healed! In the name of the Father and of the Son and of the Holy Spirit, I pronounce you well and strong and at peace through and through." The woman was instantly healed when these words were silently spoken.

As we all have a right to be free within our own Spirit, and as we all are indeed free within our own Spirit, this is a Truth that everyone who has gotten into the habit of unconsciously yielding to the race belief of one kind and another, is eager to receive. He will be healed at once. If not, you must treat him over again in the same way, the same hour he is with you. If not then, give him the same treatment again. Three times are not too many to give one message. If he comes another day complaining of the same thing, you must change your treatment, but I will speak of that in the next lesson.

If you have a practice of saying, every Monday afternoon, "I as Spirit do not accuse the world or myself of lustful passions or sensual desires; all is good in living demonstration before me," you will heal people before they come to you, and after a while you will never see any sick people. But you are to handle each case faithfully which does come to you.

There are moments when your healing power will be wonderful. When those moments are gone you may feel mournful, but you must not mourn even about that, for you are to be cheerful under all circumstances. Cheerfulness is a praiseful feeling. It always indicates that the healing power is acting through you. The cheerfulness may rise into ecstasy. Then it is instantaneous healing.

Will you now, each one of you, if you can think of someone you believe has a chronic ailment like deafness, or curvature, call the name now. Then put down your head with me, and let the Spirit within you say now:

It was not I that accused the world or myself of lustful passions or sensual appetites. I do not believe in the chronic ailments you say you are afflicted with. I do not believe in sickness, because I have never accused the race of living a life outside of Spirit, or different from Spirit. I believe in health in and for and through everybody now and forever. I believe in you as the perfect man of God.

Now speak again the name of the person you are thinking about, then speak it again, for there is something in a name that strikes down into the very soul of the Spirit, the deep mind and heart. This is the way of a regular formula which we will now use:

You are not afflicted with any kind of disease. You are Spirit.

The Spirit knows nothing of imperfection. The Spirit shines through all your being with its clear, holy light.

From first to last, in your real life, no error has fastened upon you, therefore there is no disease or imperfection in you.

You were not born of flesh, according to the law of the flesh, but of Spirit according to the law of the Spirit.

The lustful passions and sensual appetites of the generations back of you have not descended upon you in disease.

God is your Father and Mother. You have not inherited disease.

The race mind has not touched you with thoughts of lustful passions and sensual appetites, therefore disease does not touch you. God enfolds you round about.

People with whom you are associated do not burden you with their thoughts of the senses. You are not subject to the thoughts or feelings of others, therefore you cannot have disease in your mind.

Your own thoughts of things of matter, as to lustful passions and sensual appetites, have no power in them to give you disease. You are free from your own passions and appetites in the Spirit, therefore you are cleansed by spiritual thoughts now and are well.

My thoughts do not burden you. You are free of my error. You are free in the Spirit.

You are free from all thoughts of disease. God is your life. You cannot be threatened with death of any part of your life, nor fear death, nor yield to death of any part of your life forever.

God is your health. You cannot be threatened with disease in any part of your health, nor fear disease, nor yield to disease in any part of your body forever.

God is your strength. You cannot be threatened with weakness, nor fear weakness, nor yield to weakness in your strength forever.

God is your substance. Your health is God in every part of your body.

You are ready to acknowledge to all and to yourself that you are healed. You are in harmony with your life in every way.

I now realize that you are healed. I praise you for your life in the Spirit. I praise you for your strength in the Spirit. I praise you for your perfect manifestation of God NOW! Amen.

There is in reality no disease or imperfection whatever. When you realize this strongly I hope you will not treat anyone, for this realization is itself a treatment. We will give a treatment to this same case after the next lesson. And so much as you remember you can give twice before the next lesson.

You will notice that we have made one denial. It is the first to be made against disease. We do not deny to destroy anything, but because denial of evil is omnipotent Truth.

CHAPTER VIII

RENDING THE VEIL

The eighth lesson in Science is: "Be not deceived." These are the words of Jesus. Spirit never deceives. Matter is the only deceiver. Matter makes up all appearances. Matter is formulated, as you know, by thoughts concerning a kind of God who never existed.

The two friends of Job described one kind of God, and Job described another. Their kind of God was full of punishments for exactly the sort of character they described Job to be. Therefore, in the fullness of time, they reaped the fruits of their ideas; for Job insisted that he was not that character, and they must have imagined it in the peculiar wisdom of their hearts.

Thus it is with all of us. We look upon others in the red, or green, or blue tints of our own ideas, and see them entirely different from what they are in reality. Then exactly what we describe as their character, which is not the truth about them, must be our own type of mind in some of its ways. Then when we get the punishments we have felt honestly belonged to them, we are utterly astonished and grieved, and feel much abused. This explains why the righteous are strangely afflicted. They see more faults in mankind than any other class of people. Thus the eighth lesson is, "Be not deceived," either in man or God, for man and God in truth are Good. In appearance they may seem evil. In the Bhagavad Gita, the sacred book of Buddhism, we are told that the Spirit of God saith, "Whoever undeluded knows Me as the Supreme Spirit, worships Me in all forms." In other words, "Letting forms remain, opposing nothing, but nowise deceived, recognizes Me in all people and in all things."

This is another way of saying that Spirit is the only substance.

Thus man is Spirit. If man, or all, is Spirit, then I am Spirit. If Spirit cannot be in poverty, I cannot be in poverty. If Spirit cannot be burdened, I cannot be burdened. If Spirit cannot be sick, I cannot be sick. All these are nothing to Spirit, therefore they are nothing to me. I am not deceived by any of them. This is the only religion which will work practically with the mind, and bring out the external forms in new combinations. It is a religion which teaches us to be grateful to Spirit for all the good that comes to us, and appreciate that all the evil that comes is by reason of our having imagined something against man or God, or the universe, which could not be possible at all. We worship Spirit in all forms, and let forms alone. We do not try to change them; they change themselves by our thoughts of Spirit. There is a law of setting aside appearances by Truth. We learn Truth, and we are masters of the law.

Moses said the same thing in more symbolic language: "Let there be light in the firmament." He not only means the sun, moon, and stars of the skies, but he means the thoughts that made them.

Do not be deceived by your imaginations. Live by Principle. The reasoning based upon pure Principle is like sunlight to the mind and life. We soon learn to know the meaning of all things. We know exactly what to do. So, let the reasoning based upon a good true premise guide your life.

As imaginations arise let them alone. The simple knowledge that they are imaginations is sufficient to make them null and void. Imaginations deal with evil, matter, death, sickness, poverty, old age, pain, failure, and other burdens and bondages of the race. Truth does not deal with them; it leaves them alone. We, being in Truth, also leave imaginations alone. By this lesson you will see that you do not have to try to make your Truth work. You know it. You know the Truth that makes you free. You speak it, and it is its own working principle.

John the Revelator says the eighth stone is the beryl (in the foundation of Mind). The beryl is the stone which stands for a written record. When a form changes, by reason of our Truth, we have written a record in it. All who see it will see that we have put our seal there. Many a case of sickness would come out for more enduring health if we would write out our treatments and read them over and over by ourselves. One man, who could not feel any illumination from Spiritual teachings, became highly inspired after he began to write down the Science. It will be well for you to write out the treatments as much as you can. If new ideas come to you, put them down. They show that your mind is brightening by its own light.

There is nothing so gratifying to a teacher of Science as to see the radiance of his students' minds breaking forth. When they seize the truth for themselves, love it, and reason out each item of their lives by it, and see that no other reasoning has illuminating power, they are the true light in the firmament. When many such minds are utterly wedded to pure doctrine, it is promised that there shall be neither moon nor sun in any material heavens.

When we love our reasonings we are in the light. When we listen to the opinions of man, or side with our imaginations, we strike our darkness at once. Then our intellect is our light. It takes its premise; those are its stars. If intellect believes God is far off, then the stars, which are suns, will be far away. Of course there are other meanings to this text, but I will give you one which it is good to remember. "Let there be light" means, let reasoning, based on Truth, be your light of the sun. Let imaginations stand where your right reasonings put them. Eternal reasoning is eternal day. Night with its stars symbolizes the rest which mind takes at certain stages of its reasonings. There are halting places in mental action. Then we speak nothing, think nothing, do nothing. We have spoken Truth. We have many symbols of these halting places of the mind. There is the Sabbath. There is the halting place between childhood and youth; between middle age and old age. All these are to cease when we understand that they are symbols. Their substance is to be plain to us. We see now how a sick, deformed body will change its looks to robust beauty. But even in robust beauty, as we now see it, we are not beholding the possibilities of beauty and health at their fullest. People have as much more beauty and health and vigor belonging to them as the difference between deformity and the marvelous beauty of Hypatia. For between the night, with its moons, and the day, with its sunshine, is the difference between what we now see, and the real beauty of people and things. "Eye hath not seen, nor ear heard, neither hath it entered into the heart of man to conceive what God hath prepared for them that love him."

To love is to see God in all. This sight, or this love, puts out evil. So of intelligence. Even the greatest minds tell how limited they feel their knowledge to be. They also tell how ignorant and incompetent they feel to solve the problem of life. But such is not the way those feel who are in the light of reasoning, based upon the first principle that God is Wisdom, for Understanding Absolute is in them, and is also in all things, informing them of high Truth. Whenever man tells of his ignorance he is speaking of the formulations of his imagination. This lesson would say, "Let that which is light indeed be your light, or, let Truth be your words. Truth of Spirit, and truth of matter." It is true that matter is ignorant; it knows nothing. Are you Spirit or matter? Tell the truth about it. Reason it out well.

People have gotten mixed up with old delusions. They think they must look forward to old age. This is getting crystallized into the future. They think of a history in matter. This is getting crystallized into the past. This lesson is about the light. It is about freedom. On the material plane light is the freest process of nature. You cannot bottle it up. It will shed itself to the farthest that its nature tells it to. If you hide it under a bushel, it burns the bushel and makes a greater light than ever. If you hide it in iron vaults, it heats things red hot and melts and destroys them. While it lasts you may hide it behind some screen, but you cannot quench it by confinement. So of the eternal, unquenchable light of the reasoning based on the truth that there is one God, above you all, and through you all, and in you all — it cannot be spoken without shedding its light through the next statement of Science. And once it is set streaming through the mind, we must speak and think and write and live the doctrine.

The doctrine is a fire — an unquenchable light. It is not like the symbol, which can be put out. It is like the Truth itself, eternal, indestructible. It is along the way somewhere that you get on fire with the Holy Spirit, so that you live the doctrine. If you do not catch the fire the first time along the pathway of the Science, go over the statements again and again. The race is not always to the swift. "Come and let us reason together," saith the Lord. "The righteous shall shine like the sun." "Be not deceived."

Great doctrines have been looked into by thoughtful men, and they have turned about and seen how differently appearances work from principles first uttered. This has caused them to be silent concerning Truth, and much exercised about the effects of Truth which they have called laws. As for instance: If one becomes spiritually minded he loses his taste for certain kinds of food. Seeing this, the Zoroastrians proclaimed that all men should abstain from those foods. They mistook an effect for a cause. They tried for a long age of time to prove that fasting from food would make people spiritual. It never did, for material actions are not the cause of Spirit. The reverse is the way of the law. That is, according to the way of the Spirit in man, so will his outer actions be. Men banded themselves together saying that they would neither eat nor drink until they had killed Paul. Such was the outcome of the teachings of fasting.

There is the same idea in the use of words. We speak certain words after we become spiritual. Therefore it is said that speaking those words would make us spiritual. The effect is confounded with the cause again. In the case of words which the Spirit uses, we cease to undergo the sufferings which call more and more attention to the physical body. Fasters are very exercised over their physical feelings, and thus are as materially minded as gluttons. The same with people who beat their bodies, or freeze them, or otherwise abuse them. Their whole mind being given to their bodies, they are even more materially occupied than people who please their bodies with warm clothing and fresh and beautiful adornings, and have freedom from pain of all kinds.

In the case of using words, we find there is nothing at all in great truths to call attention to material things. The words, as we speak them, are given forth as the utterance of the Spirit of Life within us. All point to the Spirit, and go forth from the Spirit. We see them, by their mysterious ways, attending to the externals. So we obey both the Bhagavad Gita and Jesus, and take no thought about what we eat, drink, or wear as to whether it is wise to wear more or less.

Paul, very often, became much exercised in his mind over material things. At one moment it was meat, and at another it was the length of man's hair and woman's hair. These subjects are not in the mind of a spiritually minded man. He lets them alone. The man who is thinking righteously will be immaculately neat in his dress and about his person, but it will be the natural, unpremeditated movement of that immaculate Spirit he is thinking about. He will be very honorable in his dealings with men and women, but it will not be because of his thinking all the time about his duties to them. He will perform his duties because his mind is set on right principles.

These are the lights of Moses — the works of a man and the thoughts of a man. Jesus Christ called works signs, which is the same as lights. They tell where a man stands in spirituality, He said. Working to bring to pass anything is evidence of mind being on material things, for, when we are spiritual, we are not trying to bring great things to pass, yet they come to pass.

The lofty reasonings of Science are the sunshine of the Spirit. They are the works of Truth. Truth is in us. Let it shine. Truth performs great tasks. Let it shine on miracles of health, cheering, enlightening the nations.

Discussing symbols is getting mixed up in and identified with what we think and talk about. A young man was treating a lady against coughing so much. While he was treating her he told her a great many good reasons why her cough was not real, but all the time her cough troubled him. He was eager to help her. She kept on coughing for six weeks, to his dismay. One day he said the cough was nothing to him, she might cough all she liked. From that day she never coughed again. He had struck the eighth lesson: "Let forms remain, they are nothing to us."

Such an attitude toward the world of matter is the quickest way to get rid of its abnormal and ugly appearances. Those appearances feed and grow fat on our feeling badly about them, and talking and thinking about them as something that can hurt or disturb us. Notice that the cough was not cured until he gave up thinking it was his burden to cure her. He let the Spirit tell the Truth about it. Then both himself and the woman were free.

Spirit never mourns over robberies nor over deaths, nor over pain and crying. They are nothing to Spirit. He who suddenly realizes any sort or kind of evil as nothing at all, has touched the second treatment of environing conditions, whether people or things are his burden. This feeling in its genuineness comes generally by denying the seeming and affirming the real. It opens the eyes to see purely from a spiritual standpoint. There is a great power of clear sight that comes by setting yourself free from thoughts about lustful passions and sensual appetites. Next you feel that evil is nothing whatever to you and even if you do not feel that it is nothing to you, the way of the Spirit is your way of meeting appearances. By this I mean that Spirit or Divine Intelligence has one way of looking at the universe and all things in it. That way is to know the Good only. There is nothing else to Intelligence. That which sees evil is no intelligence at all. If we should let intelligence speak, we must speak as intelligence does.

If our patient, with any kind of malady, comes the second time to us, we have received statements of evil against somebody or something, as to their not seeming to be bad but hiding badness. This is a question of deception. If anybody or anything appears good it is our pleasure to believe it is genuine goodness. Do not allow yourself to believe that a man or woman, a child, or an object, hides evil but appears good, for, if you do, they will not come the second time saying in joyful affirmation, "I am entirely cured." You are being deceived by thinking either things or people are deceptive.

Whether it is affairs of business or in sickness, do not believe that there are lustful passions and sensual appetites lurking back of appearances, or that good appearances are hiding bad conditions. And do not believe that there is something wrong with a business even though it appears to be successful and flourishing. All that looks well is making a heroic fight to be God's good way in your eyes. Believe in it. Speak kindly of it.

The first strength of mind is the strength to endure. This is purity, which is long life. A good man may seem to be very frail, but he will live on and on where others, more robust looking, would falter, because goodness is a substance in man which endures. We get this by never accusing of unclean or sensual nature.

The second strength is the strength of youth, the strength of fearlessness. It comes to you by always believing everything is good which seems good, and that everyone is good who seems good. Do not think tobacco hides a poison, do not think rum hides a sting. Do not think that anyone who is kind to you, or whom you love or respect or enjoy the society of, or who looks kind or good, is bad, no matter who tells you so, or what interior feeling you have that they are. Let your conscious thoughts and words be according to the Good. This will give you a young and fearless look in the face, and keep your vigor. Childhood and youth never believe in bad where good seems to be.

A very childlike man in Massachusetts was told by some men, who were making fun of him but seemed kind and wise, to send warming pans to the torrid zone. He did so and made a fortune. His simple acceptance of their kindness was a success to him. He could not have been made to believe that such kindly seeming men were trying to deceive him. You will find that anyone who is full of certainty that what seems good is good, has a young look. Old age comes from not refusing to be deceived. Youth is kept by refusing to believe evil of people or things. Not believing evil takes out the sting of what seemed to be evil.

The character which holds its own steadily is a successful character. A certain lawyer wanted to take a boy to train who would succeed him in his law practice. He took a way to test the tenacity of the assembled boys in holding a point until it was brought out satisfactorily. He told a thrilling story of a prize rabbit, which was in a barn which caught fire. Many and varied incidents took place at the fire. Amusing speeches were made, and every boy forgot the rabbit except one keen-eyed boy over in the corner. "What became of the rabbit?" he asked. Nothing diverted his mind from the main idea of the story. "You are my boy," said the lawyer and dismissed the others.

In healing your patients your mind must be kept to its first intentions. Whatever comes up to divert your thoughts, go back again and again to your purpose. If you have determined to set anything right by mental action, let nothing turn you from it. You can train your mind so that even while you chat and laugh about various matters, it is running along like a mighty river within you, singing great truths of Science. If you are by seeming accident of circumstances put where it seems impossible to carry out your honorable duties, and you will keep your mind on them, without saying much but not being diverted from your original intention, all will be fulfilled.

Fretting is being diverted. Crying is being diverted. Where there's a will there's a way to cure your cases, and to straighten out your affairs, in the Science of Mind. Even your dreams tell you the state of your mind. Everything that happens tells you how you stand toward your premise. Being diverted from a purpose is being deceived. It is getting mixed with things and people, when you ought to be clear and light.

A certain lady always cures her patients by looking steadfastly at a beautiful Madonna which hangs in her room. She talks to it as if it were the living patient, expressed in that buoyant young womanhood. Nothing turns her mind away. If it seems to do so, she talks very fast, as thinking quickly compels her to be attentive.

Jonah kept his mind on the memory of how Jerusalem looked, while he was shut up in the whale. It acted as a rope to draw him out into freedom. Greatrakes, the Irishman, never let his popularity at houses of prominent people make him forget to attend to his healing. He finally was turned out of favor because he would cure animals as well as people by his healing powers and out of loving-kindness. In shutting him away they shut away their own health, but he did what he felt was his duty before God, regardless of the favor of the rich or great. This steadfastness is being true to Principle.

Pericles would walk on only one street in Athens. He never dined out socially. He gave his time, his life, his attention to his study of right government. Therefore, he is handed down as the wise governor of Athens. Michelangelo said, "Art is a jealous God. It requires the whole and entire time." He shut himself away from everybody while painting the Sistine Chapel. Newton was of no marvelous mind, and one of those who had been his early companions asked him how he succeeded so astonishingly. "By intending my mind," he said. Upon entering the land of true thinking I call your attention to this high principle of action.

Nothing will return satisfaction like the knowledge of God. Nothing widens and beautifies character like a trained mind. Nothing trains the mind like the daily reiteration of noble propositions of Good and Truth. Mind is not quickened and satisfied by the study of music or mathematics. It is apt to give way under the pressure of years. But the study of Spirit brightens the mind as the years roll on.

Healing by pure reasoning is healing by an ever increasing energy. Healing by pure reasoning is far better than healing by keeping in mind the face of the Madonna. Is not that a material picture? Still, we are not to condemn any practice, you must remember. We are not to speak ill of anything which has brought ease from pain or weariness to mankind. It is good. It is good to show us its best side.

In the Catholic Church it was said at one time that nothing is evil which brings forth good, but that led to their doing very cruel things, hoping to bring about good results. In Science there is no cruel pathway to some future good. There is no real advantage in surgery. Nobody ever gets wounded to help someone else. The angels of mercy and goodness fly ahead of the true Scientist and keep his pathway free from hurts. In Science there is no call to be brave, because there is nothing to fear. It is a sign of having stood true to Principle if we come out of the lion's jaws safely. It is a sign that we have been steadily true if we never get into the lion's jaws or sore afflictions.

So, it is not a signal that we have been absolutely true to our Principle if our patient comes to us a second time without the perfect cure. It is a sign that we can cure him, however. For, if we had entirely yielded to being deceived, he could not have come. Keep on with your reasonable doctrine in his presence. If he tells of evil symptoms, like pain, or if he tells of what happened to him, like restlessness or unhappiness, do not think you need to believe it. Many a case has been cured by mentally saying "No" while people were talking of ills. At any rate, it is nothing from beginning to end. As it is to Spirit, so it should be to you. It is nothing.

One practitioner who caught this idea of persistence to the true idea, being not diverted at all, takes only one case of healing at a time and practices for that one constantly until he heals him. You sometimes hear practitioners telling of having nothing to do. Ask them if they have one case on hand. "Oh yes," they tell you. And I tell them that it is the call of the Spirit for them to attend to the duty they have in hand, and the next duty will be attracted as to a magnet. If you do the best you can think of with such material as you have at hand, you will be sowing a principle as great in bringing you out successfully as if you had repeated the multiplication table by putting five more to each statement.

So with healing. Tell off each bead; it is a living blood drop. It will stir your pulses faster; it will throw out the fires of your soul. They will warm the cold blood of your patient. They will warm your affairs. They will make you a healer whose power will increase and increase.

Each man, each woman, each event that comes to you, will be to you the signal that you are to think a certain way. There are cases that touch your mind like electric batteries, and suddenly you think with vehemence. Sometimes you think so rapidly that it seems more like feeling than thinking. Many people will say that they did not utter any words, and yet their cases were cured, because they felt such a strange hot rush pass through them. This rush of feeling came because the words they had been speaking were just ready to work, and they worked fast. This is a cheering and delightful principle of the right thoughts. They strike you in their strength at such unexpected times. If you devote most of your time to healing, you will most likely heal many cases suddenly. You must know it is because of the ideas you have been holding. Do you suppose that if some great good thought had not been started in you once, such fruits could have come to you?

This Truth has ideas which are going forth and changing the mind of the entire race. It is the subtlest doctrine ever sprung upon the race. You are at home and maybe bruise your foot. You immediately say, "It is nothing; there is nothing to fear; there is no pain; I cannot be hurt. I am Spirit." Maybe you just put out your hand with a motion that means "No". The whole pain is gone immediately. Do you suppose that those words ever stop going? No, they are still traveling around in the air, and wherever they drop down upon a mind that thinks its foot or its head is hurt, involuntarily that mind repeats some part of your idea.

The poem, "Beautiful Snow," was thought of by two people simultaneously. As one thought it out, the other caught it flying. It is the same with inventions. There is no knowing which man really thought out any of the great inventions. Many times it is the second thinker who gets the name for the invention, or discovery, as America was named for Americus instead of Columbus.

The main principles of this Truth are old and have long been in the world, but some years ago there were a great many invalids suddenly inspired with the idea of Christ's everlasting healing presence, and thought the same treatments that we now use. They did not think them all; they felt them, and used such ones as came first to mind. For instance, about thirty-five years ago a lady was sitting by her friend, who was very ill. Suddenly she said, "You are healed by the power of God." And it was true. The friend arose at once, entirely well. When asked what she said mentally, before she spoke aloud, she answered, "I thought, 'You are well now, not sick, only you don't know you are well. You must know it.'". You see, to her the acute illness was nothing. It was not there. If she had held on to that principle as the truth of every seemingly sick one, she would have made a great healer.

Many people feel the idea of health so thoroughly that they cannot feel anything else, even if a man seems to be very ill. Their touch is full of their feeling of health. The touch of Jesus was full of healing. If you put your hand on your patients they are apt to think that it is your hand and not the idea that heals them. This new presentation of Truth is the information to the world that all healing is done by ideas and by nothing else. Therefore, ideas might just as well be given without symbols or carriages, as with them. The good religious man of old times kissed the cross and thought the cross would save him. He ate bread and thought it would make him spiritual. It was the meaning of the cross and the bread which helped him. They meant, "Nothing is evil where Christ is. All is good where Christ is, and He is here now." If he held to these ideas and left out the cross and bread, it would have been all the same.

You do not need symbols — you do not need carriages in order to carry your ideas to people. Ideas will go and light wherever you send them. If you call the name, James Brown, he will hear you, even if he is one hundred miles away and you only call mentally. Then if you tell him over and over exactly what you want him to know, he will catch the whole purport of your ideas. If your ideas are the Truth about his health and his life, he will brighten up and get well. Maybe he does not know you are speaking to him. He simply thinks as you think, and feels that he has gotten well without a doctor. He has caught what you said, as the inventor catches the idea of a machine.

The whole race is feeling very differently about religion. They deny the existence of Satan. They deny that God made any devil. They deny that God put Bunyan in jail through wicked men, in order to make him write Pilgrim's Progress. They deny that God puts us through great afflictions to see what stuff we are made of, to test our character. They deny that children are born with wicked or naughty tempers. They deny everything that the world used to believe. It has a very strange effect upon mankind. They get up strange inventions, because their minds get so clear after feeling those denials blowing in the air about them. In many new and unexpected places gold suddenly appears. It came because somebody said, "There is plenty of gold for everyone." He did not think that the plenty was right in his own hands. He thought it was afar off somewhere. So, afar off, in a remote spot, the gold was born.

What is wanted is a doctrine of NOW and HERE. You must take up this Truth in a stronger fashion than it has ever been taken up before, with the idea of Now and Here.

If the man one thousand miles off from you gets well when you tell him his pains are gone, why should not the poor man over there in the place five hundred miles away from you get hold of some money to meet his obligations when you tell him that he has not lost his property, and that he is supplied bountifully. God is just as much the Provider of his children as He is the Healer. "The Lord will provide" is as much Scripture teaching as, "The Lord is thy Healer." While healing is very well demonstrated now, supporting is not so well demonstrated, apparently. You will have to see that poverty is no reality. You must not get mixd up with the idea of poverty any more than with the idea of sickness. They all belong alike to the realms of nothingness. You must not be deceived by your seeming to be ignorant or unhappy. Ignorance and unhappiness are as much negation as sickness. Let us all together say to all the poverty of the world, "Poverty is unreality; there is no such thing as poverty; it is nothing to Spirit. Spirit owns all things." Let us say to unhappiness, "There is no unhappiness in Spirit. All is joyous peace." And let us say within our own minds, "Now! now!"

All things evil in seeming, that come to us at first for healing, come as the formulations of our talks and thoughts about other people or ourselves being in the flesh senses. We say we do not, as Spirit, believe in sensual formulations. This is our first treatment. All things evil which come to us the second time, come as the formulations held there by our talk or thoughts, since we first saw them, about how hard things are to bear, and what poisons and stings and hurts the world has in it. We may have accused our friends of being deceitful or dissimulating or hypocritical. Maybe we have thought that we ourselves are not truthful. Whenever we have agreed with something as being an evil which was not evil, we may be sure something or someone will come the second time for help.

We have a law of morning statements of Truth which we might call prayer. These treatments are all prayers. Our afternoon statements are prayers. The only difference between our prayers in the Truth and the old orthodox prayers is that we pray as if we had already received the blessings instead of begging for them. We say the man is healed. We do not beg for the man to be healed.

In the Buddhist temples they have been striking on the sounding rims of great bells for generations, crying, "O let the good come." There is such a pathetic intimation in this prayer that the good is not already here that it is no wonder the good has never appeared in the way they wish. They ought to name in certainty what good is already here. That will cause the good to appear, for indeed health is already in our midst, so we may say it is well. The good is in our affairs, and if we tell the truth about them, it will exhibit. We make nothing by our words; we only exhibit what is already made. Therefore Jesus said, "Pray as if ye had already received." Of course we have already received, and why should we not be truthful and say so? Through truth the good is visible. Good waits for truth. Good will not show you good health, good strength, good provisions, good life, except through the glass of truth. Do not expect answers to begging prayers.

Look over all the answered prayers you have ever heard of and see how suddenly the beseeching hearts stopped and said, "Thy will be done." The will of God is for health, for life, for prosperity, for peace, for friends, and peace in the home. So, when they ceased begging they were one with the Divine will and it was so their will that their prayer that moment was the kind of which Jesus spoke.

In Truth we begin at once to acknowledge the will of God about all things. We become aware that what is not well with us is not the will of God. Through the ages there has been an unprincipled laying of sickness, pain, deformity, and poverty to the will of God. We now cease in this Science from such mistakes.

Persistent thought about the laws of physical force has given man an extraordinary energy of body and mind. He has not yet learned how to use the force intelligently. If he keeps on thinking of how to use the force he had stored himself with, he certainly must come to the knowledge that he needs to use the force.

Persistent thought about healing general sickness, or, as it was said of Jesus, "He healed all manner of diseases," will give you so much healing force you will draw multitudes of sick people to you to be healed. Your persistent thought that there is no sickness will put sickness away from people before you can see them. Persistent thought about prosperity, and how prosperity is brought to us, will make you a magnet for prosperity. Your prosperity will not be the highest prosperity, it will not be useful prosperity, unless you know how to teach others to be prosperous. The pressure of your great riches upon you will make you stiff and sickly unless you can let the spiritual Principle flow freely through yourself to others. There must be a draft or the fire will not burn. There must be a valve, or a piston and wheel will wait forever before pulling the cars. There must be a free giving of your Truth, or the world may wait another million years for the wretched poverty of its people to be gone.

So you are to think your truth and not be diverted from speaking what you know. You are to write your truth and not be diverted from writing what you know. The beryl stone signifies the need of putting your truth into everyday tasks. While you are at work say some mighty word into the fabric of being, as a ventriloquist throws his voice into his wax figures. In your case you are only speaking aloud what the spirit of the fabric is now saying. It is the great I AM.

Do you remember the promise of David that even the night shall be light about thee? And of Eliphaz in Job, that the stones of the field shall teach thee? This is because it is written in them what you ought to say.

It is the province of the pen and paper to hold in eternal place certain things. You cannot afford to write very far off from what the Spirit is whispering through the white sheets of paper. And whatever subjects are touched by the writing you make shall have fastened into them native tongues of truth, and nobody can handle them without wondering how he came by such unexpected ideas. What you set your pen to tell is the beryl stone. Not until you have written the Absolute Truth have you gotten past the beryl stone. If you have written only a little you have not even begun to polish that stone. Maybe it is still covered within the earthiness of long years of thinking the first error concerning the I AM, and also the first error concerning environments.

The more truly you speak of things, the more clearly stands out the meaning of each one. Its countenance gives you its light. Jesus, stooping down, wrote in the sand, and now everything has felt the handwriting He sent under the waters to be sung to the ends of the earth, for all things are to be ready to say "Amen" when we also shall write down what He said of them. Make your record in all things. Bring out the record in all things. Thus shall all things shine. The night shall be light. The moon is to have the light of the sun, and the sun is to be seven times brighter than it now is.

All things are truly written full of such deep and wonderful messages that we should not be deceived by what is said against them. The air is filled, packed solid, with everlasting record of what we ought to have demonstrated. This is the unchangeable handwriting of God. Here is the science of music waiting in the silence for someone to express it. Ages have gone by and still this silent music is waiting for someone to read it. Mankind has never gotten beyond Handel, Hayden, Mozart, Beethoven, in music. Why not, when there is music beyond their highest and noblest?

Here is the science of mathematics packed into the airs, with computations beyond Euclid, Le Gendre and D'Alembert. Why does no one read the marvelous handwriting on the solid air walls, and teach us the science of numbers aright? Here is the science of happiness and bliss. Its truth is written in beautiful letters, clear and bright, and legible like the angles and facets of the beryl stone of Revelation. Why does no one read off its easy directions, so that "There shall be no more death, neither sorrow, nor crying, neither shall there be any more pain."

Right here is our truth whispering in our ears. That is our eighth lesson. It is so audible to our ears, its voice is so distinct. Having ears to hear, why do we not hear? Its writing is so plain, so legible. Having eyes to see, why do we not see?

The coming of any patient a second time, the appearance of trouble the second time, shows that we have to put down our heads and let the Spirit speak over us:

"I have not been deceived into seeing evil in anyone or anything. I see good in all things and in all people, always, without delusions. I never accuse anyone or anything of seeming imperfection in any way. I never accuse myself of seeming imperfection, or of hiding imperfections. All is the light of Truth in Jesus Christ."

This is standing aside in the mortal for Spirit to speak. You ought to wait a moment and see what treatment comes to you strongest. If you have devoted yourself to letting the Spirit speak of never accusing of deception, you will suddenly find a treatment spring into mind. You will feel very bold about giving it, for taking off the veil of hypocrisy is very emboldening.

Afternoon thoughts should be all about your environment. Morning thoughts should be about your own nature. "In the morning sow thy seed, and at even withold not thy hand, for thou knowest not whether shall prosper either this or that, or whether they both shall be alike good," said the preacher in Ecclesiastes.

Now if you call to mind the name of the friend you have treated, you may follow with me along the line of a second treatment. We will not stop to think whether we have treated him or her before or not. We know one treatment is enough for one day. We know that this is the second treatment which Scripture teaches, and we give it. Say to him or her exactly what I am saying to the one I have seemed to be deceived into believing to be a diseased person:

I am not deceived into believing in you as diseased.

You have not inherited the formulations of deception. You have inherited Truth only.

You have not been deceived by a race mind formulating deceptions around you.

You have not been deceived by people around you formulating disease by the falsity of their beliefs.

You have not formulated self-deceptions. You have not formulated deception between yourself and me.

I do not believe in the formulations of deception either by mesmerism, magnetism, psychology, auto-suggestion, or hypocrisy. I believe only in the clean handwriting of God on every part of your mind, and standing forth from every part of your body.

You are now showing forth perfection through every manifestation of your being. You have heard the Truth of God. You express the Truth of God. I see through you, and in you, and by you, perfect health throughout. You are every whit whole.

You are therefore ready now to acknowledge that your health is perfect. You acknowledge it to all around you, to yourself, and to me, now.

In the name of Jesus Christ I pronounce you healed now and forever, Amen.

You may give this same treatment before sleeping tonight. Write it out as well as you can remember it. Read it aloud. It is not what the flesh saith, but the everlasting voice of the Spirit.

These treatments react upon ourselves, and do us as much good as they do our patients.

Around us and before us, in the plain sight of our mind, our spirit, and our soul, is our perfect power, ready to rise to accomplish the works of God.

Join with me now in saying:

The words that I speak unto you, I speak not of myself, but the Father that dwelleth in me, He doeth the Works. God works through me to will and to do that which ought to be done by me. Amen.

CHAPTER IX.

RIGHTEOUS JUDGMENT

It has always lain heavily on the mind of the race that holiness and health, sin and disease, bear a logical relation to each other. "I have been young and now I am old, yet have I never seen the righteous forsaken nor his seed begging bread," shows that not only health of body, but health of affairs has been laid back to the doorway of righteousness.

"Envy is rottenness of bones," says one. "My words are life to them that find them and health to all their flesh," says another, when speaking for the words of the Spirit in man.

"The sins of the Fathers shall be visited upon the children unto the third and fourth generation," said Moses. And Jesus said, "No man is your father upon the earth." Who then is visited by the sins of his parents? The Adam man. Who is it that shall have no consequence of sin visited upon him? The spiritual man. Did Jesus believe in sin? "Neither hath this man sinned nor his parents." Did He often address himself to the mortal man? Just enough to make it nothing. "Go and sin no more," He said to the man whose good sight sprang forth as a strong arm when the love of Jesus warmed it forth.

He put away the fleshy appetite, He left the Spirit free. He put denials and affirmations together for a right and left wing of the law of demonstration.

It is often supposed that innocent young children are under the curse of their father's and mother's evil thoughts and character, and many have lain down under the burden of scrofula and consumption because they thought it too heavy to carry, if their parents had lain down under it. Many have lain down under bad dispositions and kleptomania and intemperance because they believed their parents had left these things to them as their inheritance.

What kind of a God would visit His own people with such a law as that? Where have the followers of Jesus been tarrying that they have not risen out of thinking such things inevitable with His commands ringing down through the written gospels, "Call no man your father," "The flesh profiteth nothing." "Follow Me." "Keep My sayings." What a strange imagination against the Lord of hosts to think He sent our evil tendencies in the first place, and the consequences of them in the second place.

Where have we been lagging in the lesson of Mind, that we have overlooked Jeremiah's information that a man's word is his only burden? And the proclamation of Jesus that by our words we are justified and condemned? Could God, the principle of thought and speech, invest His people with a richer heritage than the power of the word? Is there anything more majestic than this great principle of every word being full of divine potency when true, and gifted with only seeming greatness when false?

Can a law be more stupendous than that a lie must *seem* to be reasonable in order to seem anything at all? If there is no law of flesh, because there is no flesh, must not all we say of flesh seem to be true, or not give us any claim on itself? Would it make any difference to you if an insane man told you that your mother stole his watch, when you know he never had one, and your mother is good and upright? But if a noble looking gentleman told you that a shabby woman carried off his purse you would believe him at once, whether he is lying or not, because his story seems plausible.

So when great and learned preachers stand in high pulpits and talk about a great being called God, who made a terrible Satan to tempt good little children to steal and lie, we have felt that it seemed plausible. They were very wise indeed to describe the other side of such a God by saying that He sent His only Son into a swarm of wicked men, who were none of His kind, though He had created them, to be badly used by the only wicked creatures of His own hands. But the whole thing from beginning to end is false.

God is the principle of Holiness, Goodness and Truth. Truth about God is expressing Principle. Lies about God express the opposite of Principle, thus the opposite of Holiness and Goodness.

The experience of the mind of the race concerning holiness and sin has been that they have been indeed the creators of their own destiny by their imagination. Some of the very great lovers of God have been mighty living demonstrations of the power of words. One woman whose mind had become very quick in demonstrating words through constant praise of God, like the mind of Kurosumi, the Japanese, went through a hospital of plague-infested patients, and said: "In the name of Jesus Christ be ye healed," and many of them arose at once. Then she would say that if God pleased to afflict her with smallpox and other-wise torment her as He did His dear Son, Jesus Christ, she was at that moment ready to receive the calamities. She put up such an expectant mind that she drew those very things to her-self. Her words were quick and powerful.

"By thy words thou art justified and by thy words thou art condemned." For what the heart feels and believes, the words are sure to speak forth. Words are mighty signals of the heart's beliefs. Even if you say the man is healed, while your heart aches because he does not show forth health, you know you say he is healed because you believe he is if the Science is true. So, even in this case your belief is in your words, and if you say he is not healed, you speak from what you feel most strongly at that moment. So words are flags.

Jesus did not believe in having even our most vigorous belief in evil come forth expressed before the world. He said what to us means: Suppose you have said some violent words, expressions of your strong emotion, like "What a fool I am," or, "I am terribly abused and an unfortunate person," and it actually appears today as if you had made some bitter mistakes, or were going to ruin. I say unto you, you may blast such words as Jesus blasted the vigorous fig tree, and never see any fruit of mistakes that bring hurts or misfortunes.

Right here let me tell you that if you are going to remember in your mind how sick your patient looks, you must turn that memory right out of doors. Look at a picture of some beautiful character, or speak some lofty principles over and over, for the memory of how your patient seems while sick will bring out that sickness plainly expressed.

If you are given to imagining how something would seem if it came to hurt you, get right away from the imagination at once, for an imagination is determined to come out some way. If you have taken some good premise in mind "late in life," as we hear it expressed, you have struck a hard blow to the fears and imaginations you formerly held.

Possibly they may come out in your dreams. Be thankful they get no farther than your sleeping time in their exposure, for they were making ready to come out before all mankind in your affairs.

All evil is blamed to sin, but sin is only a mistaken idea of life, a mistaken idea of who you are, and what world you live in. This is all the sin you or anybody ever committed. You made your mistake in mind, and have lived out that mistake. This Truth erases that mistake. Then your life is free from the cause of its suffering and trouble.

You may often wonder why the Truth student, who claims to believe the doctrine of no sin, no sickness, no death, does not immediately show peaceful, satisfied conditions. "Suppose the rain and dust have beaten against the plate glass windows until they are very dirty; do you think the mere cessation of the rain and dust will make the windowpanes clean? So it is with the mind that is covered with years of habitual imaginations. It ceases from imaginations, but practical daily washings of the dust of years must be made. This does not make the sin of imagination, the mistakes about life, a reality, but explains how real it seems to us."

The ninth stone is the topaz, which stands for harmony between thoughts and externals. The world in which we live is the exact record of our thoughts. If we do not like the world we live in, then we do not like our thoughts. This is discord. There are thoughts which we can love greatly while we think them. They make conditions which we love. This is harmony. He who loves his thoughts greatly and loves his words greatly is sure to be a musician of some kind. There is much joy in his life. Let no one be surprised at his not being perfect in his science of music while he does not love his thoughts and enjoy the environments they have made.

Within each of you is the song of the Spirit. By thinking out that song within your mind, it will break forth over your affairs. Some Truth students sing their treatments, they sing their ideas. You can sing mentally until a joy of heart takes possession of you. This joy will come to pass in happy surroundings sooner or later.

Some of us fret because it takes so long to bring out thoughts of good into our environments. This is discord. If we are given to discords, let us often say:

"I give thanks and glad praise that God hath given to the Holy Spirit all the joy and song of the universe, and she does not have to pray for it, beg for it, work for it, nor struggle for it; she is joyous and sings because she is joy. I am glad that the

Holy Spirit is joy and harmony." You will uncover your spring of joy that lies within you, and soon you will sing and be joyous without trying to do so.

It is noticeable in almost all religious people that their first idea of goodness is to make life in some way harder for them selves and each other. They drive themselves to get up at five o'clock in the morning, with their families, and to go without sleep until one or two o'clock each morning, saying that as Spirit needs no rest and is strong enough to do all things, they are as able as Spirit to do that which is most harrowing to the whole family, without murmuring. This may be what you will be tempted to agree to on one subject or another. It is forgetfulness of the way of Jesus, who slept and ate, drank and clothed himself exactly like other people, and only did differently when it pleased Himself to do so, never even asking his disciples to share any of his self-elected hardships.

The yoke of Jesus upon you is easy. God is rest. The violets do not strain and struggle to be in harmony with their life. The mountains do not groan and labor to be great. The hurricane and the simoon of the desert do their mighty tasks easily. It is not being in adjustment with the Divine Mind to be thinking hard lines to travel on. Because we are Spirit, we do that which our own judgment prompts us to do, and lay no burdens on each other because of our ideas.

If it is hard for you to cure your case, you have made the mistake somewhere of believing in hardships for somebody or for yourself. A mistaken idea about God and your own life will break out somewhere.

Jesus Christ would not cast Himself off a pinnacle to show how mentally powerful He was. He moved at the dictation of Spirit along lines not laid down by men or historic precedents. If you watch very carefully you will see that there is not an item of your life in which you are not guided by the Spirit into ways of pleasantness and peace. Any other way is one you have chosen, independent of Jesus Christ principles, and is the sin of your life, that is, the mistake upon which you move about.

The ninth stone is the topaz — harmony in peace, and delight with the pathway we are walking. There is one treatment which results in efficiency to manage environment easily. It is this:

"I do not accuse the world or myself of sin; all is well."

You have no idea how much of the inefficiency of mankind comes from thinking about the wrong-doings of others, and of ourselves. There is nothing more miserable than to feel that by some mistake in life you have not amounted to what you might have, and that your misfortunes all hinge on that mistake. Now while a mistake seems to be so much, its right name is nothingness. God never made any mistakes in Spirit. Your family never made any mistakes in Spirit. None of you can possibly make any mistake in Spirit. As Spirit is all that is real of you, the facing of the worst trouble of your life with the words that the mistakes that brought them being nothing, the troubles are nothing, will have a marvelous effect in putting them in a new relation with you. I do not mean that you will be hardened to bear them, I mean that they will be gone.

The day of the Lord cometh as a thief in the night, silently. God, the Truth, taketh away the grief and sickness as a mother comforteth. God is merciful. Be merciful with your people. The Good acts only through mercy. Efficiency comes with letting the goodness of the merciful and tender Spirit speak, instead of your condemning tendencies, wherever evil seems so plain. It is a sign of being farther on in Truth when you can make sin as unreal in your mind as matter. If Spirit is the only substance, matter is no substance. If holiness is the only presence, sin is not present.

You will be sure to be faced up with your case uncured the

third time if between seeing it the second and third times you have harbored feelings of how wrongly people have acted. There are a few claims of wrong-doing, or sins, which always bring a case in the third time. There is selfishness. We see that plainly in certain people, we say. By what right do we see selfishness? By right of the Spirit or of the carnal? We speak of enviousness. Who has envy? The Spirit? If the Spirit has not envy, of whom are we talking when we speak of enviousness in others or ourselves? Of nobody, most certainly, for Spirit is all. Then there is no jealousy. Have we accused ourselves of jealousy? We are the Holy Spirit. Do you wonder that accusation brings great infirmity to represent it? If we call anybody malicious, revengeful, or cruel, we have spoken of Life, Mind, Spirit. That fairly ties our own thoughts in chains so that they do not heal well, manage environments well, or do anything in the way of skillfulness that we so much wish they would.

If sin seems so real to you take every Wednesday afternoon and deny the reality of every sin you have ever heard of. Thus will your Spirit stand out in its uncondemned holiness, and, unchained, will do great works for you.

Plato taught that the whole world is a colossal system of shadows. The deepest shade is the belief in wrong-doing. Its shadows throw long stretches of desert and forest over your pathway, which in Truth is all light with the glory of Goodness. It is said of elephants that they sometimes, in eastern countries, fight shadows on the rocks and beat themselves to pieces. Thus our missionaries and philanthropists, fighting the huge shadow of belief of somebody doing great wrongs in the universe, lie down with the feeling of how gigantic the monsters are who have the poor world in their jaws.

Learn that there is a divine harmony between the Mind from whence the true world is springing, and your mind; such a harmony that you yourself are that mighty and good Mind. Isaiah pictures that peaceable kingdom where the wolf and the lamb, the calf and the young lion shall lie down together; and the child shall play with the serpent, and the sting of all that seems to be hurtful shall be removed.

"Behold the Lamb of God, which taketh away the sin of the world." The lamb is meekness, and the lamb is not suspicious. The lamb trusts to your goodness. The Lamb of God is Jesus Christ, who condemned none, forgave all, suspected none, believed in no evil, feared nothing, loved everything. Therefore He healed instantaneously. Therefore He said, "All power is given unto Me in heaven and in earth."

If you feel all the time as though you ought to be protecting yourself from mankind, either financially, or as to reputation, stop and think over these Wednesday afternoon words. You must not put up umbrellas against things which do not exist. Umbrellas are a burden in pleasant weather. By this I mean, if God is your world, what have you to fear? So your fears are a burden. Belief that I have made a mistake terrifies me. Belief that you have made a mistake terrifies you. And so with all the world. If now we are told so strongly that it takes effect in our blood and our bones, and if we are convinced that it is true that we never could make any mistake, then our fear is gone.

"Thou wilt keep him in perfect peace whose mind is staid on Thee." "I will fear no evil, for Thy rod and Thy staff they comfort me." Rod means *activity*, and staff means *rest of mind*. We act wisely and rest comfortably, therefore we are comforted. Deny the inheritance of sin. "The son shall not bear the iniquity of the father," saith the Lord. Deny the race iniquities. "For am I not God? Do I not fill heaven and earth?" Deny contagion of sin. Fear nothing from suggestion of evil. "There shall no evil touch thee," "Thou shalt be hid from the scourge of the tongue." Deny the personal sin. "Neither hath this man sinned, nor his parents." Deny that you ever wronged anyone, for in you is God only.

Socrates, on being asked, "What is the most troublesome to good men?" answered, "The prosperity of the wicked." People who have made certain mistakes do not touch their finances or environments with those mistakes. They touch only their bodies. Some people's mistakes touch their environment entirely, while their bodies are very well indeed. There has been no statement of cause and effect yet given forth which has been entirely accurate in describing how a selfish disposition or an envious one should affect the business of a man or the health of a man. Injustice in money matters does not always bring financial disaster to the actor. It may break out in his children instead of himself.

Each one of us has all he can do to look to the ways of his own heart, and make his harmony between his own heart thoughts and his world, by thinking as his heart is really thinking at its spiritual center, instead of from the mistakes of his thoughts about life and God, which are not his heart but his imagination. Let us imagine nothing, let us speak Truth. Sometimes people feel that all the talk about even the presence and character of God as Good, as Life, Truth, Love, Omnipresence, Omnipotence, Omniscience, is pure imagination, because nobody has seen or heard or felt such a being or such a principle. They resolve everything into imagination. Well, if imagination can take its choice between imagining life, holy and omnipresent, or death, evil and pain, and can bring into outer manifestation according to its ideas so imagined, we will see that it is a higher and nobler imagination to conceive of Omnipotent Good, than to conceive of evil.

Man naturally thinks there is a God. You think so. If every book that you picked up said there is no God, you would dispute it. It is not in anyone to dispute, however, if we point out the truth that there is no such God as some have imagined — one sending afflictions and pain upon the good and innocent of the world. We are ready to give up such an imagination at once when the reasonable idea is presented that Almighty Goodness did not create a Satan, nor create passions and appetites and deceptions. He made only the good and the holy. The bad and the wicked are not made — they only seem to be made. They are the shadows of the substance of the Good.

A good trait in you, like generosity, is seen to throw down a dark opposite to itself. You show jealousy. There was hardly ever a generous person without the opposite trait called jealousy showing its dark streak. Jealousy is the long headlight of generosity. The jealousy is nothing, it is not there. The generosity is something. It is God's presence. So, of all that is not desirable, the pure goodness being called substance, and the bad called shadow, the goodness comes into plainer sight, and the badness disappears altogether.

Moses took a figure of speech to illustrate principles. Paul told his friends to take a little wine instead of so much water. He means to take strong statements, go forward in thought, instead of thinking the old religious ideas. Each mind naturally clings to its former idea of God.

In spite of their high reasonings, often you will find some Truth students falling into begging a great being on a throne in the air to help them, even after they know that there is no such God, but that instead there is the Almighty Principle of Truth and Goodness. Paul's young friend, Timothy, was inclined to think sometimes in the old ways. It is a weak way to think. Take some wine of doctrine, stronger and warmer ideas of life.

Moses in this ninth lesson says, "Let the waters bring forth abundantly the moving creature that hath life." Waters mean thoughts. The living creatures of the thoughts are the environments alive, the people, the friendships, the society, the children. Let your flowing thoughts, warmed at the fountain of pure reason, be rich in affection, love, life, joy, harmony. Swedenborg said that Moses meant affection by living creatures.

The eighth lesson was about having light. The true religion is the true light. Light is warmth. The brighter the sun the hotter it shines. The hotter the sun the surer the rivers are to bring forth living creatures in abundance. So, the hotter your religion, the warmer your love for the world, for God, for Truth. The warmer your love, the more friends and pleasures and conditions of joy surround you. This is confidence in your doctrine. It might be called self-confidence.

People who lack self-confidence are those who have not warmed into confidence in their doctrine. They are given to accusation of sin, but they as often accuse themselves of sin as their neighbors. Nothing alive and solid with success ever stays in the hands of people who are given to accusing others or themselves of sin. By this I mean, prosperity will always seem just ahead of you if you think of people or yourself as selfish, envious, jealous, revengeful, or cruel. Your health will always seem just out of your reach. Your healing power will always be slipping through your fingers. Just as you think your case is cured it is not cured. Every time it can be traced to your accusing of sin. Stop that, and your waters of mind will gather prosperity so tangibly that you cannot mistake judgments. Your waters of mind will breed new healing power. New affairs, new schemes in some line, will please and satisfy you.

If anyone tells you of there being a principle of evil, deny it. If anybody tells you of there being a Satan, deny it. If anybody tells you of there being a fall of man from his God estate, deny it. If you read of sin, deny it. You must not have a poor opinion of yourself. Your substance, your intelligence, your nature is

God. If the Spirit of you arises in its strength, you will have great confidence in your own mission, your own work, your own powers.

General Taylor, during the Mexican War, called a council of Mexicans. They told him that in numbers and artillery his enemies were so far ahead that he stood no chance of victory. "We will dismiss this council until after the battle," he said. His confidence in his principle of action was so aroused that he brought forth substantial victory.

Your principle of life is worth believing in with all your soul, or it is not worth believing in at all. Come, make up your mind decidedly. Do you believe there is any sin in the whole universe? If you do, but wish you did not, then you have light on your waters, but not heat enough to create good, tangible success.

People who ignore the sins of their neighbors the most are most beloved, and they love most. They are our best healers. People who believe in their own doctrine with all their might and main succeed every time. Make up your mind about this sin question, and you will settle the ninth point in Truth. You will polish the topaz stone of harmony with your life. Discords and strife will cease. New creations will spring forth as the result of your new thoughts.

Klopstock, the German poet, who wrote "Creation," was waited upon in Hamburg by some students who walked all the way from Gottingen to ask him what he meant by a certain passage in his composition. "I do not just now recall what I meant, gentlemen," he said, "but it would pay you to spend your lifetime trying to find out what I meant." He had such implicit confidence in the accuracy of the genius that inspired him, that he saw it must have burned with a glory out of the reach of his own ordinary mind to have spoken beyond what, in calm moments, he could comprehend. Rogers, the poet, always read his own compositions. He believed in his own genius. He was greatly honored. Wordsworth always wanted to have his own writings read to him, for he trusted and loved his own genius. He was greatly honored. Michelangelo, Dickens, Pericles — all believed in their own inspiration. "If I said it, it is so, and if it is so, I said it," said one who never opened his lips carelessly, never exaggerated, never misrepresented, wrote what he meant about God, human reason and Satan, so that even his contemporaries listened to him.

Hannibal swore eternal hate to Rome, and he believed so implicitly in the genius of his oath that when the Romans wanted to scare their children, they cried, "Hannibal is at the gate." On every plan of your campaign believe in your principles, whatever they are. Hannibal's principle was destruction of the Romans. Poetry records of him that "The pages of his history with tears of blood are wet." It shows how confidence in the principle with which you work will work it out in your life. Moses calls works of religious confidence "living creatures of good things that make glad." No crying, no killing, no sickness, or death in them. Religious teachings at their best have no pain in them. They have living Good. So when you once wake up to conscious confidence in your religion, you bring forth works, with great prosperity for yourself and for everyone.

Jesus Christ taught the making of gold by this law — stopping the conscious waters of mind with hot words full of substance. He taught the making of bread by the conscious confidence of mind in the Spirit that flows through it. You must believe that God works through you to will and to do some peculiar mission. Have confidence that if one man does to you what seems to be a wrong, your genius, your Spirit, your God is that moment working good for you. The man is the instrument. This is your religion taken exactly word for word from

Jesus Christ: "For if you love them that love you, what reward have you? Love them that hate you, and do good to them that despitefully use you." God is then working the reward in the new delight right at hand.

Despise not the creatures of the sea. The rivers of Mind, flowing with true rewards, are legal creations. You have a right to rewards, said Jesus. They are the product of confidence in your religion, says Truth. Certain ideas produce certain conditions. If you believe that something evil is going to happen to you because you once committed an injustice against somebody which you do not forgive yourself for, and you have not confidence in the Spirit of God as having made that wrong nothingness, your confidence will bring it forth, especially if you feel keenly about the matter. You won't like it, but you believe that way. Of course you know that fear of a thing is confidence enough in it to bring it to pass. Job said, "The thing that I feared hath come upon me."

It is a singular fact that people who lament much over anything always have liver complaint. Jeremiah wrote, "Mine eyes do fail with tears, my bowels are troubled, my liver is poured out upon the earth." You see he speaks of three maladies from lamentations, viz: poor eyesight, bowel trouble, and liver complaint. This may often be a hint to you in denying the cause of these three sicknesses. But back of the lamenting there must have been something believed worth lamenting about, and that is always some wrong done by somebody. That wrong never took place in God's Kingdom, so there was nothing to lament about, and the Spirit never laments. Therefore, there is no disease. This reasoning put mentally to your patient is the flowing of a river of Truth through his dry lands. It will wash away the history of his disease. It will bring out living health in his organs. In the Scriptures you can find many instances of reasoning like that of Jeremiah.

The early practitioners of healing always got a history of the case of their patients, then they negatived it by saying: "You had no cause to mourn; having no cause to mourn, you never could mourn; therefore you have no failing eyesight, for there has nothing transpired to affect your eyes. You see with spiritual vision, which no mortal condition can interfere with." If, now, you remember somebody with failing eyesight, stop and repeat this treatment.

For these three maladies, so-called, we use a scientific argument for the whole race. Take yesterday's treatment, nullifying hypocrisy, deception, lies, psychological influences, and give it to the whole world. And when your patient arrives for the second time you will not have to treat him against deception and its effects. Something will come very strongly to you, and as you are bringing out your healing river by a scientific process, you can explain how others can heal as well as yourself. Tell that the whole world is absolutely well. "The inhabitants shall not say, I am sick, any more."

The reason so much is said about bodily cure and not about moral reformation and prosperity is because if the body is well the man can catch the tones of Truth on the larger and more intricate problems of life. Bodily healing often depends upon moral rectitude. It often depends upon prosperity. So you must focus your mind to the word "Health" for the world, expecting to touch each separate need of a man the moment you look at him.

It is a great principle to understand that if you know the law of the Good, how it works when truth is told, that health and intelligence will spring forth from the face and through the bodily frame of whomsoever you speak to, whether mentally or audibly. The moment you see that the Good is really working through you, everything looks different to you from what it did before. The man's voice does not seem so rough as it did before. The child's cough seems free, it acts as if it were passing away, soon to be forgotten.

You have no idea how soon you forget evil when you have sight of the Good. The sight of Good surely acting with you makes you love it. Then you have confidence in it. Then you do good work. This is formulating Truth. When you see someone who seems to be selfish, what will you say? You will say, "Spirit never formulates in selfishness." Or you will say, "Truth never expresses in selfishness." And you will be sure to say, "I do not accuse myself or my world of selfishness."

Why do you say, "I do not accuse myself of selfishness"? Because every person you see is the expression of your own traits of character. When he is set right, you are set right. The business man you know best represents your business matters. Get him prosperous and satisfied, and you will be prosperous and satisfied. The musician you know best expresses one of your ideas on some subject. Get that idea right and he will be a fine musician. The singer whose voice you do not enjoy is one of your own thoughts out of chord with God. Tell her mentally that she is the voice of the Holy Spirit to you, and that you will not feel her imperfection. She will be gone from your ears, and her mission to you will be plain. You will feel a love, a warmth towards the Spirit that will soon bring the good news about something quite different from singing.

A woman was eating her dinner, and a telegram about the death of her son came to her. The hardness with which she received the news hardened the food in her stomach, and for years afterward she had dyspepsia. A healer told her that Spirit never received bad news, never was shocked, was always free and strong. She was cured of indigestion that day. So this doctrine, always telling of God and life and health and prosperity, does not seem to be a tangible machine like a grist mill or factory, yet it grinds out the desires of the heart in happy, satisfying conditions by its own mysterious lowliness and power. We have new circumstances by its mystic fingers. It loves to feel you in harmony with it, for then it works freely through you to will and to do. All the time it is your own mind speaking that which you call spirit. Let this be clear to you: "There is a spirit in man and the inspiration of the Almighty giveth him understanding." It is your own breath of Omnipotence when you think forth great thoughts of God. It is your own in-breathing of Omnipotence when you are pleased with something in your life. That pleasure came to pass because from the deeps of your spirit along the way somewhere you spoke truth or thought truth.

People think more truly than you give them credit for. The grumbler has some great truth which he speaks or thinks often. It makes him successful. He has many happy moments. The rest is shadow, vanity, absence. The evil is nothingness. He would change his habits entirely if you would think the truth toward him, that he is searching so restlessly for the good. The thief would drop everything and praise and bless Jesus Christ if you would breathe toward him the thoughts his mind is restlessly searching around for. The sick man would be well at once if you would breathe toward him the thoughts his heart has fainted for lack of.

"Who shall save us from our sin save he that seeth no sin in us?" If we punish sin by any other method then denying its reality, we make it more manifest than ever. So the Jesus Christ method of a blameless life, free from condemnation, peaceable, forgiving, mild, gentle, unpretentious, all the time shedding a fine radiance of inner light abroad, is the only way of setting free from sin. If you have a steady habit of thinking high thoughts, your presence will be helpful to people.

It was said of Socrates, you remember, that his presence, even without speaking, would regulate a man's judgment. If you have a strict moral rectitude, you can balance a man's health without treating him. You can clarify a man's ideas without speaking to him. Often you will have an entirely different effect upon people from what your treatments read. For instance, you might treat one for deafness, and turn his thoughts into new channels, yet not touch his deafness. This shows that your mind works that way. You must be pleased with whatever way your mind works. Pleasure at even a remote good will bring other good into your manner of action.

I have been speaking to you about a supposed case of disease. You know very well that there never was any disease. Why, then, do I speak of one, and tell you to take a case of some kind to cure? Because we take all the appearances in one lot and tell the truth. We look at the child's arithmetical problem and say "No" where it is not true. We say "Yes" to what is true. So we meet the children who are working out their life problems. We know wherein it is not the truth they speak by the sight they show. We know wherein we have not spoken the truth by the life we lead. If I am in bondage, I have had some extreme error about God and His relation to my life. The truth tells me how to erase that error. Jesus Christ erased errors very rapidly. You and I will erase errors rapidly or slowly according to our nature. If we stumble at the calling of sin nothingness, unreality, absence in this sea of omnipresence, we shall be slow in demonstration. We shall not be joyous. Our singing will be poor.

We cannot be like God until we speak and think of sin as God does. You do not believe that God looks at sin. You know that "His eyes are too pure to behold iniquity." You believe that God sees everything. Then He would see sin if there was any to see. What is this that looks like a man striking a child? In Truth there is no such action taking place. What was that when a man shot his little son? In Truth he never did. It is all the figment of the imagination. You have dreamed the stories. "Awake, thou that sleepest," shouted Paul. There is a spirit in those you have spoken of that knows nothing of those actions which you name. Look toward the Spirit. Fix your eyes there. Hear now the direction of the Almighty as to what you are to do while you are looking toward that Spirit. "Their sin will I remember no more against them forever." *You need not harbor the memory of sin if God does not.*

A woman was greatly persecuted, as it seemed to her, by people who wished to get her position from her. Suddenly while she was riding in a street car amid the smoke and noise of the city where she lived, she said, "How would God regard persecutions? Would He cry and mourn about them, or ignore them? He certainly would not know anything about them. Neither will I." This treatment took away all her grief and fear.

Is it not to you a great rest that your true and real substance does not know anything about sin, sickness, or death? When you are tempted to mix up with misery by feeling miserable, remember your noble spirit, which knows no sorrows, no pains, no sickness, no unkindness, no burden. Is it not a joy to you that you have the power right within yourself to annul every evil thing? If there is no reality in sin, rise to agree with the principle and love it. There have, as yet, been only a few to whom sin was as unreal as matter. They have had great power in healing where matter was the first unreality to them. Stopping at either of these milestones you do not harmonize with the world around you. Stepping past them, by the leading of the spirit, you harmonize your life.

If you will notice the topaz stone you will see it has a happy light. It is the peaceful light of satisfaction with your thoughts as they fold themselves around you in good friendships, good healing power, and reformed conduct of men. I use the word "reformed" in the same sense that I use "healing." God needs no healing, therefore there is no healing to be done. God needs no reforming, therefore there is no reforming to be done. What then? We tell the truth, and as the whole and perfect man steps forth, he looks on the sense plane as if he were being healed. We tell the truth, and on the sense plane it looks as if the upright son of God were reforming his actions.

I know and you know that there is no work to be done. Does God work? Is not all finished in God? Yet this very saying that there is no work to be done, gives us the appearance of accomplishing miracles, because as the signs of the heavenly estates appear they push the earthly estates aside. The rolling of the earthly conditions away looks like activity. It is really the rest of God. Have you ever watched a star come into sight on a summer evening? It was there all the time, in solemn repose, but as the night deepens the star seems to be shot towards you. At first it is startling. Thus with the last day of earth. The heavenly land swiftly speeds into our sight, the earth rolls aside her curtains.

The topaz light of your thoughts bringing out your word swiftly, is the leaping up of the heart into the mouth with joyous song. The joyous heart is a healing presence. Do you remember how Solomon said, "The merry heart doeth good like a medicine?" "Smile and sing ye the songs of Zion." Sing the thoughts of this truth you bring out. Spirit can heal the whole world if it never yields to lamentations. Will you now take the case you remembered yesterday, and call his or her name? Bow your head and let the Spirit say within you: "*I have never accused the world or myself of sin — all is Good.*"

Now to the patient, your friend, speak as I am addressing my friend:

You are not covered with formulations of sin; therefore you are not diseased.

You have not received an inheritance of sin in disease. You came forth from God.

You are not surrounded by a race of sin; you are surrounded by God.

You do not hear sin, see sin, feel sin, fear sin, from anywhere; therefore you are free in purity.

There is no gathering of the consequences of sin around the Spirit; therefore you are free from the consequence of sin.

You have not gathered your own sins together in disease. You are free from disease.

There is no cause for disease in Spirit.

I do not lay any burden of belief in my own sinfulness upon you.

The sins of carnal mind I do not believe in. I do not believe in selfishness. I do not believe in envy, I do not believe in jealousy. I do not believe in revenge. I do not believe in cruelty. I do not believe in the outshowing of these claims against mankind.

I believe mankind is God and God is mankind, without sin, sickness, disease, or death.

Therefore your life is Good, and cannot be threatened with death, nor yield to death, nor fear death in any part of your being.

Your health is God, and cannot be threatened with disease, nor fear disease, nor yield to disease in any part of you.

Your strength is Good; it cannot be threatened with weakness, nor fear weakness, nor yield to weakness in any part of you.

You are ready to acknowledge that you are healed. You say this freely to all, to yourself, to me, now.

In the name of the Father and the Son and the Holy Ghost, I pronounce you every whit whole.

Give this treatment three times before you sleep tonight. While you give it, write it out as nearly as you can. Sing it to yourself. Have confidence in it. This is what Moses meant by, "Let the waters bring forth living creatures."

CHAPTER X.

All seeds have their seed within themselves, the Scriptures tell us. Their seed is their ego, their vitality, their meaning. If you are treating a case you may discover that you can see with another set of eyes than the ones you ordinarily use. You might be half awake and see something appear in your presence, yet not in your conscious presence. Thus, while treating a man for lameness, you might see a star shining before you. Its meaning would be its seed. You are to take that meaning for your own use. It means that your word shines steadily like a star of hope to the man's helpless mind. He is feeling a little ray of hope. Its seed is the kindness of the law to you. It is your business to stop thinking about your treatment, about the man, and give thanks that your words have worked so well. If you are pledged to a principle it will work for you in loving kindness.

The tenth lesson of Science is the gift of skill in handling things with thoughts, so that they record your thoughts perfectly. The instrument must record the singing and joy of the musician. The scroll must teach others what music can do. The instrument must vibrate to the touch of the fingers. Your practice must tell the world what your genius can do. Everything you do must have its process of demonstration, which, by being recorded in plain sight, can show others how to do likewise.

While Paganini lived, he made the violin give forth tones and semi-tones of harmonies unheard of by the ears of man, till, swinging his heaven-tipped bow in the fourth dimension of space, he thrilled multitudes to awed inspiration. But there is no record of these harmonies. They were not inscribed on scrolls, nor did any pupil receive them. He had no skill of instructing in his science.

The tenth stone is the chrysoprasus, which is described as "of quartz, a variety of chalcedony, apple green in color and sometimes used as a gem." It is the color that stands for the true earth. It is the Heavenly City that descends. It is the bride, the Lamb's wife. The green fields and white gleaming mountains of Paradise are the new land into which we set our feet, if we have polished the ninth stone of our foundation, the topaz of harmony between our thoughts and our outer world.

If we have discovered how to be joyous and grateful, while yet on earth, which seems so dark and unreliable; if we have learned to smile and praise, while there was nothing, seemingly, to smile about or to be grateful for, there will come a moment when everything we are able to do we can teach others to do, and this is the stone of companionship — the chrysoprasus — for dwelling among equals. The green stone polished and smiling with answering goodness. The chrysoprasus stands for understanding how to handle things without effort.

Everything is as good to us as we have been to it. It records our skill. It tells of our ability to put our Soul life into words. It tells of our ability to discard symbol and realize reality, while we are giving forth thoughts, words, writings. Things and objects and people are the records now of ways we have thought in the past, also of ways we think now. We think new and joyous thoughts of people, of things, of life, and they presently begin to respond to our thoughts. The joyousness you persisted in has recorded itself, and answers back to you, as face answereth to face in the glass. This is the chrysoprasus stone.

When people and things respond because of your words, because of your thoughts, it is to your honor, your credit, your skill, that they have come forth. It is quite different from having things seem to be mysteriously good, unexpectedly kind.

You must know that all the lessons in Science are lessons in consciousness, lessons in your pure intelligence. It is not the chrysoprasus stone of your works when you heal blindness suddenly, or as it were, accidentally. You must know how to heal when you heal; be able to teach others how to heal, and understand keeping your cases well after they are healed. You must *know* how to make a permanent work. You must play upon all the chords and anvils of appearance with the touch of one whose words will endure after him — endure forever.

Jesus taught His disciples how to keep alive, but Paul says they preferred death. In an old French book there is record of a man who pledged himself to the Holy Spirit, and became so quick and efficient with his thoughts that there was nothing he asked for, as a child might ask for a cup of water, but what he got, as quickly as the child would get the water from its kind nurse. After a time he became tired of dwelling among symbols and asked that he might fold himself round with the mantle of death. He never seemed to have any idea of how to teach the process by which he entered into such union with the Spirit of God. He never seemed to have fixed his ideas into the surrounding conditions of his human lot, so that others were greatly benefited because of his conscious intentions. He did not seem to be selfish, but only unconscious on this question.

The stones, spoken of in Revelation, all stand for living stones, as you know, by which is meant that your living Mind is your God. There are twelve evidences of entire consciousness. You must not be asleep on any point of doctrine. Every faculty must be awake and alive. Unlike the Frenchman, who helped himself by the consciousness of the presence of the Spirit, but who seemed to have been unconscious of the needs of others, not through selfishness but through not realizing; these lessons teach us to realize and to do, leaving nothing undone. This tenth lesson is on the subject of making your work tell, making it stay by you, making it as definitely good, and as alive in its good, as your own soul.

It has always been noted by metaphysicians that people who have diseases as the result of their sinfulness do not get well as quickly as those who simply catch maladies from surrounding mental belief in disease. The whole process is unreality, and the idea that people do not give up sin readily is only an imagination. When one imagines that there is a mixture of good and evil in the universe, he is sure to see a great deal of good and evil. If he lets his mind balance on the gloomy side, more than on the joyous side, he will see more evil conditions than good in his lot. He will not touch the tenth lesson. He will not see his world record joyousness, if he does not put joyousness forth from his mind as a steady stream into the world.

Moses said, "Let the earth bring forth cattle and creeping things." Earth means mind when it is formulated by persistent thought. The bringing forth of mind is "cattle" — which is a symbolic word for larger human relations, like governments, schools, homes, friends, family. "Creeping things," is a term signifying affairs like business, daily tasks, eating, drinking, sleeping. These things, says the text, come forth in a new beauty by the persistent thinking of new truths, cheerful breaths from the Spirit of the Supreme Cheer.

All the world, and our close family relations, are Good beyond good. Let the mind see good step by step. From mountain peak to mountain peak let lofty ideas spring, never forgetting the splendor of one peak, but ever onward. Thus it is with the lessons of Science. One lesson seems to be all. The next takes us to another statement of Truth. The next still on, till the twelve gates of Truth are opened.

Our conscious, wide-awake thoughts, never off guard, must

smile, and rejoice that our obedient world may be at last compelled to return our smile. Gentleness, love, cheerfulness, these
may seem to be slow in conquering the world, but they have
Deity, in all its enduring force, behind them. So Moses here
would say, "Stand here and see your mighty principle, carried
out into government, churches, schools, homes, friends, family
life, into daily tasks, eating, drinking, sleeping. Let everything
that hath breath or that moveth, praise the Lord."

You know there is a natural strength within your mind to be
your best, and do your most creditable thing. You choose to do
and be successful. Some have chosen to be known as very rich.
They would have that for their high ambition. Ward McAlister
chose to lead society life in New York; Lady Vanderbilt wished
to take Mrs. Astor's place as social leader. Mendelssohn chose
to be known by his "Elijah" in music. Hayden will be forever
honored for his "Creation." Raphael will ever be known as the
Divine Raphael because of "The Transfiguration." So, at the
height of your genius, there rests some masterpiece of splendor,
laid out for you to do from the beginning, before ever the world
was. It is the making of your goodness or your Christ character,
whose glory rests ever in the center of your own being, manifest
in your own world. Things are plastic substance which your
skillful fingers mold, as Angelo molded the marble. They are
as receptive to your finger touches as the canvas to Perugino,
who taught Raphael to paint.

You must find out the secrets of every creature, and make
them speak. Your mind is a greater work as the follower of
Christ than Mendelssohn's, for there is music far beyond his
masterpiece, but there is no music beyond that which you bring
forth from the earth when you have proved that, to you, there
is in Truth only God (or Good).

In setting forth to heal a man of his mental formulations,
called disease, you disintegrate his accumulated ideas by true

Principle. You reason his ideas right out of his mind. It is very much like ungluing them. His ideas fall all to pieces, and there is nothing left of them.

There is always a spot of time, a little moment, when it almost seems as if a man would not let his old ideas go. If at that moment you are true to your Principle, stronger than ever, and ignore his conditions with more skill than ever, you will see him yield his false position without another struggle.

A very lame man was at a political meeting when slavery was called a "divine institution." This so stirred his mind that it held his body free from lameness and he jumped to his feet. The people laughed to see him forget his lameness, and when he saw them laughing he remembered it again, and sat down, as lame as ever. There was a time when this text would have been his entire healing, "Touch not the earth." His mind should have kept him from the earthly condition, and soared away on the ideas he knew were divine. So, when a woman who was being healed kept shouting how much worse she was, the healer took less notice of her than before, and praised God in her secret mind with harder praises than ever, till the patient ceased screaming, and after a few moments cried, "I am entirely healed."

If a patient comes before us the fourth time for healing, it shows there is a conflict going on within his mind and body. It shows that, before we saw him, we had been somewhat disturbed on the question of which is more powerful in the world, good or evil. Maybe we had been wondering if, after all, there was not a Satan. Maybe we had thought it might be, in the long run, that good, and right, and justice, would prevail, but at present things were pretty dark. Things must have seemed very much mixed up to us. So on comes the patient for the fourth treatment, and up comes the undissolved trouble again.

Well, the first thing to do is to bow the head, and let the

Spirit speak of faith, confidence, steadfastness. We have come to the middle wall of partition. We are where we must let the Spirit say, "*I do not believe in mixtures. I do not believe in failure. I believe in success.*"

If you will take Thursday afternoon and say all that the Spirit does not believe, and all that the Spirit does believe, you will not have a long treatment with a case when it appears the fourth time. You will see the good health stand out very plainly, right then and there. Or, if, when you begin to feel so mixed within your own mind on the question of evil, and good, you will say strongly, "*I do not believe in evil, I believe in the Good. I do not believe it takes time for goodness to prove itself powerfully; I believe goodness demonstrates itself instantly. I do not believe in sickness, I believe in health. I do not believe in trouble, I believe in peace.*" You will bring the patient's good health out with great skill.

Let us stop the lesson right here, and rally ourselves and say, as strongly as the Spirit speaks it, "*I do not believe in evil, I believe in the Good. I do not believe it takes time for goodness to prove itself powerfully; I believe goodness demonstrates itself instantly. I do not believe in sickness, I believe in health. I do not believe in trouble, I believe in peace.*" If your business troubles face you after you have treated faithfully three treatments, you certainly have been doubtful in your mind whether you could settle them by mental process or not. Doubt is sure to haul your lame business back into its lameness again. What you want to do is to refuse the lame side of the question. Don't touch it. "Touch not the earth," means keep your eye on the mark of the high calling.

God's prophet once told the Jews that it would not do for them to number the soldiers, or the people, because it was at a time when it would have discouraged them to know what a small army they had. So it is sometimes best not to think how your patient is at all, not to ask him a single question, not to talk to him at all, not even to answer his questions. Keep your mind only on one side of the argument. Keep it on the side of your faith. Ignore the rest. "I do not believe a word of it — not a word," you say while he mourns, or cries, or complains, or describes his ailments. So, too, you say to your affairs, when they keep facing you with what looks like disaster, "*I do not believe it, I do not believe that side of the question. I believe in success, victory, prosperity, for myself in the name of Jesus Christ.*" You say it to all that troubles you. You say it to everything and everybody that comes for a fourth time. You say it every Thursday afternoon. The old conditions must unglue, must go. God reigns. Believe it.

"God lives in me in His strength and glory,
He lives in me as my strength divine.
By the light of His love I read life's story,
And the key of the world is mine."

The Good Mind is your God. Let the Good Mind speak when you speak. Let the Good Mind speak its own glorious Truth through you. We all see things according to the mind we use. If we use the Good Mind which is in us, how can we help seeing how true the world looks? How can we help turning the key into every tree and rock and animal, by the light of the topaz stone of cheerfulness, till its goodness stands out in eternal visibility? The ego of the stone is its God life. When it is plainly visible to you, by the use of your own consciousness, then it is visible forever. When you cure your case by your wisdom, you will cure him for all eternity. He cannot have the malady again. But you must remember that you are to make all mankind every whit whole. All creatures of the earth are to be obedient records of your conscious calling of their names.

The waters form the land. The waters of your mind must be left free to form your natural world. The land of your being is your present condition; it is your circumstances. The land, being once formed, it takes great and unusual force of the waters to change its shape and appearance. So the land might be called the doctrine of fate, as indeed your circumstances have been called your fate. Whatsoever you have thought consciously, your mechanical and obedient conditions of life must unresistingly record.

The land adhesion of your natural state of affairs is undermined, disintegrated, dissolved, by the true way of thinking. The true way of thinking, which we set to flowing through us, seems, sometimes, to be long in accomplishing its mission, but it comes to pass that our conscious thoughts get greater and greater impulse as we think on, till our whole earth falls to pieces. Friends change marvelously. Home reinstates itself. Maybe we seem to have no home. Business falters. Maybe we seem to fail. But this is the point where we are at the sepulchre in the beautiful garden of resurrection. We need not say, "They have taken away my Lord," simply because things look as if they were failing us. We must look up — up! Touch not the earth, touch God! We do not believe in material ways of thinking any more, and old conditions, manufactured by our material ways of thinking, must unglue in order that the conditions formulated by our true new ways of thinking may come forth.

"If the earthly house of this tabernacle be dissolved," no matter what part of our circumstances it represents, there is a spiritual house, eternal, not materially thought, not materially born, but spiritually thought out, and now showing its seed, its germ, its face, through the ungluing particles of the old disturbed conditions.

Scientific Christians, who have been very strong and steadfast, have seen everything change around them, because they have so entirely changed their thoughts. Holding steadfastly to some one principle, some one idea, they have gone through many seeming trials with victory. Once a lady saw that her husband looked as if he were passing into another sphere. She said, "God is Love." She did not treat her husband at all. Over and over she repeated the words, although not conscious that in Science we never treat anything violent directly, but turn our mind entirely to Spirit. She did this very way. Soon her husband rallied. Another woman saw her family in great trouble and knew that she could not endure circumstances that were dissolving around her. She could think of no words to say except, "Jesus Christ," and they all came through safely.

Whenever any disturbed condition arises, do not believe in it enough to notice it. Behind you, over you, near you, there is a voice saying, "Touch not the earth, touch Me." So you look away from your environments, and with just the assertion, "I do not believe in evil, I believe in Good," you will put your mind entirely on the Spirit near you. All acute cases of sickness are signals for saying firmly what you do believe, and what you do not believe.

One woman had so much trouble that she felt that she was losing her mind. She said, "I do not believe it is Thy will that I should be in trouble. 'Thou wilt keep him in perfect peace whose mind is stayed on Thee'." Then she kept looking away from her troubles. She would not allow herself to think of them. Over and over she repeated Isaiah's promise, "Thou wilt keep him in perfect peace whose mind is stayed on Thee," till help came to her. She was saved, not only mentally, but conditions adjusted themselves. After you have determined to breathe toward you the spirit of cheerfulness, the unbalanced and distracted state of your affairs will seem to make it impossible to hold your own in the midst of your changing and disordered seeming world. "Be steadfast," said Paul, "Unmovable, always abounding in the work of the Lord." He also noticed that it was just the same in a man's affairs as in his mind. If a man has determined to follow this path, he finds himself sometimes very ecstatic, very happy, then he gets despondent. He feels doubtful whether it is true, whether he can make a success of his life on the spiritual plane. This is his mind in relation to doctrine. He must tell himself that he believes every word he has spoken, and believes it will all demonstrate exactly as he has spoken it.

The same thing happens with your cases in healing. They delight you one day and discourage you the next, if you let them move your feelings by their ups and downs of conduct. This is where you must state that you believe your doctrine is working itself out in its own way, and there is nothing in the man working against your doctrine. Tell what you believe about your case, and what you do not believe. His actions are only the exposure of some doubts you yourself have been having, where you ought to have spoken: "I DO BELIEVE IN THE GOOD."

You cannot help noticing how chilling and depressing doubt is. It comes up and shakes you. Its name is fear. Many people call their doubt of the Good now working out with them in safety and power, fear. They speak of their fear, or they shake within themselves and hide it. Maybe some of you call it apprehension. Maybe you call it the blues. Its honest name is *doubt*. It is the dark shadow cast by the figure of faith, which stands so near you. You feel fear shake your hopes. Faith stands near. You know she can do anything. She can raise your hopes to highest heaven. She can fulfill your slightest wish. She is warming, strengthening, comforting. You can choose faith, or you can choose doubt. Both are near. One is the reality of life, the other is unreality. One or the other is chosen by what you say most vehemently. I have heard of people passing through those seasons of unhappiness, caused by doubt of the Good working with them, and almost without exception they have lain down and given up to dark and dismal feelings first, and then feebly struggled to lay hold of faith. The fact is you have to choose faith the first thing. Your first words determine your future.

But, you say, "I had my house burned down, my husband at the point of death. My two boys ran away. My money is all gone. My acquaintances deserted me. It is not possible to say that I believe this all good." Here is where you are mistaken. This is where so many make their mistake. The Science does not say death is good. It says there is no death. The Science does not say the deserters are good. It says there is no such thing as desertion. The Science does not say poverty is good. It says there is no poverty. The Science does not say the changing ugly conditions are good. It says there is only Good. "Look not toward the earth, look unto Me."

It is a very important turn of the wheel of the law, this one of trying to make out that misery and death and poverty are good. They are not here. How can they be good? Their absence is good. That which is present is Good. If anybody abuses you (in the seeming) do not say it is your business to say abuse is good. Say rather, that it never transpired. Do not speak to any person mentally; speak to God. It is God who is Good. "There is only one Good and that is God," said Jesus Christ.

When you tell me your husband was so and so, your money was so and so, your children were so and so, and you could not say they were good conditions, you are at this important stone of your journey in Science. You must not think of a single one of these appearances. They are not there at all. God is there. Touch not the earth with thy mind. Touch Me. Not an evil is here. Not one. God is here. If you feel the shakiness of fear, you can say, "*There is nothing to fear. I am clinging to the loving God.*" You can say, "*I will not doubt the Good. I believe in the loving God.*" You can say, "*I do not believe in appearances. I believe in God here present in loving kindness."* In such a seemingly hard set of circumstances as mentioned, you will find it the most comforting thing in the world to say, *"I do not believe in the power of a whole army of evil conditions. I believe God is bringing us all through safely."* Why should you write a letter to your mother, or your uncle, or your brother, begging for help out of your misery, at a moment when the universe stands waiting for you to touch not the earth at any angle, but to touch God? This is called "The valley of decision." The whole world finds it so much easier to talk and think and write on the dark side that Joel said, "Multitudes, multitudes, in the valley of decision." The worse the condition, the less you are to turn your mind toward it. "Touch it not. Touch Me."

Goethe, the mighty thinker, writing of choosing between your pathways of feeling, said, "Here eyes do regard you in eternity's stillness. Choose well; your choice is brief and yet endless." That which comes over us about whether we believe in God in us now, comes over us when we put our cheerful doctrine upon the world. It seems as if our world all turns against us. But we have no right to agree with what comes. The Jesus Christ Spirit within us, and shedding its radiance around us, judges not after the sight of the eyes, nor after the hearing of the ears. There is no combination of circumstances so hard, so black, so complicated, but what God can work a miracle in them.

Now, if we examine doubt a little more closely we shall see that it is not doubt of the Good at all. It is fear that the Good won't work NOW. We think the Good lets evil run on so long, and multitudes of good people pass away before their good deeds are respected, and ages go on before their character is believed in. You will see how we all have a sneaking feeling that we would like to know what good it will do us if our wrongs are not set right now. Come, face this adversary right up. Its name is belief in time, belief that it takes time for God to work. "No," you say, "I don't mean that I think God *needs* to take time, but that He does take it." This is the adversary, then, belief that God always takes a long time to work out our cause for us.

Did you ever see people who, when they were in great trouble, never touched it with their thoughts, but touched only the God side? Did you ever see anybody who faced up that little sneaking fear that it would take a long time to set his affairs straight, and took the fear by the throat, saying, "I am not going to believe that the Almighty needs an instant of time, as I reckon time, to bring forth right conditions here and now." You must know by this time that it is the Jesus Christ doctrine that by a man's word he is justified and condemned. What can I expect but time, if I believe in time? What can I expect but fear, if I believe in fear? What can I expect but hatefulness, if I say hatefulness is good? All these things are my own imagination. Looking toward the Heavenly City, I talk of the desert. Lo, looking toward the joyous peace of God's presence, I talk of trouble!

The chrysoprasus is the stone which stands for your sight of the Good, where others see evil, your speech of God's blessed kindness, where you might feel deep bitterness.

It is singular how all the green-tinted stones of John bear up on seeing the True Kingdom through the false appearance. In the midst of what seems to you to be your degradation, when you look old, feel sick, fear poverty, cry at failure, if you cease to give way to all this for an instant, the green stone teaches you that the ego, the seed, the meaning of it all, is for you to know that you are a transcendent being, with transcendent powers. You were born of God. You go toward God. You know God. You have the power of God. It is the same with your patient. He is a transcendent being coming into your sight. It is the same with your affairs. They are Paradise coming into view.

When the storms come thickest (according to the seeming) the peace of your soul is nearest. In the heart of the cyclone is the intensest peace. The ship only needs to make one turn to be in the heart of the cyclone. We have only to look away from turmoil, "Look unto Me," and the great storm will calm down, the sorrows will have nothing to exercise themselves upon. You have heard that the Brahmins once taught that the flower of the soul springs soon after the storm, but the soul's flower will not bloom if it chooses to be in the storm.

There is nothing can shake your patient's cure out of sight, except your own fears. You need not be afraid of his sickness, you need not fear you will fail; you have only to be afraid that your family affairs will not come out right, and this will be quite enough to show a disturbance in his conditions. It is quite enough to bring him to you for the fourth time. All sudden attacks, and all our cases when they seem to be worse, need our fourth treatment for outside conditions. You need to be filled with the tenth lesson of Science. They all show we ought to be polishing the chrysoprasus stone, which means taking our mind away from the earthly things entirely, fixing it upon heavenly themes, so that our world, with which we in particular deal, may show here and now that our practice of joy is being responded to by our world.

All the lessons of Science turn to the side of joy and peace, strength, and happiness. There is not one that gives sanction for despondency on our part. Jesus was so cheerful and joyous that He was called a glutton and a wine bibber. He was so full of confidence in the good of all people that He was accused of associating with people of bad reputation. He was so firm on the side of good that He walked around among the most wicked circumstances. He went without food, without friends, without home, so much that they called Him a poor man, and said He was a man of sorrows, and acquainted with grief.

All the time He was the owner of the universe. He was the Prince of Peace. He was the Central Fire of Holiness. He was the Joy Bringer. It is His doctrine that the world today begins to realize is its greatest need. We have only to give it forth day by day, in order to see it demonstrate itself.

When evil conditions appear we do not have anything to do about them. We have only to see the presence of God above them. The child's diphtheria is not diphtheria at all. It is the signal that, by the right words now spoken, you can bring out a perfect character, a renewed intelligence, a beautiful health. You may say promptly, "I do not believe in diphtheria. I believe in the Holy Spirit. I believe in peaceful health, here and now."

If you have thought seriously of some great point in Science for a long time, you will be faced up with its mighty effects. All the opposition of your lot, your human nature, everything in your disposition, will meet your statement somewhere.

Take your premise that the Holy Ghost will teach you all things. Treat your own self for freedom from stupidity and ignorance. Commence at the very day of your birth in the flesh. Deny that any cause, or result of any kind, leading to folly, or sickness, or trouble, has existed in your life. Pronounce yourself a spiritual being, with spiritual powers, untrammeled, unhindered, unrestrained, sealed from the beginning to preach the gospel, and to demonstrate it through the universe; that the Spirit of Jesus Christ is salvation from evil for mankind.

There is no salvation for mankind except by the Spirit of Jesus Christ. In yourself is that Spirit. Let it always speak. Let it always think through you. By taking yourself in hand to be wise, you can quicken your understanding, exactly as you can cure yourself of bodily sickness. When you treat yourself, begin at the beginning, and come down to the present moment, always calling yourself spiritual and not material.

Jesus said that the Father would send the Holy Ghost, in His name, and that the Holy Ghost would teach us all things. How true it is that only the early disciples ever tried to prove this. Men have studied books and languages, machines and trees, but they have not practiced hearing the Holy Ghost through the name of Jesus Christ. So it is that we have nobody on earth who can answer all the questions that are asked in science, art, and literature, through the expression of pure spiritual wisdom, as secured by speaking the name of Jesus Christ.

Whoever follows out this Science discovers that something about himself is soon healed. You will find that already you can point to different ways in which you are better for knowing this Science. If you have been healed of something, you can see that all things may be healed. One or two conditions may not go out except by persistence. You have to stick faithfully to something. There is a part of the doctrine that practically fits your poverty, for instance; but poverty does not go out with a little dose of that part of the Science. You have to take a great quantity of it. They tell us that some people have to take a great deal of the water of Lourdes before they are healed, while others get well very soon after a little of it.

Jesus Christ told His disciples that they could not cure epilepsy except they prayed so earnestly that they forgot to eat. We often see Scientists leave their cases, and leave their important work, for the sake of their dinner, or their beds, when it is evident that, if they do so, their whole interest is not devoted to their doctrine. There is such a thing as forgetting all about everything, because you are so absorbed in your doctrine. You do not do this all of the time, but you surely do some of the time. Jesus said there were cases which would not yield till after we had been absorbed just so powerfully.

A mother got down on her knees to pray for money to send her boy to school. She was so deeply absorbed in prayer that she did not eat or sleep for three days. Then, suddenly, she came forth, her face radiant. She had received a mental assurance of answer. That very day the money came. Go by yourself, alone with God, sometimes, and speak alone to Him. Reason with the Almighty, as Job did.

A beautiful nature once wrote a little pamphlet about how he took every little item of his life to the Holy Spirit, and talked with God as a man would talk with his friend. The consequence was that he knew what he needed to know, and was helped all he needed help. His requests were very simple. He never asked for healing, and he never asked for the fullness of wisdom, which Jesus Christ commanded. I speak of him only to show you that if a little of the Christian doctrine, believed in, would do so much, if the short practice which people give to the Holy Presence will heal and help so much, what may you not expect from a life absolutely dedicated to the Spirit. If God will support a man who spends all his time in spiritual devotions, why not give all your time to the Spirit? If God will teach all wisdom to the man who converses with God continually, why not make God our Counselor, our Guide, our Friend?

When a physical or mental disturbance arises, as the effect of opposing Truth, it is called chemicalization. It is always met by keeping right on with the Truth. It is always the sign that Truth is working fast. It shows that we are to welcome the Spirit. If our friend seems to fall down in a faint, we speak rapidly: "*I do not believe in fainting and failure. I believe in life and activity.*"

In a public dining room in a western town, a man struck

a waiter. The waiter struck him back. Instantly, the guests rushed back and forth. There was great confusion. A Scientist present never looked up at all, but said within her own mind: "*It is nothing at all, peace is here. I do not believe in disturbance. I believe in harmony.*" It was amazing how quickly people picked themselves up, and the man and the waiter settled the matter.

You can quell the very roughness of the ocean storm by sending your steady word of peace over the waters, as Jesus Christ demonstrated. They will respond. Response to constant treatment, on the part of people and affairs, is typified by the chrysoprasus stone. The whole Kingdom of God is here, ready to break into your sight. When one seeming thing comes forth, through seeming trials, as the result of our treatments, we have touched the tenth stone of our City.

The oftener you bring order out of chaos, the oftener you touch the tenth stone. The oftener you ignore mixed-up and grievous states of affairs, the oftener you touch the tenth stone of your character. To stand still and hold on to one statement, when another statement seems to have the whole battle, is to become a skillful workman, approved of heaven. While there is no great issue at stake we do not seem to have a great test of our skill. When the storm faces the ship, if she is a good one she ignores the storm, and pulls all sound and clean into port.

The man who is on the point of bankruptcy and saves himself by his Science, touches the stone of his assurance. He hits upon his sure way of life. He knows how to work his Science. The man whose eyesight fails him, and his treatments only seem to put him into deeper darkness, knows, if he holds to one principle till it pulls him safely into light, just how to make everything yield to his treatment. Difficulties never daunt him.

The chrysoprasus stone signifies the type of mind seeing land ahead — whether anybody else sees it or not. Columbus, driving on in spite of opposition, is the Scientist ignoring terrible appearances, and driving on with his doctrine. The chrysoprasus stone stands for increase of seed, for enlargement of germs, for greater manifestations from lesser ones. One idea of Good, held in mind, is a deathless seed, for if it is in mind, it is outside in your affairs also. What you are thinking about is surely in your surroundings. They are obedient to your suspicions. Your doubts are on the shade side. They are obedient to your confidence, your faith, your steadfast ignoring of your own evil feelings. When a case comes the fourth time, tell mentally what you do not believe, and what you do believe. When a disfigured state of affairs comes up, give this fourth treatment.

When you feel grieved or frightened at what is said or done in your world, give this fourth treatment. You may be interested to know that chemicalization means that things are coming out in a better state of affairs. It never means anything else. It is like alkali and acid in chemistry. When they mix they form a new base. So, when Truth goes singing over the thoughts of men, they have to begin to think in a new way. There is nothing to fear, there is no pain in chemicalization. There is no sorrow, if you do not believe in such things. You need not have a patient come to you the fourth time, but if he should come, you yourself are in chemicalization, and so is he. You have been mixed up and troubled about something which did not need to take an instant of your notice. Please, now, take your case you have been naming with me, bow your head, and let the Spirit of Jesus Christ say:

I have not believed in a mixture of good and evil.
I do not believe in evil of any kind. I believe that all is Good.
There is no reality in trouble. All is peace.
There is no reality in sickness. All is perfect health.

I do not believe in anything wrong. I believe all is well.

Now, call the name of the patient and speak to him or her in this way, while I speak to the one who has been called diseased.

There is no mixture of good and evil in you. All is Good.

I do not believe in an inheritance of any kind of sickness, disease, or pain. I believe in an inheritance of Good only.

I do not believe in a race of beings partly good and partly evil. I believe in the universe of God.

I do not believe in contagion of evil through the mixed and confused thoughts of the people round about us. I believe in their God Mind only.

I do not believe in your evil thoughts. They affect you not at all. Your mind is God.

I do not believe in my own errors. They are not real. They cannot affect you. My mind is Good. I believe in God.

You are every whit whole.

Your life is God. It cannot be threatened with death, nor fear death, nor yield to death in any part of your being.

Your health is God. It cannot be threatened with disease, nor fear disease, nor yield to disease in any part of your being.

Your strength is God. It cannot be threatened with weakness, nor fear weakness, nor yield to weakness in any part of your being.

You are showing forth to the people around you that you are healed. You acknowledge to yourself that you are healed. You acknowledge to me that you are healed.

In the name of the Father, and the Son, and the Holy Ghost, I pronounce you healed now and forever.

I assure you that if you will focus all your mind to such

a treatment as this, if you repeat it over and over, you will be so confident of the Good and the right coming forth victorious, that nothing can distract your attention at all. By such treatments as this you will see the whole world healed of grief, of sickness and pain, and of poverty and sin. It is, as you see, an orderly way of telling all the highest Truth you know. For my part, I feel it is a doctrine that needs only to be once heard, to take an everlasting hold on the heart.

I believe it is so reasonable that when we think it over all alone by ourselves, that even then the universal Mind of man responds, and unconsciously they are all believing it. It is the perfect doctrine of prophecy. Let us once more bow our heads and proclaim to the universal Mind:

I do not believe in evil. I believe in Good.

I do not believe in poverty. I believe in the bounty of God.

I do not believe in sickness. I believe in health for all the world now. Amen.

CHAPTER XI.

THE WAY OF WISDOM

Confucius, the Chinese sage, who lived 550 B.C., said, "A man filled with truth hath power over heaven and earth, gods and devils. Nothing in the universe can injure him. Water and fire cannot cause him to fear." Nothing can harm one who actually believes himself safe, though the one who tells him he is safe does not believe it. Then how much more will he be kept safe who, himself holding the Truth, believes what is true, despite lack of faith about him. This is what is meant; possessing life, and thereby calling to one's self the life of heaven and earth,

The eleventh lesson has for its subject one of those experiences of mind where, having taken the basis, or premise, that a man is perfectly well because he is a spiritual being, not subject to material conditions, you come to an experience where it seems as if your premise, which has pleased you so much and had so much reasonableness in its appeal, is, after all, much feebler than the premise or mental position of the man who claims to be sick.

You will notice that the last lesson showed the importance of holding your highest thoughts while the man's or woman's condition gives the appearance of holding on to evil. It is no kind of position to take, in mind, that sickness is more powerful than health. The strongest position you can take is on the side of the happy and peaceful state, as the real state. Even if a man tells you he is well when his liver is being destroyed (so his doctors say) and you cheerfully and innocently believe him, he will be recovered from his malady and his life prolonged (to use old terms) awhile, because of your simple faith.

In the Andover Review for June, 1889, you may read of an aged man who went through the most extraordinary experiences, at the command of people he thought were superior beings. His faith was so simple that it held his life unhurt, springing from pinnacles, or diving under seas.

Confidence, or faith, is a life principle. Always after taking a premise there comes a time when it seems as if it would not work after all. Paul said: "Stand, and having done all, stand." He also said that God is able to make a man stand firm to his highest premise, after he has once taken it.

You have not forgotten the fourth axiom, that mind will demonstrate as much Truth as it has courage to stand by its affirmations. The tenth lesson matches the fourth — only the tenth relates to the environment. Its axiom is like the fourth, viz., the world will persist in exhibiting before you what you persist in affirming the world is. All dissolving, ungluing conditions come from your giving up your old affirmations.

If now you have become shaken up, and fall back to your old thoughts that scientific statements sound better than they demonstrate, your new affirmations must come from your warm feelings, or the world will set itself to the old tune again. Paul said that God is able to make us stand. He means that those who have recognized that within themselves is God, must live the life which that knowledge kindles. We cannot possibly go back to affirmations of evil, when we know that by affirmations our premise of life is made just as we choose.

The Japanese have a teaching that the divinity within your own soul may set aside the question of God, and by faith in itself work all the miracles ever thought of.

If you have heard this tenth lesson, of the law of the spirit of life in Christ Jesus that maketh free from the law of sin and death, you will certainly know what to think and to do in a time of special excitement, or in the time when you would persist in showing some ugly condition over and over. You persist as hard as it does, only you persist in ignoring it, and living on your side of the question. To you there is only one side of the question. Persistence is a wonderful manager. Daniel ignored Nebuchadnezzar's insanity three and one-half years before it fell into nothingness.

The call in Science is for you to take the position that your life, health, strength, support, defense, are from God. As God cannot fail, so these cannot fail. Cannot you persist in believing in your side of the question a few years? There is no need of its taking a few years to bring out your ideas, but if you have to stand by a premise, that Elisha and Daniel and Jesus and Kurozuma demonstrated, you can do it. Think that being true to your idea will be as wealth straight from the Spirit of God, so that you can feed all the seemingly poor people in the world; health straight from the Spirit of God, so that you can heal all the sickness in the world; wisdom straight from the Spirit of God, so that you can impart wisdom to all the seemingly dark minds in the world. You know by this time that this is only a mode of expressing that by your wisdom you see wisdom; by your health you see health; by your provisions you see bounty everywhere.

The eleventh lesson has for its axiom: *Judgment is as great and competent as will and meekness can agree.* This axiom, like every other one, is universally true. For instance, you have a strong will. Naturally you feel like having everything go your own way. This is well, if you have meekness of character enough to yield your point instantly when you see you are wrong. Such a combination will make your judgment quick and accurate. In the first place, your mind will unconsciously be trying all the time to protect your strong will, so that it won't have to be yielding to another man's quicker judgment of the case than yours. Secondly, you will be consciously directing your will along the right so far as you can see it. We may always count upon it that we have exercised our will to carry out our notions, wrong or right, if we come to a particular point where we do not quickly know what to do. Or, we may have let ourselves yield to doing something we did not have a will to do, when our will was set right and the temptation was set wrong. We call this unbalanced condition of mind, foolishness or ignorance. Nothing discourages a man like seeing what bad judgment he has used. Bad judgment always comes from turning to the way our best judgment disapproves, or, comes from carrying out our own will, regardless of everything, forgetting and ignoring judgment, or calling our vigorous will judgment.

Science teaches that you may take a base in your mind that you have consumption, and regardless of God's good presence of health, you may stick to it until consumption shows up and ends in its own habitual way. Or, you may take a base that you are sound and well, and hold out on that line until your health is a miracle.

Some people can see this law better by calling it a premise which people take in mind. For instance, you take the premise that you already show signs of breaking down in your health. Every other thought you have will bow down to this one. When you think you will work hard, your premise shouts out, "No, you must look out, you are breaking down." So, you knuckle under to a premise you yourself made up. What made you take that premise in the first place? "Oh," you answer, "because I felt my years." Who said you ought to feel your years? Mortal man or God man? How do you know but that these feelings you had were the quickening renewals of a spiritual influx of new strength? Was it necessary for you to take your premise with mortal man instead of God man? The siding with the low and dying side, instead of the high and living side, was not meekness, it was simply foolish yielding against your will, which blunts good judgment. I assure you that you can make your judgment perfect by living up to the highest spiritual premise where your natural will leads you.

You can give birth to the divinest decision by compelling your meekness to unite with your will, as to your health, as to your strength, as to your prosperity.

Things look badly against your affairs — do they? Do you will them to be bad? No, a thousand times no. Your will is for good, but your poor will cannot carry the day alone. It has to be married to meekness. Meekness means yielding. This word "yielding" has gotten a good many Christians into misery. It has seemed to them to mean yielding to the evil and hard side of the appearance, when all the time it meant yielding to the spiritual doctrine, although appearances argued louder than spiritual realities.

A young man who had looked into the intentions of God with respect to man found he had been thinking that he must yield to his poverty as sent of God. He saw his mistake. God does not send poverty. Whoever has said that the bountiful God is a giver of poverty has lied. He has been badly tempted, and has foolishly yielded to the temptation to judge against his will on the material side, as much as any person who ever dropped into lying or stealing.

All weakness of the body comes from yielding to appearances, when the man or woman ought to have yielded to spiritual doctrine. Therefore, when a man or woman asks you for help from weakness, you may know the mainspring to touch is foolishness and ignorance, and these being unreality, nothingness, shadow, you can easily say, "Your will never fell through temptation." The doctrine of the fall of man came from believing in the reality of temptation, on the material side.

When the will is set to carry a point, whether the Scriptural doctrine says one way or another, you will have more crosses than you can count, for it is materiality which you formulate yourself. You compelled what you know to be nothing, to seem real. This is foolishness. It is said to be harder to get rid of than ignorance. You can see this by the way an idiot and an ignorant child act. With the latter you have pleasure in the speed with which he responds to your instructions, and with the other your heart fails, when you have labored as long for no response, apparently. Both these children are the full bloom of the weed which you may call belief in foolishness and ignorance, or perverted will. It has both names in the Bible.

Solomon said: "The foolishness of man perverteth his way." Way is a word often used for will. When one does not respond to four treatments, he must be treated a fifth time. If he comes a fifth time, what makes him come, if that time does not find him joyously acknowledging his health? He comes because you have not touched his judgment. You have not struck the chord of his will. Why not? Because your own judgment has a veil before it. What veil is before your own judgment? I will tell you. It is your persistent habit of detecting ignorance and stupidity in people, and wailing about your own stupidity and ignorance. If you have seen that you did not know something, you have called yourself ignorant. If you have seen that somebody else did not know what you thought they ought to, or failed to be quick enough to please you, it was on your tongue, or in your mind, that they were either foolish or ignorant. It is the fall of man. It is all the fall there is.

It is yielding to appearances. Spiritually, you have the power of discernment so strong that a child, man, or woman can tell you anything you ask instantly. Judging that they cannot, and judging that you yourself cannot, keeps a veil before your mind. And you can tell when it is thickest, because your problem comes up again and again, and your patients come the fifth time, or they appear very weak and discouraged.

Many a practitioner has felt very discouraged when her patient has talked hard on the dark and feeble side. But it was only the final throw of the mind of old belief to hold its own. It is the last grasp of the patient's belief in sickness, when he complains and whines in a discouraged manner; but it is the very best sign to you that his belief in evil is on its last legs.

How does your will want the case to talk? Of course it wants him or her to talk buoyantly and cheerfully. So marry your will to the spiritual facts of the case. Rouse your judgment. This is the man of you. Notice the eleventh text. "Let us make man — and let him have dominion." Then put it with this one: "The Father hath committed all judgment unto the Son." The Son is man, whom the Divine will and Divine meekness bring out as Jesus Christ. His will, He said, was omnipotent God. His meekness, He said, was to God. There is the almighty judgment of Jesus Christ in you.

If your environments come the fifth time troubling you, let the powerful judgment of Jesus Christ speak of the Spirit of the universe, and take down the evil that hides your prosperity. You can say, "*I do not accuse the world or myself of foolishness or ignorance; therefore, I see clearly the prosperity of my new life now.*" If your patient comes the fifth time, tell him the same principle. If a person seems very weak or feeble, say these words mentally, before you attempt to treat him.

I know that if you take every Friday afternoon to insist upon the Jesus Christ judgment within you as knowing mankind to be the expression of the wisdom of God and therefore intelligent and wise at all times, and if you positively take the premise that you do not accuse the world, or yourself, of foolishness or ignorance, nobody will ever come the fifth time uncured, and your affairs will never seem to wilt or hang heavy. Your own mind must be this man having dominion. Your own judgment must reign supreme. It must have no evil before it.

Do not let another man's discouragement pervert your judgment. Touch the chord of his will. Does he not will to be free, wise, and strong? If you mentally unload him of all the yielding to appearances he has ever done, he will spring up and respond to that touch of your judgment.

All discouragement, all feebleness, all fainting, halting, stopping, are signs to you to come forth with the fifth treatment. Come boldly forth. The powers of omnipotence are on your side.

John called the character which man exhibits after making the fifth treatment of his environment, the Jacinth stone of his character. Mind is composed of twelve powers. When mind exercises these twelve powers it has twelve characteristics, which shine like polished jewels. They make a perfect foundation for an absolute demonstration of Jesus Christ Spirit. The first time you go the rounds of these twelve powers, you may not show much difference in character. The second time, the third time, the millionth time around the statements, and how shining your life and mind become.

It is written that "Our daughters shall be like precious stones fitly polished." "Daughters" are meek statements of the spiritual side of our lives, when the material side tells a different story.

The first six statements are the beautiful powers of your mind as to your own looks, your own judgment. The last six relate to your surroundings. So when I say fifth treatment, I mean the eleventh lesson, or point of doctrine. Some call it the eleventh perfect premise.

The perfect jacinth is the ruby. The son of man is ruddy — is red with ruddy health, robust strength. His judgment is warming, kindling, reviving, like the wine fires of the ruby.

When he speaks he helps you. The wine of prosperity is handed to you in the good news from your business. "Drink ye all of it," said Jesus. "It is my blood of the new testament." If you will bear in mind that the Spirit of Jesus Christ was health, life, prosperity, red with the reviving as the wines he gave at the wedding feast, you will understand the results of taking eleven right statements. You will have the judgment of the transcendent being that you are. You will be awakened. If I say to you that this is the only manner of thinking which has any practical effect in the life, on the triumphant and joyous side, you will have only the truth from me. It is in justice to this doctrine that I acknowledge it is the only way you can think that will be every day safety for you.

There are twelve conditions of human life which may be met by twelve truths. These twelve conditions being met by Truth, you may be sure that your life will be free, glad and powerful. The Brahmins had a teaching which read: "So dwell on the highest thoughts; this is the life of the awakened."

There is one thing which good judgment awakens, that has been brought out by some Scripture writers, and that is beauty. The perfect in judgment are perfect in beauty. The beauty of Jesus Christ is because of His judgment. The ruby is the beauty stone. The polish of meekness — that is the angel of beauty, who measures the City. He is bound to no traditions. What others believe he must be in order to be beautiful, he needs not. That which his own judgment decrees is his own charm.

So, no matter what others believe about the portent of your dream of the night, you must judge that it means something good for your surroundings — something others might call evil. Your judgment yielding to the good says some blessed good is coming to you. If you see symbols, speak of their good for your own surroundings. They all come for your benefit. They tell you that your environments are good. Then your ideas will be recognized as good by others sooner or later.

There is one universal Mind which is the perfect intelligence from whence all ages of men draw their stock of intelligence. Man may draw all this intelligence for his own use and not decrease it at all, as he might know all mathematics, and his neighbor might know all, and all the town might know all of mathematics, and not rob each other, nor exhaust mathematics. The more you speak according to this judgment, the more judgment your neighbors will have. They may not see at first that you are wise with the Mind Divine, from which you are drinking each day by taking these twelve lessons home to yourself, but after a time they will acknowledge the excellency of your judgment. Indeed you yourself may not always see why you say and do certain things, but afterwards you will see that it was your wisest course.

The refusal to call any man, woman, or child ignorant or foolish will uncover your dormant chord. You will leave the strings of your soul exposed for the winds of God to blow over, and bring out the tones of music, the radiant beauty, given unto your judgment from the foundations of the universe.

When you lay your judgment to the line, and your righteousness to the plummet of the highest truths you have heard, then, says the prophet, your old covenant with death will be annulled, and your agreement with hell will not stand. You give up your old ideas in meekness, you talk aloud your new ideas, after you have thought them, and after you have written them. They are the outgrowth of solid soil.

Sometimes you will be astonished to hear people speaking rapidly and lightly of the lofty Truth that you could not speak until after it had been sown into your deep soil of profound meditation. Sometimes you yourself may speak this way. The fruitage of lightly handling these mighty principles is light.

By the deep thought of the mind the word of the lips is solid judgment in ripe fruitage.

Isaiah told the City, which typifies us, that when they had gotten themselves into captivity through careless speaking of their Science, they would be glad to have money to redeem themselves with. But they should not be redeemed with money, they should be redeemed by their fidelity to their religion, entirely independent of money.

So, once in a while, you may find that nothing you do yourself causes your patient's cure. So far as you see, he gets his cure by reason of somebody else's treatments, after you have practiced with him. Or, you may find that money is not given to you to get out of debt with, yet somehow, by one deal or another, there are no debts there. This is really your will married to a kind of weak yielding to scientific statements. You did not make them your deep life, and therefore solid assistance.

The whole of demonstration is the fruitage of your own judgment: "Ye have sold yourselves for a thing of naught, and ye shall be redeemed without money," is the voice to a half-hearted, insincere, timid, unprofound acceptance of Science. Even writing the Science glibly brings out the redemption, without substantial, solid aid coming. Even thinking the Science lightly does the same. Living it comes from thinking it deeply, writing honestly, speaking sacredly. When the outward life accords, then is judgment risen in her beauty. Then is healing instantaneous. Then, if you ask for help, it comes exactly as your perfect judgment would indicate. The point is to get your perfect judgment forward. It comes forward by handling this eleventh lesson. It is signaled to be handled every time the fifth treatment is necessary. Judgment, when it is good, touches the loftiest ideas and the plainest themes with equal respect. One often finds that his demonstration waits for him to give up his prejudices with respect to what is high or low. All must be alike to him, when they are names and descriptions of Spirit.

One woman, whose grief was that she was so ugly to look upon and could not make herself highly thought of, insisted that her affirmation must be a high one. So she took, "I am absolute Love." A friend, to whom there was no high or low name of Deity as used by Jesus Christ, told her to use the interpretation of her own name for a constant affirmation. It was a meek one, "I am the King's daughter." It was the right one to soften and refine her face, and win her way for her. But it sounded so low to her that she refused it. Yet it was the only treatment of meekness belonging to her, as the one of Jesus, "I am meek and lowly of heart," belonged to Him.

Perfect judgment touches the life chords of each situation with the right word. Lofty ambitions are evidences of belief in high and low places. In reality there is neither high nor low in Christ Jesus. To the Spirit, all that is, is Good. That which is evil is not, never was, and never will be. So they who believe in high or low will have to take some statement which to them seems low, as that lady will have to speak her simple one in order to carry her point.

Scientific statements, held along in their order, will bring you to where you will see, no matter how unsuccessful you may appear, that you are not unsuccessful, because Spirit is not unsuccessful. You have fairly to seem to be unsuccessful, practically, before you can see that it is so. The instant your judgment is accurate with respect to success and non-success, all things, will work out to your pleasure, even in the old way of looking at them. The mind must agree with the Spirit; then comes perfect judgment. This is man. Judgment hath dominion. The keys of heaven and earth are given unto perfect judgment.

The law and the Gospel must be one. In the Gospel there

The Way of Wisdom

is no material remedy for disease. In the law, Truth is the healer. In the Gospel there is no disease, and not even Truth heals disease. In the law disease seems very real, and the law that Truth is its remedy seems so rigorous that it is accounted a terrible thing to take a pill for neuralgia. Whoever thinks anything is terrible must certainly believe in it greatly. It must have great power in his eyes. He may have to take a pill to see how unreal it is, how simple, how far from terrible. The law is against hating anything. Even stealing must not be hated. Why not? Because there is no stealing. We do not need to hate what does not exist. What is stealing? It is delusion of imagination. Is not God the only living being? Can God steal? This is a very awakening activity of mind. Thinking this way will bring forth wise judgment. Then this judgment will balance all things. Thieves, as they are called, will find there is a way of support preferable to stealing.

When judgment is come forth, you will find you are not bound to methods of curing the sick, not bound to the modes of eating and drinking, sleeping and dressing. As judgment ripens with yielding the will to spiritual ideas, over and over, you will see great events and great circumstances yielding to very simple actions on your part. One man felt suddenly, after long practice of thinking spiritual ways, that he could as easily make gold as cure bones, but a voice seemed to say to him: "You would act foolishly with gold if you had it." He yielded the point at once. It looked meek and good on his part to yield to a warning voice, but no voice from the Spirit ever accuses a mind of foolishness or ignorance. Here is where he should have used the eleventh lesson, or the fifth treatment of environments. Here was one of his self-accusations formulated right close to him, and audible as a human voice. It had bloomed in order to be refused for the sake of Spirit.

Judgment comes of compelling yourself to believe just as

much as you hope for. If you hope to cure everybody that comes to you, you are able to believe all that you hope. If you only hope that you can cure them, you will be disappointed. Hope needs faith. If you cannot believe you can cure all, take a night or day for the statement of what you believe in Truth. Covenant with the Spirit for the Spirit to do all your cures for you. The government is on the shoulders of perfect judgment we are told. Therefore, let perfect judgment be born in you. The strong man says "I can!". The strong man says "I will!" The wise man says "I know!" The perfect man says, "*I know what to do, and I am able to do it, therefore I will do it.*"

The state of mind that calls for you to state what you can and will do, is when you have steadily ignored the harsh and hard side of life, as it has been showing itself to you. When things looked dark and hard, you did not allow your mind to think about them at all. You thought only of God, the Spirit. You kept hold of the highest statement you had. You ignored the appearance. Then, after you had won the battle, or seemed plainly to have things coming out right, you had a feeling of blankness. You felt devoid of power, devoid of ideas. This is the blankness of a clear paper, upon which you may write what you like. Declare, that as the Mind of Jesus Christ, you do not believe in foolishness or ignorance. Declare, that as the Mind of Jesus Christ your judgment is perfect judgment. Declare, "*I know all things. I can do all things.*"

The blankness is like a smooth mass of protoplasm, out of which some idea will arise, which will govern all other ideas. Nothing can stand before that one idea which comes up when you feel blank, absent-minded, vague. If you can make it strongly enough felt that your main idea is on the side of Jesus Christ in you, then you will do the work of Jesus Christ in wisdom and strength.

There is no more potent opportunity for the use of judgment

than this one. Have you not had something of this feeling lately? Let us take the fifth treatment together, to rouse your judgment away from the clutches of the old temptation to believe in foolishness and ignorance as belonging to us. Let us, as Mind, now state the eleventh premise:

"I never accuse the world, or myself, of foolishness or ignorance. I am the judgment of God. I know all things and do all things well."

This idea is a living amoeba, that arises from the protoplasm of mind, that lies still as the sea waiting for the winds to blow over it, like the waters which the angels troubled or stirred. So the mind is still, until the angel of Truth stirs it.

Right near at our hand is the Heavenly City. While we have called it distant, could we expect it to be near? Right here, visible to us, is the Heavenly Land. Could we expect it to show us its beauties if we talked of its being invisible? Right now you are wise and immortal, free, strong, and at peace. Can you expect to feel your own true nature and delight in your estate, if you keep talking and thinking of how little you know, how mortal flesh and blood are, and how unhappy you are?

Buddha taught that Self is the Lord over self. If you and I do not speak from the spiritual Self of us, it will not act. We are the arbiters of our own destiny. The Spirit is truthful and takes us at our word. If we say, "I am foolish and ignorant," it lets us be what we say we are. Having endowed us with wisdom to know that we are the sons of God, with free will, does it suppose we could be telling we are something we do not want to be? The Spirit supposes nothing. It believes all things. Spirit brings its fountains of power to all words of *"I am,"* and *"I will."*

Buddha says, "A fool does not know when he commits evil deeds." Then there are no fools, for there is a Spirit in all men which pushes them away from all evil. The wise man breathes his breaths as airs of omnipotence. He drinks his waters as cups of strength. He eats his food as the Spirit renewing itself. He knows all actions as spiritual, and so knows no decay, no failure, no death. The wise know no evil. They know there is none. They know no sickness. They know there is none. They set their faces like flint to know the ways of God.

This is the true foolishness, namely: determination to know nothing among us save Jesus Christ. This is the true ignorance: ignorance of evil, through knowing it is not reality.

The fourth strength of mind is the strength of inspiration. It enables one to see what ought to be done. It gives one wisdom to know how everything ought to be done. It gives him quick skill to do it. There is the fire of wisdom and beauty in the sunshine of inspiration. John calls it the strength of the eagle, which is always a symbol of inspiration. We have no treatment which equals the denial of accusations of foolishness and ignorance for causing the inspiration of wisdom. Buddha taught that all deeds wrought out by mind, and carried into the life as far as we can exercise our thoughts, bring happiness. "All forms are unreal." He said, "He who knows this becomes passive in pain; this is the way to purity." He advises the repetition of prayers. Repeat them often.

When you take your life in your hand, to speak of your own spiritual nature as it was at the time of your supposed birth in the flesh, do not stop short of six day's repetition of your treatments. Deny that there are any causes, or results of causes, in you or around you, that could lead to disease, poverty or failure. Take yourself for each year. If you set out upon the journey of treating a case, even if that one is cured of his malady the first day, do not let his high welfare escape your faithful mind for six days. This is a training process. Each day send your high blessing.

The ancient Bible taught that it is good to tame the mind,

which is difficult to hold in and very flighty, rushing whither it listeth, but once tamed it will bring you great happiness.

One who had dropped all thoughts of evil from his mind, for a certain period of time, found out that if we are given to detracting from the merits of our companions, easily picking flaws in them, we get weaker and weaker, and cannot possibly destroy weakness in others. He found that there is no path to peace through outward acts. We must truly not see the faults of our neighbors as reality. We must not see ignorance or foolishness hiding the intelligence and freedom of our neighbors. This is called taming the mind.

We cannot crush out criticism. It will not be crushed. We can deny it, and this erases it from our mind. Being free from criticism, the mind runs only to recognition of Good. It is then perfectly tamed. The unity of mind is a great fact to recognize. There is but one Good Mind. All the good and the wise render this same verdict as to what is just and right, when their accusation is laid aside.

Accusations are prejudices against people, which keep the highly efficient judgment from speaking. They do not emanate from the One Mind. Prejudice against a religion will act against your business judgment just as possibly as your health. Prejudice against people will very likely hit your business affairs. It does not always strike at your bodily health the first thing. The feeling we have against alcohol, tobacco, opium, is a prejudice against an imaginary substance. That prejudice held on to is foolishness. That prejudice taken hold of, as a principle, because appearances teach us to fight the poor little ideas, is simply ignorance. So on the same plane every prejudice is found to be a tacit accusation of others or ourselves as to foolishness and ignorance. We could not possibly hold out intolerance to anything if we were not accusers of that which brings about feebleness and failure.

Therefore, we will take our cases and meekly say now:

I have never, as the judgment of Jesus Christ, accused the world, or myself, of being foolish or ignorant.

Now we will speak to the case by name:

You are not the result of inheriting foolishness and ignorance. You inherit the wisdom of God, your Father.

You are not surrounded by a foolish and ignorant race. You are surrounded by the wisdom of God.

Your daily associations do not burden and darken you by the weight of their foolishness, or the darkness of their ignorance. All is wisdom, from which you draw wisdom every moment.

You do not weigh down your own mind with wilfulness in thinking evil. You know no weakness or failure of any part of your being. You are the spiritual light that cannot fail.

I do not persist in thinking of you as faltering or feeble in any part of your being. I see you as strength, freedom, light.

Your strength is Good, and cannot be threatened with weakness, or yield to weakness, in any part of your being.

Your life is Good. It cannot be threatened with death in any part, nor fear death, nor yield to death.

Your health is of the Spirit and cannot be threatened with disease and sickness, nor fear disease or sickness, nor yield to disease or sickness in any part of your being.

You are ready to acknowledge to all around you, to yourself, and to me, that you are every whit whole.

In the name of the Father, and of the Son, and of the Holy Ghost, I pronounce you healed, now and forever. Amen.

Repeat this treatment before you sleep. If any other words come to you while you are treating the case, be sure to use them, for every new way of thinking that springs up out of the good soil of the old way, is the new plant which the Heavenly Father hath watered. For this reason every teacher ought to be glad to hear of the success of his student — each in his own way, though all agreeing with the foundation Principle.

CHAPTER XII.

THE CROWN OF GLORY

To the Romans, Paul wrote the twelfth lesson of the Science of Christ: "Love worketh no ill to his neighbor: therefore love is the fulfilling of the law."

Jesus Christ said at the Last Supper: "Henceforth I call you not servants but I have called you friends; for all things that I have heard of My Father I have made known unto you." His life was His doctrine. Having so regarded it, He said, "Greater love hath no man than this, that a man lay down his life for his friends." Giving all His doctrine to His friends, He gave them His life. Seeing their heavy miseries, He descended into heavy miseries to show them how to ascend out of their miseries. A fireman goes into a burning building to bring out the people who are in danger, as a good physician goes into a plague hospital to cure the patients.

Jesus was so full to overflowing with love that the plagues and dangers of this world did not terrify him in the least. He was not hurt by a single one of the miseries He threw Himself into. Love is stronger than death. He that hath love hath freedom from every ill. He that hath abundance of love, wherewith God fills the whole universe, can save his friends from every ill. He is an atmosphere wherever he walks. Love diffuses itself with all its powers. Having love we have life, so we radiate life. Having love, we have strength, so we radiate strength. Pure love for a child will save the life of a child; so the life of all is saved if a man loves God, for God is all.

Jesus loved God. Thus He had all of life, all of love, all of truth, all of substance, all of intelligence, all of beauty, all of health, all of inspiration. He, therefore, saved the whole world. Even to look at Him would cure, when He was manifest in the flesh. He, never having gone away from our side, we can look upon Him now, and be cured of whatever ailment we cry about. Some people cry with lonesomeness. He will cure that entirely, if they look upon Him. Looking at Him mentally is the way we look nowadays, though it is certain that some people even in this century have seen Jesus, the Healer, as present before them as He was before the two Marys at His tomb.

Looking, mentally, upon Jesus Chirst as present, will cure poverty; it will cure blindness; it will cure deafness; it will cure palsy; it will cure rheumatism; it will cure insanity.

The amethyst is the symbol of the miracle-working power of love. It is the love stone in the sense that the chalcedony is the love stone, and in a still further sense than that stone. It is the stone of the resurrection, of ascension, of the New Kingdom, where love is filling man's mind and overflows to the world, and awakens the same love to shine back. It is that love that is stronger than death, and when it enters into man's love death is not possible. It is that love which, being entered into man's, is stronger than hate, stronger than poverty, stronger than swords, stronger than crucifixion and the tomb.

The amethyst stone has the hues of all the stones. There is no stone which, as you look into the heavenly face of the amethyst is not seen shining in beauty. Twelve works of God as Holy Spirit are all manifest in the amethyst. John said the twelfth power of the gospel, showing forth in you, would be like the amethyst stone.

Whoever gets into the state of overflowing unquenchable love is manifesting Jesus Christ. He sees no evil in anybody or anything. He sees their Good only. He receives no injuries at anybody's hands. He rejoices at everything that occurs. Everything has a light and a life and a joy and a renewal of pleasure in it for him, which nothing that happens to him can destroy.

If things grieve you, then you have not touched the twelfth sweetness of the Science. If things hurt you, then you are not in love with the Science. You are not alive with the ecstasy of the Science. If you are afraid of anything, you do not know the twelfth feeling of security. "Love casteth out fear." If you are poor, or in debt, or old, or discouraged, you have not touched the resurrection stone of love that is stronger than death.

I told you that accusation would make somebody come to you looking sick and unhappy. Well, a joyous praise, felt in your heart, will bring somebody well and grateful to see you. If somebody comes the sixth time for help, you may be certain that you have been complaining and whining about something or somebody.

Complaining and whining are only exhibitions of great desert spots in your character. You must fill up deserts with rain and fertilizer. So you must transform your moments of complaining by praise and descriptions of the Good in the universe. The desert has not had rain enough, so you have not charity and mercy enough, if you feel like complaining. If things in your past have made you feel sad and hard, you must say the good they have done you makes you thankful. Give great thanks.

Nehemiah told the people not to grieve or mourn at all. They must eat the fat and drink the sweet of their lives, just as if it had come to them. Jesus Christ taught that we must look upon our life, just as it has come to us, and beautify and inspire it with the red wine of gladness. Both Nehemiah, 445 B.C., and Jesus Christ Himself, knew that you and I need not mourn, if we do not choose to mourn. Jesus took the six stone water jugs and inspired the water to become wine. So you and I can take our conditions and inspire them with the twelfth lesson in Science.

At the sound of the twelfth lesson on the sands of the

Sahara, roses and corn and grapes will spring up. At the sound of the twelfth lesson on the desolation of your heart, happiness will spring up within you, and radiate around you. The twelfth stone is the amethyst, symbol of happiness. We may see that the twelve lessons of Science are all intended to bring supreme happiness to the world.

Carlyle says there is a higher condition than happiness. He calls it blessedness. But blessedness and true happiness are identical terms. Nothing is left for us to wish for, when the twelve lessons of Science have poured out their twelve results upon our life.

It is gratification to know that if an accusation will bring a sick person, a thankful and praiseful word, felt sincerely, will bring a happy and healed case to our sight. It is a good thing to know that there are healing thoughts we can think which will fill our mind when it gets to complaining and whining. We need not deny, if we feel low-spirited and dissatisfied — we need just describe the Good of our lot. We have lost sight of our Good for a moment. Describing our Good will bring it to our sight again. One thing remember: you will feel less spiritual inspiration when you are mourning, whining, and complaining, but when you praise and describe the Good you will feel full of spiritual fervor.

If a case appears the sixth time, you must praise him for every virtue, every power, every beauty you can think of. You need not deny his disease. You need not deny your complaining. You must just praise and describe the Good in him. The denials you have been giving have made some good chinks in his cottage, through which your sunlight can penetrate. Happiness will bubble over and glisten from you, through a mind that comes the sixth time for treatment.

A deaf and blind person stands for some wilfulness of yours. You would not see a plain truth and you would not hear what somebody told you, once upon a time. You persisted in seeing things your own way. But now your daily denials of accusation will break down your stubbornness. You will listen meekly, gladly, willingly to every voice. You will be quick to detect the true and the false ring in what you hear. The false will not count with you — you will forget it.

Now, you know that accusation takes different forms of expression, or writings, on faces and in people. You remember that yesterday's lesson spoke of the jacinth as standing for beauty and judgment. Good judgment marks the face with lines of beauty. Falling short of good judgment marks the face with weakness and homeliness. So, if you see a homely face, it is certain that you have been accusing people of being foolish and ignorant. If you yourself are homely, you have accused yourself of being foolish and ignorant. Homeliness and weakness may come down to disease, they are so dependent upon accusations of foolishness and ignorance.

You see an immense herd of plain looking people in our cities. They do not look much diseased. This signifies that you have, all your lifetime, been accusing people and yourself in a general way, not at all maliciously, but enough to show forth. You see many elderly and old people. They show your accusations against certain ones, that they know little, or nothing. Your own accusations against yourself will have the same effect as against others. The effect of praise of the spiritual intelligence is to bring beauty and good judgment to view everywhere.

We look at a strong man, and, if we remember how his strength looked to us, we catch his strength. There is a text which reads, "In thy light we shall see light." It can be carried out also in the strength which people show. It can be the same with beauty — "In thy beauty we see beauty" — which means that as we recognize beauty, we soon show forth the same beauty.

There is a story of a child who kept a picture of a beautiful woman in her room and looked at it and talked to it so much that she became like the picture. A young woman found an ideal face of Jesus Christ, and carried it around with her. She looked at it and loved it so much that her face began to resemble the face of Jesus Christ remarkably — even to the fine shining light which always transfigures it when we think of it. Ingratitude is a painter of hard lines on the face. Soon all the curves and smiles will change. We must have a grateful feeling towards everybody and everything. In the story of "The First Violin," by Jessie Frothergill, the hero, who was supernaturally handsome, is pictured as always grateful for everything that anybody did.

Cynicism is a species of ingratitude that brings the most extraordinary people around us. Give thanks to the universe, to your ancestors, to your neighbors, to yourself, to animals, to everything that you have dealings with. Its spirit is your good, loving provider. Sometimes you must stop giving thanks to the supreme God and name everything as giving you bounty, for God seems afar off sometimes, and not speaking and breathing through our world and every object in it. By stretching the mind forth to be grateful to our idea of God we do well, but we do well to look at the God near at hand also.

The Divine Intelligence marks the orbit of the distant Canis Major and rounds the little moons of Mars with the same tender care. Divine beauty paints the North Star and the violet with impartial tenderness. So, you will be grateful to the man who steals your purse as well as to the father who provides for your youth. Why? Because God is the Life, the Spirit, the Intelligence of each alike, without difference of goodness from the hand of the Lord. If you have not seen this, it is true just the same.

Did you ever see a calm, benignant countenance? It shows how once you said calm, peaceful words, and thought that way, in harmony with your words. Look over your list of acquaintances, those you can call by name, and see what there is that is lovely in them. Then remember awhile how that loveliness looked. "Bring all the tithes into the storehouse," said the prophet to the Jews. If you gather all the beauty of one woman into your memory, all the smiles of a friend into your memory, you will have all the tithes in your storehouse. The prophet said that whosoever should do this would spill over with blessings, for he would not have room enough to keep them to himself. This constitutes happiness. Happiness is the stone of freedom. The amethyst touches the blue of the sapphire, shines aglint with the red of the ruby, gives the white of the diamond, last; as it has all the colors in one — it is the last stone of Revelation. It leaves out most of the green, for green stands mostly for works.

With the last polish of the lessons on your character, you see that there is nothing whatsoever to do. All was, and is, and ever will be, the finished work of the Divine Mind. "God saw everything He had made, and behold, it was very good." Divine Mind never sees any evil, and sees nothing to do. While we see evil, or see something to do, we must think according to denials and affirmations. When we love greatly, love supremely, we see nothing to do; and finished, beautiful life satisfies us, everywhere we walk. Like the clear innocent amethyst, we let the happiness of the Divine Mind sift its innocent light through us.

As you look through the amethyst you see all the colors of the rainbow. As you look through the topaz everything looks laughing yellow — even the shadows look happy. As you look through the amethyst the happiness of the topaz is accompanied by the intelligence of the sardius and the inspiration of the ruby. The green of green stones symbolizes completed work.

Now, do not lay too much stress upon stones, nor upon any

other kind of symbol. Money is a symbol of the riches of God, the bounty of God. The topaz tells you to laugh, because everything is supplied with its natural good. The amethyst tells you everything is good and wise and satisfied, as well as able to do all things. But none of these is the thing itself. Gold is the symbol of the bounty of Jehovah. When you look at gold, speak its meaning. That is its life and substance. If it does not increase for you, then you are ungrateful, cynical. Its nature is hidden from you as deeply as Lazarus was buried.

Do you remember how Jesus Christ gave thanks, when Lazarus was cold and still? Well, when your conditions are cold and unyielding, after you have been treating them faithfully, you must go into a room by yourself and give thanks to the Spirit that it always does everything good for you, that it supplies you, pays your debts, and in every way blesses you. Then speak to the gold, or to your affairs, or to your sick neighbor, or to your family trouble, with a loud voice, praising its real meaning, and call it to come forth with new life, new kindness, new bounty, and good conditions.

Read over the story of how Jesus raised Lazarus, in the eleventh chapter of John. It tells how Jesus tarried, when He knew that Lazarus was sick, in order to symbolize or tell how people sometimes neglect to give thanks and feel grateful so long that things get, seemingly, very bad for them. We have all the hardships because we have been neglectful of the vitalizing power of right words. But, even here, said Jesus, there is a way to make things into new life. It is the highest evidence of power to be able to take seemingly dead conditions and wake them into happy life.

"The last enemy to be overthrown is death." When you have learned the last lesson you will not only have power, but ALL power. You are not free from one accusation only, you are free from accusation utterly. You see the whole ground of the

law beneath your feet, so, "Love is the fulfilling of the law."
George Herbert sang the twelfth light of Revelation:
"Oh, now I know how all thy lights combine
And the configuration of their story;
Seeing not only how each world doth shine,
But all the constellations in their glory."
You have run with the winged feet of mind from mountain
top to mountain top of the shining lessons of Science without
halting, but at the twelfth lesson you are like an eagle that folds
its wings over the earth, so far beneath, and surveys the land-
scape in peaceful security. There is absolute security, if you
understand and feel the twelfth lesson of Science. The amethyst
stands for security. Only the heart that is above condemnation
feels secure from condemnation.

The axiom of the twelfth lesson is: He that knows Me, tran-
scends Me. It means that whoever truly knows Me is tran-
scendently beyond the God he imagined Me to be. You know
that even you feel that those who love you find in you virtue beyond what you feel yourself to possess. The man who sees
in his neighbor great virtues, has in himself those very virtues.
It is himself he sees. He may not appreciate goodness and greatness as rich germs in his own nature, needing only to see
goodness and greatness outside of himself to be fed with increasing good. Within yourself is the germ of beauty. If you see
beauty outside of yourself, without carping at it, or complaining
that you have it not, your germs are fed, and beauty begins
to show in you. You have touched the twelfth lesson in Science.

This is the old art of animation of the particular from
the universal, sought after by the ancients, but not found.

It is recognized good that makes us good enough to show
goodness. The great wisdom-power within you is ready to spring
up, fed with the increasing principle, when you see wisdom
expressed in a book, or a man, or, even if you see for a second the

wisdom expressed by the flies and the spiders in your house.

If you look straight into the face of the all-pervading wisdom of the universe, you will feed your germs, which are like little mouths waiting for food, with their own kind of aliment, and your wisdom will increase rapidly. So with happiness. You look into the child's happiness, and do not lament because you are not happy, but just thank the happiness you see for showing itself to you, and your germ or love of happiness, innate within you, will be fed.

If anybody speaks to you critically, listen carefully. There is a ring of Divine Intelligence at your door. You will get a piece of news about your faults, and you will take those faults and deny them. This may leave you a little melancholy. Now you want to thank God for speaking to you. Give thanks for His wisdom expressed to you. This causes your love of wisdom to feed in delight.

When you see adversity as the hand of God bestowing bounty, and give thanks to God, and call to the bounty of God to come plainly to your sight, you have touched the lights of all twelve lessons at once. It is not that God chooses adversity through which to give you riches. No, it is that, having neglected to give thanks and be grateful at the right time, you have covered your prosperity with a cold shell. But, there is no death of prosperity. It is alive in your adversity, and by your dealings with this state of affairs, you can bring out your prosperity.

It lies within adversity to bring your bounty to feed your love of prosperity, innate within you, like a hungry germ. It lies within criticism to feed your love of wisdom, innate within you, like a hungry germ. The love of strength, the love of health, the love of security, the love of skill, the love of harmony — all abide within you. When you see health or strength or prosperity, or see power of any kind, and do not whine or carp or complain that you do not have them, you are fed instantly, and soon will be all that you see. Also you will see more. It is the beauty of health that if you see it, it increases to your sight.

Have you ever noticed that if you see a lame man on the street, you soon see half-a-dozen lame men? Things increase by seeing them. It never rains, when you let things come without ugly feelings, but it pours. When you see health, peace, prosperity, everywhere, you are in the absolute Mind of God. If you practice every Saturday afternoon praising your world, telling you are satisfied with it, describing it as the perfect creation of Divine Mind, you will soon see more good than you have been accustomed to seeing.

So, I believe there is a "Don't" in the Science which has no denial with it, but only silence, and that is, "DON'T COMPLAIN."

The word of the Lord came to Haggai the Prophet "The desire of all nations shall come; and I will fill this house with glory, saith the Lord of hosts." You can see that, like the rest of the prophets, he saw that a time would come when the doctrine preached by Jesus would be understood. You can see that if the air, skies, trees, men, women are all filled with the Spirit of Good, we shall increase our love of God by seeing this Good. It is the opening of our eyes, ears, mouth, to be filled with satisfaction.

Sometimes it is wise to say that everything we see, hear, smell, taste, feel and think, delights us, we are satisfied utterly. This is breaking the barriers down. Our eyes have power to see much beyond what we use them for, and it is so with all our faculties.

Ibsen wrote a play called the "Master Builder," in which his motive is to prove that man is a limited being, and must not aspire to get beyond his limits. This is quite opposite to Jesus Christ's instructions: "Behold, I have set before thee an open door and no man can shut it." "To him that overcometh will

I grant to sit with Me in My throne." "I in you." "That where I am there ye may be also." The twelfth lesson sets aside the doctrine of limitations.

You can see for yourself that if a man sets his mind steadfastly to the premise that he is a limited being, that word "limit" will stop his career somewhere. You have seen great men rise to heights of knowledge, like Emerson and Ruskin, and then drop suddenly to nonentity. All the powers of intellect, which intellect is the simulation of spiritual Intelligence, fly to sustain any premise put by mind. So the world intellect has flown to support the ideas of limitation. But the spiritual nature of man has no doctrine of limitation. Take your choice which nature to take your premise from. By the spiritual law you have no bars put anywhere to your expansion. The love of harmony within you may be fed with harmony itself, till the great masters are left far behind.

The wisdom within you is the love of wisdom. Feed it by sight of wisdom itself, and your wisdom will expand and multiply to the omniscience of God. If you are capable of eating some of God, are you not capable of eating all of God? Jesus Christ said: "God is within you," and "I am within you." Then you are able to take in all of God. This is only one form of expression which gives a different turn of the mind. It is not that you eat God in a material sense, but Jesus Christ called it "bread" which He would have all the world eat of — speaking figuratively.

We have a marvelous birthright. We do not show our intelligence, our judgment, until we lay hold upon our birthright. We can hold this knowledge within our mind and then it will work through all the mind of the world. A false idea falls somewhere and fails. A true idea lives on and on forever. If we take the premise, within our mnid, that there is no limit to our power, even though each day we see things seemingly acting against us, we nevertheless have the doctrine that will triumph.

A piece of ice may be found in the crucible of intensest heat. If the ice holds its own, and increases by constant renewal the crucible heat must fail, leaving clear ice. So in the fires of the martyrs, they kept cool and steadfast. Pain got no hold upon them. Even racks and the flames could not hurt them. In the center of the blazing, violent sun there is a place that is beyond expression, absolute stillness. This stillness will conquer the violence of the sun eventually. So, the Spirit that is within you will conquer the miseries of the human lot. They shall be visibly nothing — just as they are truly nothing.

It is our business to translate the spiritual Truth within into visible manifestation. We do this first by thinking the absolute Truth, then speaking it, then fixing it into everything around us. We must mix the idea we have in our mind with the right word that expresses that idea. For instance, if you mean that a man is well, but you say that he is sick, you carry, for the time being, the meaning of the word "sick," and your mental report of it does not work with the man to heal him as quickly as the words you speak work to keep him sick. We are told by Solomon that the thoughts work, but Jesus gives us to understand that not only do our thoughts work, but words, which have certain meanings, will convey those meanings sooner than thoughts which dispute them. We must mean exactly what we say. "By thy words thou art justified."

A man said this Science was true enough, but it would take a hundred years for it to work out with mankind. So, every attempt he made to do anything was slow. He mentally thought that Spirit could act instantly, of course, but his mental reservation counted for nothing for the time being. The heart must agree with the lips. Zoroaster said, "Taking the first step with good thought, the second step with good word, the third step with good deed, I enter Paradise." If the thought and the word agree, we cannot help but enact good deeds. The lessons of Science lead you to absolute freedom from the results of the thoughts of the world, and from the material actions of the world.

Men may gather all the gold into a lump, and say you cannot have any, but by some way of the Spirit you will come out with more abundant riches than all the rest put together. They may hold arguments and try psychological processes to chain your mind or change it, but the Spirit will make a way with you to keep you free from all such attempts. You will elude every mental opposition as easily as you elude material things. Jesus came through their belief that he was dead.

Spirit does not need to go to school. It knows all things. If we speak and think from the Spirit, we are also wise without schools. The Spirit does not need commandments not to lie or steal. It is out of reach of commandments. The Spirit does not need to be told to be Good. It is above even goodness. The goodness that man deals with is badness under some circumstances. For instance, you can hate stealing so much that your goodness in not stealing is no virtue at all. It is a very subtle form of badness.

An old lady said she thought it very wrong to drink tea at church suppers. She did not drink tea, she hated it. Many people hate tobacco, until their hatred is far worse than chewing and smoking, for their own health and the happiness of their families. Sometimes people hate the wrongdoing of others so that they cannot possibly see their virtues. It makes an acid in the blood and eats up the strong gray particles of the brain. Hate is the premise we have to let fall entirely. Hate nothing. God sees everything good. What are we that other peoples' actions are so bad in our eyes? When we have a notion to which we would like to tie all the world, we are tied to that notion. It is as much bondage to be tied to an idea as to a stake. Martin Luther believed in freedom from other people's ideas, but he wanted to tie all the world to his ideas. In Science we do not get chained to a single statement. They are all good, but we do not drag ourselves around by any of them.

As you know, faith is good. Faith is the salvation of man. The idea that faith will save man is a good idea, but when Luther would not shake hands with Zwingle because he did not think faith would save a man, he needed an idea beyond the idea of faith. He needed love. He needed the idea of love as the greatest of all. He tied himself to the stake of an idea and would not go on to the mountain of love.

The twelve lessons of Science are all ideas. The ideas have living meanings. Luther's idea of faith had a living meaning, which he never got at all. The living meaning of salvation by faith is that faith in the Good enables us to see Good everywhere and in everything. Faith is God. God is Mind. Mind is Good and Mind sees Good. Mind knows God. The mind that has not the living essence of its ideas is as dry as sticks. Zwingle did not believe in the doctrine of faith, so Luther wanted to lift him out of salvation. So, our ideas of God have kept us chained. God is free. He is the skill of the healer. God is the Spirit that works out the health of the sick. God is the skill of all things. All action has a skill about its action, and that skill is the moving Holy Spirit. God does not see the outer actions. God sees only the heart.

The springs of life are fed by the meanings of words. Some people do not quite feel the meanings of the words they use, but the use of the words, by and by, breaks their meanings out over the mind. Precious ointment was shut in the alabaster boxes. Striking the boxes broke them, and the precious ointment fell out. So, striking the right words together breaks them open, after awhile. It is the meanings of the words that go over the world like angels of mercy, changing all the thoughts of men. The higher the truths we tell, the finer and more precious their meaning. Breaking open the twelve lessons of Science, and receiving the ointment of the meanings, is getting at the actual teaching of Jesus Christ.

Looking at your state of mind, you will see how full you seem to be of heavy ideas. Your breath seems to have brought in anxieties. Now hardships meet you at every turn — you think. The ancients advised people to breathe outward, to entirely empty their lungs of breath, and then draw in the breath with some affirmation of Good. Then, when they breathed outward again, they would only have a healing breath going through their bodies and affairs. The breath, they said, is vitally connected with our happiness.

You will sometimes find yourself praising and blessing your affairs for your prosperity, their life in God. You will find yourself consigning all your affairs into the hands of the Spirit. Whatsoever we do, we are not to lament, not to wail, not to mourn. There is nothing that will slice out of your feeling of power like grief. You cannot cry and heal at the same moment. Shakespeare said: "Grief, that's beauty's canker," and judgment is beauty. People make the worst mistakes of their lives when they are wailing. All the time the Spirit sits in calm security — in perfect happiness.

When we are happy, through some accomplishment directly from the hand of our doctrine, we have the amethyst stone of character. We are in intelligence and peace. They together make happiness. All despondency, all melancholy, all depression of feeling, must be met by breathing in and out words of praise of the great realities of life. The spiritual nature of man is his reality. The reality is understanding. Understanding is formless, but it formulates. This is very metaphysical. Let me repeat it: "My understanding has no form, but it formulates me and my affairs. I have no affairs and no substance except what my understanding formulates."

Now, those affairs formulated by pure understanding are not visible to my fleshly eyes, which see things imperfectly, since they are limited. This sight in itself is a fine piercing ray from my understanding. Let me give the right word, and that sight will extend to touch perfect objects. So with hearing. It is no good to limit my hearing by not giving my understanding its absolute sway with me. Understanding can radiate through us till our faculties touch things in an entirely different way from what they do now.

The more freedom we give our understanding, the more delight we have in life. Our understanding being set free, it feeds upon the great universal light. There is enough understanding in the universe for feeding our faculties forever. The step toward setting free our understanding of the world in which we live, and the understanding of ourselves at the same time, has been taken when the eleventh lesson of Science has been practised. It is being set free from accusations of foolishness and ignorance. There is no acid in the mind that has no condemnation, either of itself or anybody else. It is the acid of thinking evil that makes the blood corrode, and the bones and skin and sinews to fail. It is possible to nullify all our strong feelings by some exactly opposite idea. If you find yourself thinking that somebody is entirely wrong in using material remedies when you know that the word of the Spirit is the only healer, let the idea fall out of your mind. It is the same with not using them. You will find you are free as God is free, if you depend upon nothing at all for your health. Your simple freedom is enough of a spread of the Truth.

Some find themselves having new diseases, new pains, new trouble every day. They can all be traced to the bondage of the mind, to some one idea or another. The Sunday affirmation of

Science is good for such people. It is one you also must keep
for Sunday. It is: *"While knowing all things and doing all
things, I am independent of all things. I am absolutely free."*
This will take you out of the clutches of your old drugs. It will
take you out of the clutches of your idea that it is wicked to
use drugs. You will be free from the need of remedies bodily,
and free from any idea of remedies mentally.

It is the same with old age. The word of the Spirit is eternal
life. There is no old age in Spirit. The knowledge of this
will set you free from the clutches of old age physically, and
from the clutches of old age mentally. The same is true of
riches. Outwardly you will be well provided for, then you will
feel free. Mentally you will never think of coming to want.
You will never get to imagining what you would do if you
should come to want. This is real freedom.

We must get free from our ideas. God is freedom from ideas.
God is the free substance that penetrates and pervades all things.
If you are afraid to do anything because somebody might not
like it, you are tied to their ideas. You must do as it is right to
do because you are pleased with the right, or you have not
learned the twelfth lesson of Science. You are not happy if you
are not free.

You must begin the description of the perfection of the world
in which you live. You are glad that the free Spirit is flowing
through the airs. Tell it you are glad. You are glad there is a
way to speak to the Spirit to bring it into your being. Tell it
you are glad. You think your neighbor is a beautiful soul.
Tell her soul, mentally that you are glad it is so beautiful. The
skies are lovely. Their loveliness is spiritual. Tell their loveliness how glad you are that it is visible to you. The stars resting
on their black beds are wonderful. Their wonderfulness is
spiritual. Tell them how glad you are that it is visible to you.
The deep night, half towards morning, is stately peace.

Though you stand on bare sand, there is Mind whispering rich secrets. You do not need to be lonesome. Jesus Christ is whispering every instant some wonderful message into your ear. It would be a good plan for you to listen to the Voice of the Spirit. No matter if you are riding in the street cars you can be listening to what the free Spirit is speaking, as plainly to you through the earthquake as through the stillness. Only we do not think we can listen to a voice within a sound as well as to a voice within stillness.

There is a chance for the most unhappy person among you to breathe out your unhappiness and breathe in descriptions of the things you are glad about, till you hear the finer voice of nature, till you see the finer side of all things. You get above the ideas of your world. You are free from them. You get above even the idea of freedom. You see, the idea of freedom takes with it the idea of bondage of some kind. So you are neither free nor bound. You are not on that plane. You do not talk about riches, for that idea conveys the idea of poverty. You are neither rich nor poor. You do not live on that plane. You do not say you have dominion over all things, because the idea of dominion is the same as the idea that somebody is inferior in some way. You are neither inferior nor superior. You do not live on that plane. The Spirit never gets caught on any of those hooks. It is not inferior to your understanding, nor superior to it. The Spirit is one with your understanding. So the Spirit has no dominion over you. It is one with you. You do not talk of destroying your temper. You have no temper to destroy. You do not talk of getting free from poverty. You have no poverty to get free from.

This is the effect of using the twelfth statement of Science. You sometimes hear Scientists make these statements and they sound dangerous. They only show that they are thinking just as the twelfth lesson led them. Every Saturday afternoon you ought to have a special proclamation. If you have a good realization of the meaning of what you say that afternoon, you will keep free from complaining about your disappointments or troubles, even within your own mind. Why should you tie your mind to a stake and swing back and forth like a rag in the wind? If you tie your mind to a single idea, you will miss the twelfth lesson. There have been many people who have missed the twelfth lesson, because they have stopped to whine and to wail. They tied themselves to an idea that they did not like one thing, and howled all night long over it. Of course, these cases came for a sixth treatment and said they were not cured. Of course the same old affair faced them again for the sixth time.

You must not tie to an idea of anything being bad. If we speak of it, let us quickly give the twelfth lesson law to our mind. That is, *we say nothing more about it. We think nothing more about it.* We ignore it utterly and talk about something we like. We think about the true premise we have taken, whereby we propose to think that, if evil is not a reality, we do not mean to deal with it.

Now, whatever proposition you have made up your mind to, can you not stick to it? Of all things, if it is true that there is a substance of delight called Mind, within ourselves, and we can make whatever thought we please by thinking that way, we shall be very silly indeed if we do not choose a noble thought about ourselves, instead of an ignoble one. It is a noble thought to say:

"I am satisfied with the world in which I walk. All things please me. Near me is the presence of Good and afar off is the Good. You are all creations of the living God, perfect, harmonious, satisfying."

You will find this is a good idea with which to work out your happiness. Having your mind filled with this idea, you cannot have another idea in it. This idea results in happiness.

It is the one to take when you feel like comparing your lot in life with what you wanted it to be. It radiates your work with the green of the amethyst stone. It will gladden your home with the yellow sunshine of the topaz stone. It will make peace and harmony among your friends, like the sapphire blue of heaven. It will redden your business with the ruby wine of prosperity.

It is what was so gloriously demonstrated by Peter and John. They sang with great songs of joy, when they might have wailed because they were in prison. If you will notice people, you will see that they can hardly be made to laugh and sing when they contrast their lot, as it seems, with what they wanted it to be. People say they would be satisfied if they had this, or that, or the other. No such thing! If they mourn now, they would find something to mourn about then. Happiness is something that must come from the mind within, being fed and renewed by the Truth of life. Nothing but Truth will satisfy the mind. Complaining kept the Israelites of old from large inheritance. "They provoked the Lord with their complainings."

The pleasant, happy mind is a health-giver, without trying to be. It knows its value in the world. It does not heal without knowing what it is that heals. Jesus perceived when He was healing people who were behind Him. It is intelligence. Nobody is so wise as that man or woman who has refused the temptation to complain, and has, in his mind, spoken the twelfth lesson of Science. The meeting of melancholy with this statement is the best mixture for happiness that can be stirred up.

If your case comes the sixth time, tell him that you rejoice that he is giving the free Spirit unrestrained freedom through him. Knock at all twelve gates of his being through which he ought to be a shouting healthy life. Say to the case that claims to be cured the same treatment as to the case that seems to hang on, because you have felt hurt or grieved or have forgotten or neglected to give the right thoughts that would have made you an intelligent healer. This latter case should have the same treatment as the one that has been cured. It is the time for you to give thanks to God, and call out loudly to the true state of affairs to come into your sight. The cured case is easily told mentally that you rejoice in his health as God. The case that you are finding fault with and so keep on the sick list, does not seem so easy, but if you have made it hard you must soften it.

I might truthfully say that the case which comes the sixth time for cure is the outshowing of your disposition. A good disposition through and through is a happy disposition, and a happy disposition will cure anything. A happy disposition, mixed with scientific words, makes a quick understanding of how to speak mentally to a sick or unhappy being, and bring him instantly out into the right state. A good disposition, mixed with these lessons of Science, will make a perfect memory. A good disposition mixed with thoughts of the truths of life, put forth while you are alone each day, will make you very good and quick at speaking and writing the Science.

If your disposition is bad, or seems so to yourself or friends, the repetition of the twelfth premise in Science will make it good. Another thing, you will be able to quickly see if a man's disposition stands in the way of his health. A lady who had trained her disposition to be smiling and cheerful had been treating a patient, who believed in sore eyes, for a long time. One day, she spoke mentally, very impetuously: "You, as Spirit, have no bad temper." The next day the patient came, all cured.

That practitioner said she would sometimes be six weeks treating a case and not stir it; then, she would suddenly say, mentally: "You never could, as a spiritual being, feel dissatisfied with your son." Or, she would say: "You, as Spirit, can say that you, as spirit, cannot be unjust with anybody." These sudden thoughts she said, seemed to cut a tough thread that was holding the patient's mind from thinking of health. These little cuts at the strings that hold a case in pain or sickness are what come from your mind as naturally as seed comes up into corn and wheat. No teacher can tell what to say in particular to a case. They can only give the general treatment. The general treatment leads up to the particular one. There is a verse that has helped a great many people into good courage. It is this:

"He who hath led me to this way,
Still on the way will show.
He who hath taught me of this way,
Still more will make me know."

It means that if God, in His infinite kindness and mercy, has put this Science before us, and led us into it, He will see that we go on to its end. It is as with David when he was taken from the sheep-cote, from following after sheep, and put into the king's palace. God elected him and fitted him for this place. So, if you have chosen to learn the Science, chosen to practice it, God, the Infinite Mind, will give you strength and fitness to fulfill each task set before you. Sometimes you will seem to be in great trouble, but you will never go under. Calamity will never overtake you. Probably the most prominent practitioners have had the very hardest troubles to encounter, but they never go under. They are always lifted safely over. A ship on the ocean dips low, and rides high. So you are built, if you have these lessons in your mind. They have gone out, like angels, to prepare your way for you. They have taken deep, eternal hold on your mind and body. Jesus said, "Fear not, little flock," and so I say to you, be faithful to the lessons. Be faithful to this last lesson, which goes down into your deep nature, and takes hold of your disposition to make it divine.

If a case comes cured the sixth day, it is a sure signal that you have gained a victory over your disposition. You have won the amethyst stone. A very simple, trusting practitioner who had entirely given her life to the spiritual doctrine, had an amethyst given her. She took it as a signal that she had been victorious over her disposition. She thought, to herself, "It is a sign that, when I wanted to complain, I promptly spoke the last treatment of Science." She had a topaz given to her. She took it as a sign that she had put cheerful, buoyant words out into her affairs, when they troubled her. "The outward conditions are so dependent on my thoughts," she said, "that I feel as if there were sermons in brooks and books in stones, telling me how I am getting on."

One teacher used to talk to herself first, as a newly born, perfect child of the Spirit; as she was when one year old, then two years old. She told the little thing what a miracle of God would be wrought for her some day. Then, when she came to the year of her age, according to the world's reckoning, she would pronounce the whole miracle already wrought. She felt that it was very important that she be every whit whole in her mind, if she was to teach Science.

No matter what that patient of yours would say to you personally, if you were to see him or her now, you may give him the sixth treatment, which is the last lesson of Science. You will be faithful in giving it to your world every Saturday afternoon, and you will treat every case, no matter how it seems, to this teaching, if it comes the sixth time. Follow me. I will speak to that one who used to believe in disease:

You are a perfect creation of the living God, spiritual, harmonious, fearless, free. You reflect all the universe of Good.

From every direction, everywhere, come words of Truth, making you know that you are free, wise, and happy.

You are satisfied with the world in which you live.

You show forth to the world health, wisdom, peace.

You show to me perfect health in every part of your being.

You are fearless, free, strong, wise, and able to do everything that belongs to you to do each day. God works through you to will and to do that which ought to be done by you.

You are a living demonstration of the power of Truth to set free into health and strength for living service to the world.

You acknowledge to the world that you are every whit whole.

You acknowledge to yourself, and to me that you are well and strong and alive through and through.

God is your life, health, strength, and support forever.

In the name of the Father, and of the Son, and of the Holy Ghost, I pronounce you well and strong.

As God saw the works of His hands Good, so I see you Good. All is Good. Amen.

NOTES

INDEX